DIAGNOSIS AND CORRECTION
OF READING PROBLEMS

DIAGNOSIS AND CORRECTION OF READING PROBLEMS

DARRELL MORRIS

THE GUILFORD PRESS
New York   London

© 2008 The Guilford Press
A Division of Guilford Publications, Inc.
72 Spring Street, New York, NY 10012
www.guilford.com

Printed in the United States of America

This book is printed on acid-free paper.

Last digit is print number: 9 8 7 6 5 4 3 2 1

Library of Congress Cataloging-in-Publication Data

Morris, Darrell.
   Diagnosis and correction of reading problems / by Darrell Morris.
       p.   cm.
   Includes bibliographical references and index.
   ISBN-13: 978-1-59385-616-8 (pbk. : alk. paper)
   ISBN-10: 1-59385-616-4 (pbk. : alk. paper)
   ISBN-13: 978-1-59385-617-5 (hardcover : alk. paper)
   ISBN-10: 1-59385-617-2 (hardcover : alk. paper)
   1. Reading disability—Diagnosis.   2. Reading—Remedial teaching.
I. Title.
   LB1050.5.M668 2008
   371.91'44—dc22
                                                          2007028268

For Joe, Justin, Laurel, and Ed . . . battlers all

About the Author

Darrell Morris, EdD, is Professor of Education and Director of the Reading Clinic at Appalachian State University in Boone, North Carolina, where he has been on the faculty since 1989. While at Appalachian State, he has directed the master's program in reading, researched the beginning reading and spelling processes, and helped school districts throughout the country set up early reading intervention programs. Dr. Morris is the author of *The Howard Street Tutoring Manual, Second Edition: Teaching At-Risk Readers in the Primary Grades* (Guilford, 2005) and the recipient (with several colleagues) of the International Reading Association's 2005 Dina Feitelson Research Award.

Contents

PART III   TRAINING READING TEACHERS

Diagnosis and Correction of Reading Problems

CHAPTER 1

Introduction

Before deciding to write a book on the diagnosis and correction of reading difficulties, I had to think more than the proverbial twice. After all, there are many books on the subject, several of them up-to-date and encyclopedic in nature. I was not inclined to produce another 600-page tome that summarized the existing knowledge base. It is true that I had taught a course on reading diagnosis and correction for 25 consecutive years, never tiring of the subject. However, I was aware from previous experience that it can be very difficult to write about a topic that one knows intimately and cares about deeply. So why did I write this book? It was because I wanted, in a small way, to keep alive a tradition that means a great deal to me—the clinical tradition in the field of reading education. Let me begin at the beginning.

THE McGUFFEY READING CENTER— UNIVERSITY OF VIRGINIA

Many years ago, after completing a master's degree in psychology and serving a short stint as a consulting special education teacher, I realized that I was most interested in the problems poor children confront in school, reading being the foremost among them. A good friend of mine, Tom Gill, was enrolled in a graduate program in reading education at the University of Virginia. Tom said that if I spent 1 year at the McGuffey Reading Center, I would learn how to teach a child to read. That sounded good to me.

My professor at the University of Virginia was Edmund Henderson. I quickly realized that he was an experienced scholar who possessed a first-rate analytic mind, but what struck me was his genuine commitment to clinical diagnosis and instruction, the applied "nuts and bolts" of the profession. In our reading diagnosis course, a child with a reading problem came to the clinic each week to be assessed. One student in the graduate class administered informal reading tests to the child, and a second student administered a psychological test. The rest of us, along with Henderson, observed this testing through a one-way mirror. In addition, while the child was being tested, a third student conducted an interview with the parents. On Wednesdays, we came together as a group to discuss the child's case. After the reading, psychological, and parent interview data had been shared, Henderson, a master clinician, delighted in "walking us through" the diagnostic process, always ending with concrete recommendations for instruction. What made a lasting impression on me as a doctoral student was the man's enthusiasm for, and curiosity about, this clinical endeavor. I sat in on Henderson's diagnosis class for 3 consecutive years. At least once per semester, he would say, with a broad grin, "Isn't this fun? Do you believe they pay me to teach this course?" I remember thinking at the time, "If this full professor, who is knowledgeable and highly intelligent, is this interested in diagnosis and remediation issues, they must be important."

As graduate students, we also tutored a struggling reader each day under the supervision of Henderson or an experienced doctoral student. The supervision was perhaps not as close as it might have been, but the important point was that we had ongoing opportunities to try out techniques that we were learning in methods courses (e.g., language-experience stories, word sorts, directed reading–thinking activities, repeated readings) and to discuss our teaching successes and failures with an interested group of colleagues. Henderson (1981, pp. 129–130) later wrote about his philosophy for training reading teachers:

> I am convinced that a year-long practicum should be required for all reading specialists. The work should be carried on under the direct supervision of an experienced clinician who can show by example both the techniques and the exercise of judgment that are needed. No formula will suffice nor will practice by a teacher alone convey what must be mastered. . . . It is only by experiencing the effects of refined teaching that students learning to be teachers are gradually able to free themselves from the false belief that it is the method rather than they themselves that must control the set for learning. . . . Such teaching skill is learned only gradually, by example and practice.

But where and when did Professor Henderson develop his intense interest in, and respect for, clinical work? Not surprisingly, it was in his own graduate training in the late 1950s under the experienced and watchful eye of another reading clinician, Dr. Russell Stauffer of the University of Delaware. Henderson was Stauffer's first doctoral student at Delaware and, in fact, took his degree in educational psychology because there was no doctorate in reading education at the time. He divided his time between taking academic psychology and research courses and helping run the university's reading clinic. When Henderson would excitedly share with his mentor some new psychological finding he had come upon in his academic course work, Stauffer, a committed scholar himself, would admonish his student:

"You go over there and take those psychology courses, but just remember that it's here in the clinic where you will learn about reading."

Henderson never forgot Stauffer's admonition, and he shared it at least once per year with his own doctoral students. *It's here in the clinic where you will learn about reading.* Does this statement simply mean that we learn to teach disabled readers by teaching them in a controlled situation while receiving feedback from an experienced coach? It does . . . but it also means more than this. Henderson believed that we could come to understand the learning-to-read process—the *psychological* process—only by engaging in the teaching act and thinking deeply about what we observe. In fact, he believed that if a current theoretical explanation of reading, however popular it might be, does not comport with what we see children do with our own eyes, then the theory should be questioned. In other words, theoretical explanations must always be grounded in the real world of teaching children to read. In a sense, Henderson was out of step with the times in the late 1970s, advocating clinical training (one-to-one teaching) when the broader field of reading education was moving toward an examination of variables affecting classroom reading instruction. Out of step or not, my professor's position made sense to me at the time, and it still does today after 25 years of working in the profession.

THE EDUCATION OF A READING CLINICIAN

In my own career as a university-based reading educator, first at National College of Education in the suburbs of Chicago and later at Appalachian State University in the mountains of North Carolina, I have tried to keep up with the latest research findings that bear on the diagnosis and teaching of reading. However, my understanding of how children learn—and fail to learn—to read has been more profoundly influenced by three types of clinical experience: supervision of university-based diagnostic and teaching practica; guidance of early reading intervention projects in the public schools; and one-to-one tutoring of struggling readers.

At both universities where I have worked, I have directed a reading clinic—a setting where teachers-in-training tutor children with reading problems under the supervision of an experienced clinician. For example, at Appalachian State, I teach the two-course clinical sequence in our reading master's program: a diagnosis course followed by a summer practicum in which 20 or more graduate students each tutor two children for 4 weeks. Although the diagnosis course is generally well received, the teaching practicum is greatly appreciated by the graduate students. They consistently comment on the value of (1) observing the reading process in a structured one-to-one teaching situation, and (2) receiving feedback on their teaching from an experienced reading clinician. As a young professor unsure of his abilities, I was pleased that my graduate students found clinical teaching to be a valuable part of their training. Now late in my career, I and my students still find the reading practicum to be a stimulating, rewarding experience. Each semester, a new crop of children learns to read, graduate students learn to teach reading, and I and my supervisory staff continue to broaden and deepen our understanding of reading as we facilitate the work of the tutor–child pairs.

An offshoot of my clinical teaching at the university has been my long involvement in tutoring programs in school and after-school settings. In the early 1980s, I helped found a grass-roots, after-school tutoring program in a poor neighborhood on the north side of Chicago (Morris, 2005a). At Howard Street, we used community volunteers (e.g., college students, retirees, suburban homemakers) to provide tutoring to low-reading second and third graders. This use of lay tutors (there was no alternative) forced me to rethink and adapt a university-based clinical training model to a real-world context. Ongoing supervision of the volunteer tutors by a reading specialist proved to be the key, for there is no substitute for expertise. However, achievement results at Howard Street (see Morris, Shaw, & Perney, 1990) showed that volunteer tutors, *if carefully supervised*, could be effective, and this finding opened up, at least in my mind, new possibilities for delivering tutorial instruction to at-risk readers.

In the late 1980s, influenced by the work of the New Zealander Marie Clay (1979), I began to help public schools set up early reading intervention programs for at-risk first graders. To Clay's Reading Recovery lesson plan (rereading little books, sentence writing, introducing a new book), I added a systematic phonics component. I also instituted a different training regimen for teachers. Essentially, I visited a school every 3–4 weeks throughout the year, each time observing 30-minute tutoring lessons conducted by first-grade classroom teachers and reading teachers. The teachers would tutor and then we would debrief the lessons as a group, focusing on teaching technique and the pacing of instruction. This practicum-like intervention (i.e., tutoring supervised by a trainer) came to be called Early Steps, and it was successful in raising the achievement of the tutored first graders (Morris, Tyner, & Perney, 2000; Santa & Hoien, 1999). Maybe more important, Early Steps training strengthened the participating teachers' understanding of the beginning reading process, enabling many of them to adapt the tutoring principles and activities for use in small reading groups in the classroom (see Tyner, 2004). The success of Early Steps in a variety of school systems (rich, poor, and in between) strengthened my belief that clinical teacher-training models have an important role to play in preventing reading failure in our public schools.

Early in my college teaching career, I began to tutor struggling readers in the clinic, taking on one or two cases each semester. I did so because I loved working with kids, and I was curious about how they learned. That is, I wanted to better understand the nature and complexity of reading difficulties and believed that hands-on experience with a variety of clinical cases was the best way to do so. Over the years, this practice of tutoring individual students (usually the toughest cases in the clinic) has served me well. I have been successful with many problem readers, and this success has bolstered my confidence in the basic theory and pedagogy that I use and teach to others. With a few children, however, I have been less successful. These "tough" cases have not only instilled humility but have led me to recognize that reading disability is on a continuum and that severely disabled readers (perhaps 3%) often need a different, more intensive type of reading instruction (see Chapter 7).

The clinical experiences described above have shaped my career as a reading educator. Moreover, they directly inform the ideas about reading diagnosis and instruction that are presented in this book. Before previewing the book's content, however, I believe it is important that I acknowledge a few core principles or assumptions that guide my work as a clinician. Because not every reader of this book will agree with these assumptions, it is all the more important "to get them out on the table" at the start.

THREE ASSUMPTIONS
ABOUT THE READING PROCESS

1. *Reading can be conceptualized as a combination of print-processing skill and comprehension.* At the sentence level, *print processing* refers to the accurate and automatic pickup of a sequence of printed words. *Comprehension* refers to the extraction (or construction) of meaning from this processed sequence of words. Obviously, one can print-process a sentence (e.g., "They fired the rock around the diamond before returning it to the young hurler.") without understanding its meaning ("They threw the baseball around the infield before returning it to the young pitcher.") But in real life, do we do this—do we process the words without comprehending? On occasion, of course we do. Think of a college sophomore's first reading of Joyce's *Ulysses* or his or her attempt to read a convoluted passage in a philosophy text. Or think of average adults who read in bed each night before going to sleep. It is often their hazy recognition that they have "read" a paragraph *with little or no understanding* that leads them to close the book and turn out the light.

Can it work the other way? Do we sometimes comprehend text without fully processing the printed words on the page? Certainly skillful adult readers can skim through a newspaper or magazine article—skipping words, even phrases—and still come up with the general meaning or gist of the article. Perhaps a better example is the below-grade-level reader who must plod through grade-level reading passages on an end-of-year standardized test. Such a child may misread 10–15% of the words in the passage, yet still attain a passing comprehension score by making "educated guesses." A little luck also helps on these standardized, multiple-choice comprehension tests.

Reading = Print processing + Comprehension

Thus far, we have considered separating the reading process into two parts: print-processing skill and comprehension. The work of Charles Perfetti (1985,

1992) takes us a step further by showing how these two parts are functionally related. According to Perfetti, the act of reading (print processing + comprehension) must be executed within the limitations of the mind's processing resources. The idea, he argues, is to automatize print processing (or word recognition) so that more mental energy can be devoted to comprehension. An analogy may help here. Think of a teenage boy learning to drive a stick-shift car. At first, every movement (starting, stopping, turning the car) requires the neophyte's conscious attention, resulting in driving that is slow, erratic, and often nerve-racking. Now fast forward 6 months. The same teenager is effortlessly driving down the road, checking out restaurants while engaging in spirited conversation with two passengers. What has happened? After 6 months of almost daily practice, the teenager has automatized the skills of maneuvering an automobile, thereby freeing up processing resources that he can use to converse with his friends. The beginning or struggling reader is in a similar situation. At first, he or she must give considerable attention to decoding printed words, which can lead to halting, inaccurate reading. With practice, word recognition processes are automatized and contextual reading becomes more fluent. This, in turn, frees up processing resources that the child can use to comprehend the text (see Figure 1.1).

The notion that reading can be divided into *print-processing* skill and *comprehension* skill—and that the former directly influences the latter—has important implications for the reading teacher that will become clear in the chapters on diagnosis and instruction that follow.

2. *Print-processing skill is distributed along a continuum.* Like many other human abilities or skills (e.g., carrying a tune, shooting a basketball, drawing a picture, playing a video game, memorizing a poem), print processing or fluent reading is unequally distributed in the population. Here I am referring to the psychological processing or "pickup" of a sequence of printed words (e.g., phrase, sentence, paragraph), not the comprehension of that sequence. The exact distribution of print-processing skill among developing readers is unknown (Figure 1.2 shows a possible normal distribution). Nor do we know how much of the inequality to assign to na-

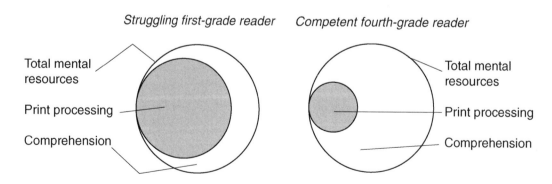

FIGURE 1.1. Allocation of mental resources to print processing and comprehension by two readers functioning at different ability levels.

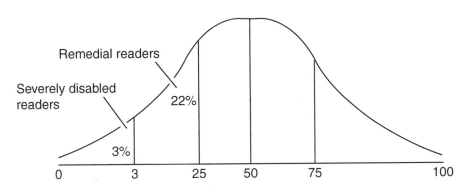

FIGURE 1.2. Normal distribution of print-processing skill.

ture (genetic predisposition) or to nurture (home literacy environment, school reading program). Still, we do know that some schoolchildren (perhaps 25%, on average) have more difficulty learning to read print than do their peers. Print processing is not just another entry in a long list of human skills and talents. Its importance is defined by the central role reading plays in our information-laden culture. If children have trouble humming tunes, shooting baskets, or winning video games, these weaknesses—at most, embarrassments to be avoided—do not significantly affect their lives. On the other hand, difficulty in learning to read can detrimentally affect a child's education and seriously limit his or her later career choices. In short, being able to read in our society is a survival skill.

There is a hopeful side to this discussion of print processing as an unequally distributed skill in the population. First, students need not be at the top end of the skill continuum to "get by." The average adult reads at a rate of 250–300 words per minute (Carver, 1990; Rayner & Pollatsek, 1989). However, an adult who reads 200 words per minute can function effectively in most literacy contexts (e.g., reading a newspaper, magazine, novel, textbook). Second, students can improve their skill level through instruction and practice. Just as professional lessons and much practice can improve the swing of a beginning tennis player, appropriate instruction and practice can improve the print-processing skill (or fluency) of a beginning or struggling reader. Referring back to Figure 1.2, it is quite possible that most low readers (see 4th to 25th percentile), if identified early and provided with appropriate instruction, could, over time, move into the average range in print-processing skill. Although it is true that the bottom 3% in Figure 1.2 will have difficulty becoming fluent readers, even the students in this severely disabled group, if provided with specialized instruction, can sometimes acquire the literacy skills they need to achieve success in school and life.

The distinction between below-average readers and severely disabled readers is an important one. Wherever we draw the line separating the two groups (e.g., 2nd, 3rd, or 5th percentile), the idea is that instruction should vary depending on the severity of a child's reading difficulty. For example, I suggest that the vast majority of children (97%) can benefit from traditional reading instruction (a judicious mix of phonics, fluency, and comprehension activities) *if* the instruction is provided at the appropriate difficulty level. On the other hand, severely handicapped readers (3%) will require more intensive alphabetic-code instruction (e.g., Gillingham & Stillman, 1960; Wilson, 1996) if they are to progress.

3. *Learning to read is a developmental process.* Reading skill, like many complicated cognitive skills, evolves over time. Whereas an average first grader can read *The Cat in the Hat*, a fourth grader can read *Charlotte's Web*, and a seventh grader can read *Tom Sawyer* or *The Hobbit*.

Jeanne Chall (1983) provided a useful description of the developmental course children follow on their way to achieving reading maturity (see Figure 1.3). In first grade, Chall argued, beginning readers are "glued to print," reading in a slow, halting manner as they attempt to memorize some words and use letter sounds to decode others. Second and third graders become "unglued to print" as their more advanced word recognition skills allow them to read in phrases. Fourth graders, having acquired a degree of print-processing fluency, can devote more cognitive energy to comprehending new ideas in a text. And finally, upper-elementary and middle school students are able to integrate (compare and contrast) ideas across different texts that they are reading—a fairly sophisticated cognitive achievement (also see the developmental sequence proposed by Spear-Swerling & Sternberg, 1998).

For most children, the developmental path is so smooth that it is difficult for laypeople (and many educators) to appreciate the complexity of the reading acquisition process. However, for the 25% of students who experience difficulty learning to read, development is far from smooth or seamless. These students may initially find it difficult to break the alphabetic code; their progress in reading may be painfully slow; or they may advance erratically without establishing a necessary skill foundation.

To help low-achieving readers, a teacher must understand how reading skill de-

---

Stage 1: Decoding (first grade). Children are "glued to print," learning the alphabet and how to blend letter–sounds into words.

Stage 2: Fluency (second–third grade). Children become "unglued to print." With improved word recognition skill, they are able to read familiar texts at a faster pace and with appropriate phrasing.

Stage 3A: Reading to Learn (fourth grade). With basic print-processing skills mastered, children can now concentrate on comprehending new information as they read.

Stage 3B: Analytic Reading (fifth–sixth grades). Children begin to read more critically, considering text information from multiple perspectives.

FIGURE 1.3. The first three stages in Chall's (1983) description of reading development.

velops; how cognitive subprocesses, such as word recognition, fluency, and comprehension, mature and interact over time. The teacher should also have a sense of what constitutes average reading performance at the various grade levels. For example, what should a mid-first-grade reader be able to do? A second-grade reader? A fourth-grade reader? This is not an uncomplicated business. Nonetheless, good training in reading diagnosis can introduce teachers to the developmental nature of reading, and supervised tutoring experiences can sensitize them to the obstacles facing struggling readers at different levels of development.

ORGANIZATION OF THIS BOOK

The ideas in this book mirror, to a degree, the content of a graduate course I teach each year in reading diagnosis and correction. The book, intended as a tutorial for undergraduate and graduate students, is divided into three parts. The first two parts, Diagnosing Reading Problems and Correcting Reading Problems, are included in most textbooks of this type. The third part, Teacher Training, reflects my conviction that a particular type of hands-on clinical training is necessary if teachers are to become truly competent in diagnosing and correcting students' reading problems.

Part I, Diagnosing Reading Problems, contains three chapters. In Chapter 2, I explain how to administer a traditional assessment battery that includes informal tests of word recognition in isolation, passage reading, and spelling. I also show how to adapt this battery so that it can be used effectively with beginning readers. In Chapter 3, I consider how to interpret scores from an informal reading assessment with an eye toward placing a student at the correct instructional level. Chapter 4 completes the diagnosis section of the book with a discussion of related topics, such as the parent interview, diagnosis through teaching, pre- and posttesting with an informal test battery, and standardized reading assessment.

Part II, Correcting Reading Problems, also contains three chapters. In Chapter 5, I describe a set of tutoring strategies (e.g., support reading, word study, writing) and show how these can be combined or adjusted to meet the needs of *beginning readers* functioning at different developmental levels (emergent, preprimer, and primer). I also note how these tutoring strategies can be adapted for small-group instruction in the primary-grade classroom. In Chapters 6 and 7, I address the broader issue of *reading difficulties from the second-grade to sixth-grade level*. In Chapter 6, I describe a set of teaching strategies (e.g., word study, comprehension, and fluency) that can be used with remedial readers in either a tutoring or classroom context. In Chapter 7, I show how these strategies, alone or in combination, can be applied to individual cases representing different types of reading problems. Chapter 7 also includes a brief discussion of severe reading disability. (*Note*: All case names in this book are pseudonyms.)

Part III, Teacher Training, contains a single chapter (Chapter 8) that addresses the education of reading teachers. I cite the goals of such training, describe the context in which it needs to be carried out, and mention obstacles that stand in the way.

Few will question this book's emphasis on diagnosing reading problems in a one-to-one context. However, the topic of corrective reading instruction can be approached at different levels—whole classroom, small-group, or tutorial. In this book, I have chosen to describe reading instruction, for the most part, at the tutorial or one-to-one level. I make no apologies for this choice. After more than a quarter of a century as a reading educator, I understand my profession's concern for, and emphasis on, classroom instruction. This is where most of the students are, where most of the materials are sold, and where "new" instructional trends have the best chance of taking hold. Nonetheless, materials and trends (e.g., word-control basals, whole language, "scientifically based" phonics instruction) do not teach children how to read; teachers do. And to be effective with *struggling* readers, teachers require knowledge and skill. I firmly believe that such craft-like skill is best learned through supervised one-to-one teaching experiences. Moreover, I believe that once teachers get a "feel" for clinical teaching—that is, realize that their considered actions can make a difference in a child's learning—they will be more effective in teaching reading in other contexts (e.g., the classroom or the resource room). These beliefs led me to write this book.

PART I

DIAGNOSING READING PROBLEMS

CHAPTER 2

Administering an Informal Reading Diagnosis

The *American Heritage College Dictionary* (1997) lists two definitions of the word *diagnosis*: (1) "the act of determining the nature and cause of a disease or injury through examination of a patient," and (2) "a critical analysis of the nature of something." It is this second definition that applies to our discussion of reading diagnosis. Our goal is not necessarily to uncover the cause of a reading problem—always a dicey endeavor. Instead, the dual purpose of a reading diagnosis is to establish a student's reading instructional level (the difficulty or grade level at which he or she should be taught), and to identify relative strengths and weaknesses in the student's reading behavior. In other words, we diagnose in order to understand the individual reader and thereby to teach him or her effectively.

For many years practitioners in the field of reading have relied on informal as opposed to formal or standardized assessments (Betts, 1946; Stauffer, Abrams, & Pikulski, 1978; Barr, Blachowicz, Katz, & Kaufman, 2002). Following this tradition, in this chapter I describe how to administer a diagnostic battery that includes three informal tests: *word recognition in isolation*, *contextual reading*, and *spelling*. For each assessment area, I provide a brief rationale, a description of the test instrument, and detailed directions on how to administer and score the test. At the end of the chapter, I explain how to adapt the diagnosis for beginning or first-grade-level readers.

ASSESSING WORD RECOGNITION IN ISOLATION

Rationale

Accurate, automatic recognition of printed words drives the reading process (Adams, 1990; Rayner, Foorman, Perfetti, Pesetsky, & Seidenberg, 2001). Word recognition skill is developmental in nature, evolving across the grade levels to provide the foundation for reading progress. Word recognition can be assessed *in context* (e.g., percentage of words read correctly in a third-grade passage) or *in isolation* (e.g., percentage of words read correctly in a third-grade word list). Both assessment formats are important, but note that reading isolated words in a list provides a purer, context-free measure of word recognition ability.

Word recognition is usually assessed by having a child read graded lists of words (first grade, second grade, third grade, and so on) until he or she reaches a frustration level—for example, misreads more than 50% of the words in a list. Although such an assessment provides a measure of word recognition accuracy, it does not address the crucial issue of automaticity. In the following example, the child read correctly 70% of the words on the third-grade list.

Preprimer	100% (Start test)
Primer	100%
First grade	95%
Second grade	80%
Third grade	70%
Fourth grade	30% (Stop test)

But how long did he or she take to read each word—½ second, a full second, or 2 seconds? Does reading words correctly after 1 or more seconds represent automatic sight recognition or decoding skill (i.e., sounding out a word letter by letter or syllable by syllable)?

Many years ago Betts (1946) offered a solution to this problem. He suggested that word recognition lists be administered in a flash/untimed presentation format (see also Johnson, Kress, & Pikulski, 1987; Barr et al., 2002). That is, using a tachistoscopic technique, the examiner "flashes" each word to the child for approximately ¼–½ second and records his or her response. If the child misreads the word on the flash presentation, he or she receives another chance to read the word on the untimed presentation. Such an administration yields two percentage-correct scores on each grade-level list: a *flash score* representing accuracy and automaticity, and an *untimed score* representing accuracy.

Although Betts's flash/untimed technique was used by reading clinicians for many years (I was taught the procedure at the University of Virginia in the late-1970s), it gradually fell out of favor in the last quarter of the 20th century for a number of reasons: The flash technique was somewhat difficult to learn; there were no agreed-upon criteria for interpreting flash word recognition performance; and many reading educators came to question the importance of assessing word recognition out of context. Today, although most published informal reading tests (e.g., Roe & Burns, 2007; Leslie & Caldwell, 2005; Woods & Moe, 2007) include graded word recognition lists, rarely is the examiner asked to flash the list words to the student. This omission is ironic, given what we know about the centrality of automatic word recognition in the reading process (see Perfetti, 1992; Rayner & Pollatsek, 1989). In an attempt to capture the automatic aspect of word recognition skill, the assessment includes a flash/untimed presentation.

Test Instrument

The word recognition test contains ten 20-word lists (see Appendix 2.1), ranging in difficulty from preprimer (early first grade) to eighth grade. The lists were developed by randomly sampling the grade-level lists from *Basic Reading Vocabularies* (Harris & Jacobson, 1982). For example, to establish the 20-word preprimer list, I selected every 5th word from the 94 words in the Harris–Jacobson preprimer-level corpus. To come up with 20 primer-level words, I selected every 8th word from the 175 words in the Harris–Jacobson primer-level corpus. And so on.

A perusal of the word recognition lists (see Appendix 2.1) shows that, across the grade levels, the list words increase in difficulty. For example, first-grade words (e.g., *go, big, saw, hurt*) are commonly used and short in length. Third-grade words (e.g., *favor, haircut, bandage, unroll*) are less common and usually contain more than one syllable. And sixth-grade words (e.g., *elevate, conservation, similarity, quantity*), drawn more from written than from spoken language, are complex and multisyllabic in structure. The graded nature of the lists gives them their diagnostic power. That is, the further a child can progress through the word lists (particularly with automatic recognition), the more advanced or sophisticated is his or her word knowledge.

A recent dissertation by Frye (2004) established the reliability and hierarchical order of the 10-list word recognition instrument. In administering the word recognition test to 124 third and fourth graders, Frye reported a split-half reliability correlation of $r = .98$ for levels preprimer through eighth grade. She also constructed a conditional frequency table to test the hierarchical structure of the word recognition test. That is, students should score higher on lower-level lists (easier words) than on higher-level lists (harder words). Frye found this to be the case. Of her 124 third- and fourth-grade students, 111 scored higher on the first-grade list than on the second-grade list; 121 scored higher on the second-grade list than on the third-grade list; 116 scored higher on the third-grade list than on the fourth-grade list, and so on. These hierarchical or stepwise results were expected, given that the word lists (preprimer through eighth) were derived from a large, carefully graded word corpus (Harris & Jacobson, 1982).

Administration

Administration of the word recognition test always begins with the *preprimer* list. This makes sense for a first grader, but why start an older student on the early-first-grade list? Isn't time wasted if a fifth grader breezes through the first four lists (preprimer through second grade) with 95–100% accuracy on the flash presentation? Not necessarily. Keep in mind that, for the older reader, administration of the first few lists accustoms the child to the task, takes little time (the words are being flashed), and provides important information about foundational, first-grade word knowledge.

Testing begins with the first word in the preprimer list. Using two blank 3" x 5" index cards to cover the page, the examiner "flashes" the first word to the child for approximately ¼ second. Johnson et al. (1987, p. 57) provided a clear description of this timed or flash presentation:

> To rapidly present a word to the child, the two cards are held together immediately above the first word on the list. The lower card is moved down to expose the word; the upper card is then moved down to close the opening between them. This complete series of motions is carried out quickly, giving the child only a brief presentation of the word. It is important, however, that the word be exposed completely and clearly. . . .

If the child responds correctly to the flash presentation of the first word, the examiner proceeds to flash the next word, continuing on down the list in this manner until a given word is misread. At that point, the examiner opens up the cards to frame the misread word and allows the child ample time to analyze or decode the word, if he or she can. This is the untimed presentation. Following the child's untimed response, the examiner resumes flashing the list words until subsequent errors necessitate the need for other untimed presentations.

The examiner should record the child's responses as the list words are being administered. A pencil and a scoresheet corresponding to the child's test list should be at the examiner's side (away from the child) during the administration of the word recognition test. *Only errors need be recorded.* As long as the child is responding accurately on the flash presentations, the examiner need not pick up the pencil. When the child does misread a flashed word, the examiner routinely:

- Opens the cards, initiating the untimed presentation.
- Quickly writes down the child's flash response.
- Waits for and then records the untimed response.
- Readies the child for the flash presentation of the next list word.

For example, if Emily, a second grader, reads "shoot" for *shout* on the flash presentation (see Figure 2.1, item 13 in first-grade list), the examiner opens the cards, immediately records *shoot* in the flash column of the scoresheet, and waits for the child's untimed response. If Emily correctly identifies *shout* when given the addi-

	First grade				Second grade	
	Flash	Untimed			Flash	Untimed
1. leg	lag	✓		1. able	0	✓
2. black				2. break	brack	breek
3. smile				3. pull		
4. hurt				4. week		
5. dark				5. gate		
6. white				6. felt		
7. couldn't	0	✓		7. north		
8. seen				8. rush	rich	✓
9. until				9. wrote	h	✓
10. because				10. perfect	per-	0
11. men	h	✓		11. change	chang	0
12. winter				12. basket	bas-	✓
13. shout	shoot	✓		13. shoot	shot	✓
14. glass				14. hospital	0	hosp
15. paint				15. spill		
16. children				16. dug		
17. table				17. crayon	0	0
18. stand				18. third		
19. head	heed	0		19. taken	take	✓
20. drove	drive	✓		20. prize	priz	0
	70%	95%			40%	70%

FIGURE 2.1. Emily's performance on the word recognition test (first- and second-grade lists).

tional time, the examiner simply records a check (✓) in the untimed column. If the child makes another incorrect response (e.g., "shot"), the examiner writes *shot* in the untimed column. Finally, if Emily fails to respond to the untimed presentation of the target word, "shout," the examiner records a *0* in the untimed column.

On the flash presentation of a word, the child can actually respond in four ways. She can (1) identify the word immediately, (2) misread the word, (3) provide no response, or (4) hesitate briefly before identifying the flashed word correctly. Only response number 1 is scored as correct. If Emily hesitates ½ second or more before saying the flashed word, the examiner records an "h" for hesitation in the flash column and a check (✓) in the untimed column. Hesitations are counted as errors in the flash column because they do not indicate immediate recognition of the target word.

After administering a list of words, the examiner quickly adds up the number of words marked incorrect *in the flash column*. This includes words misread, no responses (0's), and hesitations (h's). If the total number of errors in the flash column is 10 or fewer (50%+ correct), the examiner administers the next list. If the total number of errors exceeds 10 (below 50% correct), the examiner can stop the test. Notice in Figure 2.1 that Emily made only six errors (flash presentation) on the first-grade list. Therefore the examiner administered the second-grade list. On this list, Emily made 12 errors (flash presentation), and the examiner stopped the test.

Scoring

Scoring a child's word recognition performance is quick and easy. Two scores (flash and untimed) are obtained for each list. To determine the *flash score*, which indicates automatic word recognition, the examiner (1) counts the number of errors in the flash column, (2) multiplies this number by 5 to obtain the percentage of error, and (3) subtracts the percentage of error from 100 to obtain the percentage correct. For example, on the first-grade list in Figure 2.1, Emily made six errors (four misreads, one no-response, and one hesitation). Therefore, 6 × 5 = 30; 100 − 30 = 70% correct.

To determine the *untimed score*, a cumulative score, the examiner starts with the percentage correct in the flash column and adds 5 points for each additional word identified in the untimed column. Referring again to the example in Figure 2.1, on the first-grade list Emily achieved a 70% flash recognition score and identified five additional words in the untimed condition. This produced an untimed score of 95% correct (70% + 25%).

Emily's scores on the word recognition tests are as follows:

Level	Flash (%)	Untimed (%)
Preprimer	95	100
Primer	90	100
First grade	70	95
Second grade	40	70

Keep in mind that scores in the flash column (indicating sight vocabulary) are a better predictor of contextual reading ability than are scores in the untimed column (indicating decoding skill). In interpreting Emily's *flash* recognition performance, we use the following criteria (see Stauffer et al., 1978):

- *90% or above* on a given list indicates *independent level*. The child has sufficient sight vocabulary at this level to read independently, that is, without teacher support.

- *70–85% on a given list indicates instructional level.* The child has sufficient sight vocabulary at this level to read successfully with teacher support.
- *Below 50% on a given list indicates frustration level.* The child does not have sufficient sight vocabulary at this level to read successfully.

(*Note*: Flash scores of 50–65% are in the "gray area" and are less reliable as predictors of contextual reading level.)

According to these criteria, Emily has adequate sight vocabulary to read at the late-first-grade level (flash = 70%) but not at the second-grade level (flash = 40%). This finding, of course, is only a prediction of Emily's true contextual reading level, but it is a prediction based on an important component of reading skill—that is, automatic word recognition.

A second way to analyze word recognition performance is to look at the amount of "pickup" or improvement between the flash and untimed scores on given lists. A substantial amount of improvement from the flash to the untimed score is an indicator that the child, given sufficient time, can decode words at that level of difficulty. Conversely, a negligible improvement may signal the child's lack of decoding skill at that level. Notice, in Figure 2.1, that Emily, on the untimed presentations, was able to identify five additional words on the late-first-grade list and six additional words on the second-grade list. This performance indicates decoding skill.

A third way to analyze a child's word recognition performance is to look at the types of errors he or she makes on individual words. With regard to Emily's flash recognition performance on the first- and second-grade lists (see Figure 2.1), a lack of vowel pattern knowledge seems to be the root cause of her errors (see "lag" for *leg*; "shoot" for *shout*; "brack" for *break*; "rich" for *rush*; "shot" for *shoot*; and "priz" for *prize*). On the positive side, note that she made very few errors that did not honor the beginning and ending consonants in words.

To sum up, the word recognition test, first and foremost, provides a measure of the child's word recognition *power*—his or her ability to recognize words immediately on lists that are graded in difficulty. These flash (or power) scores are valid predictors of contextual reading level (Frye, 2007). In addition, the word recognition test provides a measure of the child's decoding skill and information on the nature of his or her word recognition errors.

Before ending this section on word recognition assessment, a note of caution is in order. Learning to "flash" a list of words to a child—and to score responses quickly as one goes along—is not the easiest of tasks to master. There is a subtle coordination involved in the flash technique that can only be picked up through practice and more practice. Probably the best way to learn the technique is to observe it being modeled by an experienced reading teacher, to practice on your own, and then to get feedback from the reading teacher regarding your proficiency. Fortunately, once the motor routine of crisply flashing the words is mastered, the skill is not lost over time. It cannot be overstressed how important an assessment procedure this is to the tutor or teacher who works with struggling readers.

ASSESSING CONTEXTUAL READING
(ORAL AND SILENT)

Rationale

Over the years, several of my graduate students (experienced teachers all) have commented that it was in analyzing children's oral reading performance that they first gained insight into—and became curious about—the reading process. This is not surprising. A careful record of a child's oral reading is the best "window" we can have into the developing reading process. For example, does a third-grade girl read the words in the text with adequate accuracy (e.g., 95%)? Does her reading show rhythm or cadence? On meeting new words, does she rely more on contextual cues or letter–sound cues? Does she self-correct errors that disrupt the meaning of the text? Does she take risks or instead depend on teacher assistance when she is in doubt? These and other questions can be answered by analyzing the child's oral reading.

In the following sections, I describe how to administer and score an oral reading assessment in which the student reads aloud a series of graded passages (easy to hard) and answers a few questions after each passage has been read. Scoring provides measures of the student's oral reading *accuracy, rate,* and *comprehension* at various levels of passage difficulty (e.g., first, second, third, and fourth grade). After discussing oral reading assessment in some detail, I briefly explain how the procedures can be modified to assess silent reading.

Test Instrument

An informal reading inventory (IRI) is a series of graded passages (each 100–250 words in length) that is used to assess reading ability. The assessment concept is simple. The examiner starts the student with an easy passage and then proceeds to administer progressively more challenging passages, until the reader becomes frustrated, at which point the testing is stopped. The highest passage level that the student can read without becoming frustrated is designated the "instructional level."

There are more than a dozen commercial informal reading inventories in print today (e.g., Roe & Burns, 2007; Leslie & Caldwell, 2005; Woods & Moe, 2007), some of these having been around for over 20 years. In my estimation, there are only two important criteria for selecting a given IRI for use. First, the passages in the inventory need to be accurate in reflecting grade-level difficulty (e.g., the first-grade passage should be of first-grade difficulty, the second-grade passage should be of second-grade difficulty, and so on). This accuracy in level produces a valid hierarchy of passages in which a lower passage (e.g., second grade) is easier to read than a higher one (third grade). Second, the passages in an IRI should be interesting to the children who read them. A valid assessment of a child's reading ability can only be made when that child is actively trying to read and understand a text. But a child will read actively (with concentration) only if he or she is interested in the passages being read. Thus, the content quality of the IRI passages is very important.

Other characteristics of published IRIs, such as scoring procedures, comprehension questions, and the author's theoretical orientation, are less important. After all, the IRI, a set of graded passages, is an *informal* assessment instrument, and its administration can be modified if an examiner sees fit (e.g., choosing to use a different introductory statement; deleting or adding a comprehension question; or deciding to score self-corrections as a word-reading error when the IRI manual counsels against this).

Thirty years ago I began to use the Analytical Reading Inventory (Woods & Moe, 1977) in my reading clinic. The psychometric data (reliability and validity) in the manual seemed sound and, by testing students, I quickly confirmed that the passages were leveled appropriately. Still, the major reason I initially chose to use the Woods and Moe inventory was the content of the reading passages. Intuitively, I felt that the realistic fiction and short biographies that comprised the inventory's passages would be appealing to elementary and middle school readers. Over the years, this has proven to be the case.

Whether a teacher chooses to use the Analytical Reading Inventory or some other published IRI, there are advantages to sticking with one diagnostic instrument. By using only one inventory, the diagnostician becomes familiar with its reading passages. In fact, over time, the passages become a reliable tool—a "trusted old friend," if you will—with which to evaluate variation in student performance. For example, once you have listened to 20 third-grade children read the third- and fourth-grade passages in *your* IRI, you will begin to build a norm set in your head. That is, you will begin to form an idea of what constitutes average, below-average, and above-average performance on these passages. Such "in-the-head" norms are best established by consistently using the same measuring tool, whether it be a graded series of word recognition lists or a graded series of reading passages.

In the following pages I refer to passages from the Analytical Reading Inventory (Woods & Moe, 2007) in describing how to administer an oral reading assessment. However, keep in mind that these directions for administration and scoring can be applied to any set of graded reading passages—to any IRI that the teacher may choose to use.

Administration

With eight oral reading passages (first grade through eighth grade), the examiner needs to know at which level to begin the assessment. Here is where the previously administered isolated word recognition assessment comes in handy. We begin the oral reading at the highest grade level where the student scored 80% or better on *flash*-word recognition. For example, suppose a fifth-grade boy (James) achieved the following scores on the word recognition test:

	Flash (%)	Untimed (%)
Preprimer	100	—
Primer	100	—
First grade	95	100
Second grade	95	100
Third grade	85	95
Fourth grade	70	90
Fifth grade	30	70

The highest level where James scored 80% on flash word recognition was third grade; therefore, we begin the oral reading assessment at this level. The idea is that if the child can immediately recognize 80% (or more) of the words on a third-grade list, he or she should be able to read a third-grade passage with ease. Note that such a decision allows the examiner to skip the first- and second-grade oral passages, thereby saving valuable administration time.

Prior to the oral reading, the examiner explains to James that his task is to read aloud a few passages and answer some questions about their content. The examiner also mentions that the oral reading will be tape-recorded so that she can go back later and listen to James's oral reading. (In fact, the tape recorder is turned on at this point and remains on throughout the oral reading assessment.) Next, the examiner provides a brief introduction to the first passage ("This is a story about a boy and a neighborhood club.") and signals James to begin reading.

As James begins to read the 149-word, third-grade passage, the examiner clicks on a stopwatch to mark the starting time. Then the examiner follows along on her own copy as James reads orally. She attempts to record the child's reading errors as he reads, but realizes that she has the tape recorder as a backup. If James comes to a word and pauses, the examiner allows 3 seconds before providing the word. When the last word has been read, the examiner clicks off the stopwatch and records the time, closes the child's reading booklet, and proceeds to ask several comprehension questions pertaining to the passage just read. (*Note:* The tape recorder remains on during the question-asking.)

At this point, the examiner has to decide whether to move forward to the next oral reading passage—fourth grade, in this case. Because James achieved a third-grade flash word recognition score of 85% (indicating a strong sight vocabulary at this level), chances are he read the third-grade passage with ease and therefore can move on to the fourth-grade passage. However, if James did experience undue difficulty in reading the third-grade passage, the examiner would then reverse course and administer the second-grade oral passage. The point is that after each oral reading passage, the examiner must make a judgment as to whether the child was reading adequately or was frustrated, in which case the oral reading is discontinued. Signs of frustration may include a significant increase in word-reading errors, a decrease in reading rate, and an increase in the need for examiner assistance in pronouncing words. But, we are getting ahead of the game. The next section provides more about how to score and interpret oral reading performance.

Scoring

In describing how to score the oral reading sample, I first discuss the issue of *coding* or transcribing the child's oral reading, and then move to *interpreting* the coded sample. Regarding materials, the examiner needs a scoresheet (an examiner's copy of the reading passage and accompanying questions), two pencils (one regular, one colored), a pocket calculator, and the aforementioned tape recorder and stopwatch.

Oral Reading Accuracy

The coding system (see Figure 2.2) is traditional and straightforward, with five types of oral reading errors to be marked. In this system, repetitions are marked by underlining the repeated word or phase (the boy was), but repetitions are not counted as errors. Self-corrections *are* counted as errors, because they indicate an

---

1. **Substitutions:** Write the substituted or mispronounced word over the word in the text.

saw

(the   boy   was)

2. **Omissions:** Circle the omitted word.

(the (big) boy)

3. **Insertions:** Use a caret to indicate the inserted word(s).

big

(the   red   ball)

^

4. **Self-corrections:** Place a check (✓) next to the marked error to indicate that the child has self-corrected. (A self-correction is usually a substitution error that the child spontaneously corrects.)

saw ✓

(the   boy   was)

5. **Examiner help:** Place an "H" above each word that has to be provided by the examiner. The examiner should refrain from providing help unless it is clearly necessary to do so—that is, unless the child refuses to attempt the unknown word or is noticeably unsuccessful in decoding it. (Wait 3 seconds before providing help.)

H

(the   boy   was)

FIGURE 2.2. Coding system for oral reading errors.

initial misreading of text and cost the reader in momentum or fluency (see Stauffer et al., 1978; Barr et al., 2002).

Figure 2.3 shows the coding of our fifth grader James's reading of a fourth-grade passage. Note that James made 7 errors—a mixture of 4 substitutions, 2 insertions, and 1 examiner help.

Having established a system for coding oral reading, let us now address the scoring and interpretation of a coded sample. The first score to obtain is the *oral reading score*—that is, the percentage of words read accurately in a passage (100% minus the % of reading error). To compute this score, we must know the *error quotient*: how much to take off for each oral reading error. This number is usually listed on the examiner's score sheet. However, to determine the error quotient for any passage, we can use the following formula:

Error quotient = 100 ÷ number of words in passage

There were 153 words in the fourth-grade passage read by James; 100 ÷ 153 yields an error quotient of .65.

Knowing the error quotient and the number of errors that James made, we can now compute his *oral reading score* or percentage of words read correctly:

Number of errors (7) × error quotient (.65) = error percentage (4.6, rounded to 5.0)
100% − error (5%) = oral reading score (95%)

The question confronting us now is: How is an oral reading score of 95% to be interpreted? Traditional performance criteria, handed down over the years, can be of help here (see Bond & Tinker, 1973; Johnson et al., 1987; Barr et al., 2002):

- *98% or above* on a given passage indicates *independent level*. The child shows sufficient oral reading accuracy to read independently, that is, without teacher support.
- *95–97%* on a given passage indicates *instructional level*. The child shows sufficient oral reading accuracy to read successfully with teacher support.
- *Below 90%* on a given passage indicates *frustration level*. The child's low oral reading accuracy indicates that he or she is overchallenged by text at this level of difficulty.

Note that just as there was a gray or borderline area for flash word recognition (50–65%), there is also a gray area for oral reading accuracy (90–94%).

What are the implications of these functional reading levels? First, if children misread only 1 or 2 words out of 100 in running text, they should be able to read the material independently. Second, if they misread 3–5 words out of 100 (instructional level), they still are in control of the process and, with a little teacher guidance, should be able to comprehend what they read. Moreover, this is the optimal

Fourth-Grade Passage (153 words)

(Introduction: Read this passage to find out why a young girl is worried.)

Jody was so worried that she had stayed in the barn all day to take care of her sick horse, Gabe. She thought his condition seemed to be growing worse. His breathing grew louder and harder.

That
At nightfall, Jody brought a blanket from the house so she could sleep near her beloved animal. In the middle of the night the wind whipped around the barn, rattling ~~the~~ windows, off splitters ✓ and the barn door shook as if it would break into splinters. She had been so exhausted that she slept through all the noise.

When the dawn light poured through the windows, Jody stirred. Bits of straw stuck in her hair and onto her wrinkled clothes. Where was the sound of the sickly breathing? She sat up with a jolt! Then she saw Gabe, healthy and strong, standing by the open door. To her surprise it looked like he was saying, "Let's go for a run."

Error quotient = .65	Total number of errors	__7__
	Meaning change errors	__2__
	Oral reading score	__95__ %
	Comprehension score	__75__ %
	Reading rate	__112__ wpm

FIGURE 2.3. James's oral reading of a fourth-grade passage. This passage is taken from the Analytical Reading Inventory, Form 4C (Woods & Moe, 2007).

level for learning new words because a printed word's "newness" (in terms of structure or meaning) is actually highlighted by the 95%+ of known words that surround it in the text. Finally, if children misread 11 or more words out of 100 in running text, they tend to become frustrated. This is understandable, for if a child misreads or hesitates on almost one printed word per line, he or she is reduced to "translating" the text, that is, overrelying on context to identify words. Reading rate slows, attention is diverted from comprehension, and visible signs of confusion and frustration often appear. Providing reading instruction at this level (below 90% oral reading accuracy) can be counterproductive.

On the fourth-grade passage, James's oral reading score of 95% is at the low end of instructional level. Before moving on, let us briefly examine two aspects of his oral reading errors: (1) how closely each error matches up orthographically with the text word, and (2) whether or not the individual errors disrupt the meaning of the text.

James made four substitution errors in reading the fourth-grade passage:

Text word	Substitution
At	That
splinters	splitters (self-corrected)
onto	on
healthy	heathing

From these errors, it is apparent that he is attending closely to the letter sounds within words that he misreads.

To determine whether James's oral reading errors disrupted meaning, we can go back and rescore the passage for *meaning change* errors. To do so, the examiner simply rereads the passage, stopping at each of James's errors to determine if it changed the meaning of the text. (*Note*: Examiner helps are scored as meaning-change errors; self-corrections are not.) In Figure 2.3, the meaning-change errors are shaded in gray (in everyday practice, the examiner should circle meaning-change errors with a colored pencil). Note that on this fourth-grade passage, only two of James's seven oral reading errors disrupted meaning (the examiner help on *jolt*, and the substitution of "heathing" for *healthy*). James's fourth-grade oral reading score of 95%, along with only two meaning-change errors, indicates a possible instructional level; however, keep in mind that we have not yet factored reading rate and comprehension into the equation.

Now let us see how James fared at the fifth-grade level. On the 171-word fifth-grade passage (error quotient = .58), he made 16 errors (see Figure 2.4). To compute his oral reading score, we use the aforementioned method:

Number of errors (16) × error quotient (.58) = error percentage (9.3, rounded to 9.0)
100% − error (9%) = oral reading score (91%)

Note that James misread nearly 1 out of every 10 words on the fifth-grade passage,

Fifth-Grade Passage (171 words)

(Introduction: This passage tells about a bicycle race.)

"Look out," Sheila Young thought as she saw her challenger's bicycle come too close.
                                          fall
"Watch out or you will foul me!"

At that moment, a horrifying thing happened as (she) was bumped by another racer at
                                                    skinned
forty miles an hour. Sheila's bicycle crashed, and she skidded on the surface of the track.
                  and
From the wreck she received a nine-inch gash on her head.
                                                against
      The judges ruled that the race should be run again (since) a foul had been made.
      wouldn't ✓   wind ✓   made ✓
Sheila would not have enough time to get her wound stitched; still, she didn't want to quit
                                                            stample
the race because she could only think of winning. "Just staple the cut together and ban-

dage it," she told the doctor. "I want to win this race."

      The doctor did as Sheila asked, and as (she) stood in silence while being treated, tears
                      inspence
rolled down her face from the intense pain. Then, with a blood-stained bandage on her
 thrōbing   a   H
throbbing head, she pushed on to amaze the crowd with a sensational victory and(a)gold

medal.

Error quotient = .58   Total number of errors _____16_____

                               Meaning change errors _____8_____

                               Oral reading score _____91_____%

                               Comprehension score _____50_____%

                               Reading rate _____88_____wpm

FIGURE 2.4. James's oral reading of a fifth-grade passage. This passage is taken from the *Analytical Reading Inventory*, Form 5A (Woods & Moe, 2007).

attaining an oral reading score of 91%. To interpret this "gray area" score—that is, to declare it either instructional level or frustration level—we need more information.

Again, in analyzing James's errors, we can look at the orthographic match between error and text word and also at the meaning-preserving nature (or not) of each error. On the fifth-grade passage, James made 11 substitution errors, 3 of which he self-corrected (sc).

Text word	Substitution
foul	fall
skidded	skinned
she	and
again	against
would	wouldn't (sc)
wound	wind (sc)
didn't	made (sc)
staple	stample
intense	inspense
throbbing	thrōbing
the	a

With the exception of two high-frequency words (*she* and *the*), almost all of James's substitutions bore a close letter–sound relationship to the text word. He definitely was attending to letter features in the words he misread.

With regard to preserving meaning, 8 of James's 16 oral reading errors (see shaded words in Figure 2.4) were meaning-change errors (e.g., "fall" for *foul*; "skinned" for *skidded*; "against" for *again*). It is true that meaning-change determinations are not always clear-cut. For example, one might question in Figure 2.4 whether "skinned" (instead of *skidded*) *on the surface of the track* should be counted as a meaning-change error, or whether the adjacent errors in line 6 (substitution of "against" for *again*; omission of *since*) should be counted as one or two meaning-change errors. Nevertheless, it is important to obtain an estimate of the number of serious or meaning-costing errors the reader makes on a given passage. In the present case, James's 8 meaning-change errors on the 171-word, fifth-grade passage are a cause for concern. Note that on the fourth-grade passage (Figure 2.3), he made only 2 meaning-change errors.

Fourth grade	7 errors	2 meaning changes
Fifth grade	16 errors	8 meaning changes

Based on this fifth grader's oral reading scores, we might tentatively designate fourth grade as his instructional level (95% accuracy with 2 meaning-change errors) and fifth grade as his frustration level (91% accuracy with 8 meaning-change errors). Still, we need to look at James's reading rates and comprehension on the fourth- and fifth-grade passages before making a final decision about functional reading levels.

Reading Rate

The rate or speed at which the child reads an IRI passage is a very important measure. Rate, measured in words read per minute (wpm), is a reliable proxy for oral reading fluency when a child (e.g., James) is reading a passage, expecting to be questioned about its content. An adequate reading rate usually means that the child is processing text in phrases or clauses (as opposed to word by word), which frees up mental resources for comprehension. Conversely, a slow reading rate indicates a disruption in fluent reading that may be due to word-level decoding problems or an inability to chunk words into appropriate phrases. (*Note*: In addition to recording reading rate, some examiners may want to assign a *fluency rating* [e.g., below-average, average, or above-average] to the child's reading of each passage. An experienced examiner can make such a fluency rating as he or she is scoring the oral reading passage. On the other hand, a neophyte examiner should score the passage for errors first and then listen to the passage again to assign the fluency rating.)

Fortunately, accurate measures of reading rate are easy to obtain. The first step is to record, with a stopwatch, the amount of time (number of seconds) the child needs to read each passage. The second step, usually performed after the entire IRI has been administered, is to compute the child's reading rates for the passages read using the following formula:

$$\text{Reading rate (wpm)} = \frac{60 \times \text{No. of words in passage}}{\text{No. of seconds needed to read passage}}$$

To illustrate, James read the fourth-grade oral passage (153 words) in 82 seconds. (*Note*: The number of words in the passage is usually found at the top of the passage score sheet.) Therefore, James's fourth-grade oral reading rate is:

$$\frac{60 \times 153 \text{ (words)}}{82 \text{ (seconds)}} = 112 \text{ wpm}$$

On average, reading rates vary across grade levels; that is, third graders read faster than second graders but slower than fourth and fifth graders. To determine the adequacy of James's fourth-grade oral rate of 112 wpm, we can refer to Table 2.1, which shows expected oral and silent reading rates by grade level.

Notice that James's oral rate of 112 wpm falls within the fourth-grade range of 110–150 wpm. This finding, together with the fact that he read the fourth-grade passage with 95% accuracy, indicates that he has adequate print-processing skill at the fourth-grade level.

Now, let us look briefly at fifth grade, where James achieved a borderline oral reading score of 91%. James read the 171-word fifth-grade passage in 116 seconds. Thus, his fifth-grade oral rate is 88 wpm (60 × 171 words ÷ 116 seconds = 88 wpm). When we check the grade-level averages in Table 2.1, we find that 88 wpm at fifth grade is considerably below the fifth-grade interval of 125–155 wpm. Therefore, James's relatively slow reading rate at fifth grade, coupled with his borderline oral reading accuracy and eight meaning-change errors, raises questions about his ability to read successfully at this level.

Thus far, James's oral reading accuracy and rate scores point to a fourth-grade instructional level and a fifth-grade frustration level. Next, we need to examine his comprehension on these oral reading passages.

Comprehension

The comprehension score is based on the child's ability to answer questions about a passage he or she has just read. For example, after James has read aloud the fourth-grade passage (see Figure 2.4) and closed the reading folder, the examiner asks him six comprehension questions. These questions, along with suggested answers, are listed on the passage score sheet (see Figure 2.5). Keep in mind that we should not expect the child's responses to match the "suggested" answers word for word.

In fact, the examiner should anticipate three types of answers from James. *First,* the child may answer the question correctly, matching or paraphrasing the suggested answer. In this case, the examiner puts a check (✓) by the question number or records

TABLE 2.1. Average End-of-Year Reading Rate Ranges (Oral and Silent) for Grades 1 through 8

Grade	Oral rates (wpm)[a]	Silent rates (wpm)[b]
First	45–85	50–90
Second	80–120	95–145
Third	95–135	120–170
Fourth	110–150	135–185
Fifth	125–155	150–200
Sixth	135–160	160–210
Seventh	145–160	170–220
Eighth	145–160	180–230

[a]Oral reading rate ranges are derived from the average oral rates reported by Hasbrouck and Tindall (2006) and Bloodgood and Kucan (2005).

[b]Silent reading rate ranges are derived from the average silent rates reported by Taylor (in Carver, 1990) and Bloodgood and Kucan (2005).

✓1. Who are the characters in this story? (Jody and her horse, Gabe)
   Jody and her horse

✓2. Why was Jody worried? (Gabe was very sick; the horse had a hard time breathing)
   her horse was very sick

✓3. What did Jody decide to do (spend the night in the barn with, or sleep with, her horse)
   sleep in the barn with the horse

④. What does <u>condition</u> mean in this sentence: "His condition seemed to be growing worse?" (his health; how the horse feels)
   Don't know

½ 5. What happened in the middle of the night? (a big wind rattled the windows <u>or</u> shook the barn door [need 1 of 2])
   barn door shook (Probe) No response

✓6. What did Jody discover when she woke up? (Gabe was feeling better)
   the horse was feeling better

FIGURE 2.5. James's answers to comprehension questions on the fourth-grade (oral) passage (see Figure 2.3).

nothing. *Second*, James may provide an obviously incorrect answer or say "I don't know" (see question 4 in Figure 2.5). The examiner scores an incorrect answer by circling the number of the question. *Third*, James may provide a partially correct answer (see question 5 in Figure 2.5). In such a case, the examiner should probe the answer, seeking more information from the child. Probes should be neutral; they should not lead the child to the correct answer—for example, "Can you tell me a little more?" or "Can you say that a different way?" Sometimes just repeating the question is an effective probe. In the present example (question 5), the examiner probed, "James, what made the barn door shake?" If the child improves his or her answer following the probe, full credit is awarded. If he or she fails to improve the initial answer, half credit is awarded and the examiner writes ½ by the question number.

After reading the fourth-grade passage, James answered 4.5 of the 6 comprehension questions correctly, giving him a comprehension score of 75%. (*Note:* With 6 questions, 16.6% is taken off for each incorrect answer: 100 ÷ 6 = 16.6.) Traditional criteria for interpreting comprehension scores are as follows:

- *90–100%* on a given passage equals *independent level.*
- *75–89%* on a given passage equals *instructional level.*
- *50% and below* on a given passage equals *frustration level.*

The gray or borderline area for comprehension is thus between 51 and 74%.
James's fourth-grade comprehension score of 75% is at the low end of instruc-

tional level. The score is consistent with James's oral reading accuracy (95%) and reading rate (112 wpm) scores at fourth grade, which were also at instructional level. On the fifth-grade oral reading passage, James could answer only three of the six comprehension questions correctly, attaining a frustration-level score of 50%. Again, this score was consistent with his borderline oral reading accuracy (91%) and low reading rate (88 wpm) on the fifth-grade passage.

	Accuracy (%)	Comprehension (%)	Rate (wpm)
Fourth grade	95	75	112
Fifth grade	91	50	88

Before leaving comprehension assessment, two points deserve mention. First, the decision to use six questions for each passage (third through eighth grade) is arbitrary. In fact, I suggest using only five questions on the shorter first- and second-grade passages. Nonetheless, I have generally found it difficult to come up with more than six good, context-dependent questions for IRI passages that run from 150 to 300 words in length. Second, it must be acknowledged that comprehension, when compared to oral reading accuracy and rate, is a less reliable measure. Children's initial responses to questions can be vague or imprecise, making them difficult to score. In such cases, the examiner must probe in a neutral manner and use commonsense judgment in awarding full, partial, or no credit for a given answer.

Assessing Silent Reading

We have seen that an oral reading assessment can provide rich, multifaceted information about the reading process (e.g., measures of word recognition in context, reading rate, and comprehension). However, we also want to examine children's silent reading, particularly in relation to their oral reading ability and grade level. For beginning readers, oral and silent reading are similar processes; for example, silent reading by first graders often amounts to mumbling the individual words. By the middle of second grade, however, many children begin to read faster in the silent mode, for now they can "read with their eyes" and do not have to pronounce each word. By fourth grade, most reading—in and out of school—is done silently; children at this stage prefer silent to oral reading because they can process text faster and concentrate more fully on comprehension when reading silently.

Administration

The examiner explains to the child that he or she will be reading some passages silently and answering some questions about their content. The child is encouraged to read at his or her normal speed. As in the oral reading assessment, the examiner provides a brief introduction to each passage (e.g., "This passage tells about a bicy-cle race.") before the child begins to read.

To identify a starting point, the examiner (1) determines the *highest* passage level where the child performed an acceptable (instructional-level) oral reading, and then (2) drops back one level to begin the silent reading. In the following example, James successfully read the second-grade through fourth-grade oral passages before becoming frustrated on the fifth-grade passage. Therefore, the examiner dropped back one level from fourth grade to begin the silent reading at third grade. Notice that this move allows the examiner to omit the second-grade passage in silent read-ing. If the child is successful in reading the third-grade passage silently—that is, with adequate comprehension and rate—the examiner moves on to higher passages (fourth, fifth) until the reader evidences frustration. If, on the other hand, the child is unsuccessful on the third-grade silent passage, the examiner goes back and ad-ministers the second-grade silent passage.

Oral reading passages			Silent reading passages
Second grade	✓		
Third grade	✓	→	*Start*
Fourth grade	✓		
Fifth grade	✗		

Testing of silent reading is discontinued when the child's comprehension score falls to 50% or below on a given passage. Some children, particularly when facing a difficult passage, rush through the silent reading, obtaining unreasonably high read-ing rates and usually poor comprehension scores. For this reason, it is always pru-dent for the examiner to intermittently check children's concentration level as they read silently. (Do their lips move as they read? Do they use their finger to track the print? Does their demeanor indicate that they are attending to the task?)

Scoring

Silent reading *rate* is computed using the same formula that we used to compute oral reading rate:

$$\text{Reading rate (wpm)} = \frac{60 \times \text{No. of words in passage}}{\text{No. of seconds needed to read passage}}$$

Refer to Table 2.1 (p. 30) for expected silent reading rates by grade level.

Silent reading *comprehension* is computed in the same manner as oral reading comprehension. If there are six questions following the passage, take off 16.6% for each incorrect answer; if there are five questions (e.g., first- and second-grade pas-sages), take off 20% for each incorrect answer. When appropriate, partial or half credit can be awarded for specific answers. The same performance criteria are used for interpreting oral and silent comprehension scores: independent level = 90% or above; instructional level = 75–89%; frustration level = 50% or below.

Before moving on to the spelling assessment, let us summarize James's contextual reading performance (oral and silent) on the fourth- and fifth-grade passages:

	Oral reading			Silent reading	
	Acc. (%)	Comprehen. (%)	Rate (wpm)	Comprehen. (%)	Rate (wpm)
Fourth grade	95	75	112	83	120
Fifth grade	91	50	88	58	94

Based on our performance criteria, we can safely say that James has a fourth-grade reading instructional level and a fifth-grade frustration level. His low accuracy, comprehension, and rate scores at fifth grade support this diagnostic conclusion.

ASSESSING SPELLING

Rationale

One might question the inclusion of a spelling task in a battery designed to assess reading ability. However, there are good reasons for doing so. Spelling and word-reading ability are highly correlated. Morris and Perney (1984) reported a spelling–word recognition correlation of .82 in first grade, and Zutell and Rasinski (1989) found high correlations between the two abilities at third grade ($r = .70$) and fifth grade ($r = .74$). In explaining the relationship between reading and spelling, Henderson (1992) and Ehri (1998) argued that *an abstract, developing word knowledge underlies the ability to do both.* And Perfetti (1992, p. 170), always straightforward, put it this way: "There is a single [mental] representation that serves both reading and spelling. It does so throughout the course of development."

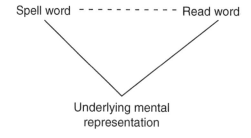

Spelling and reading may draw on the same underlying lexical representation, but they are not identical processes. Students can often read words (e.g., *cabbage, caught, slammed*) that they cannot spell correctly (e.g, CABBIG, COUGT, SLAMED) because correct spelling requires a complete, letter-by-letter representation of a given word. The following spelling assessment provides an important, alternative window into a student's underlying orthographic knowledge, and, like the word recognition assessment (see p. 14), it does so by using word lists that are graded in difficulty.

Test Instrument

The spelling test contains eight 12-word lists (see Appendix 2.2) that range in difficulty from first to eighth grade. The lists are derived from the Qualitative Inventory of Word Knowledge, an eight-level spelling inventory developed by Robert Schlagal (1989, 2007) at the University of Virginia. Schlagal had two aims in developing his spelling inventory; first, to account for word frequency at a given grade level, and second, to account for specific spelling features (patterns) that need to be learned at that grade level. Thus, the second-grade spelling list contains words that occur frequently in the reading and writing of second graders (e.g., *train, thick, cloud, stuff*). In addition, the list words include representative spelling features that second-grade students need to master (e.g., beginning consonant blends [*tr-, st-*]; short- and long-vowel patterns [*-ick, -ess, -ase, -een*]; final consonant digraphs [*-ck, -ff*]).

Looking at the spelling lists in Appendix 2.2, we see that the list words increase in difficulty across the grade levels. First-grade words are mostly one syllable (e.g., *trap, wish, drive*) and assess knowledge of beginning consonant blends and short- and long-vowel patterns. Third-grade words are one and two syllables in length and sample knowledge of less frequent consonant clusters (e.g., *scream, knock*) and vowel patterns (e.g., *noise, caught, thirsty*). And fifth-grade words, all multisyllable, pose a variety of spelling challenges (e.g., *explosion, measure, settlement, honorable*). As with the word recognition lists, the graded nature of the spelling lists gives them their diagnostic power. The further a child can progress through the eight spelling lists (achieving a score of 50% correct or better), the more advanced his or her word knowledge. And interestingly, on a given list there is a relationship between the percentage of words the child spells correctly and the nature of his or her spelling errors.

Administration

Even with an older child, such as our fifth-grader, James, it is wise to begin the spelling test with the first-grade list. It takes little time to administer the 12-word lists, and a fifth-grade child's performance on the initial lists will reveal his or her knowledge of foundational short- and long-vowel patterns.

In administering a given list, the examiner pronounces each word clearly, uses it in a short sentence or phrase, and then repeats the word a final time (e.g., "Bed. I sleep in a bed. Bed."). The child should write the words with a pencil so that he or she can erase and make self-corrections if necessary. When the child finishes spelling the words on a list, the examiner picks up the paper and quickly checks the spellings. If the child misspells eight (or more) of the twelve words, the test is stopped. If he or she misspells seven (or fewer) words, the examiner moves on to the next list.

Scoring

After the entire spelling test is completed, the examiner scores each list in the following manner. Beside each incorrect spelling, the examiner writes the correct spelling in colored ink (see Figure 2.6). She then counts the number of misspellings and takes off 8.3% for each. (*Note:* 100 ÷ 12 words = 8.3.) James misspelled 3 words on the third-grade list: 3 × 8.3 = 25. If we subtract 25% from 100%, his power score or percentage correct on the third-grade list is 75%. The following criteria can be used to interpret spelling power scores (see Morris, Nelson, & Perney, 1986; Morris, Blanton, Blanton, Nowacek, & Perney, 1995):

- *90–100% on a given list equals independent level.*
- *50–89% on a given list equals instructional level.*
- *Below 40% on a given list equals frustration level.*

The gray or borderline area for spelling is between 40 and 49% correct.

Having established a power (or quantitative) score for each list James attempted, we can now go back and examine the *nature* of his spelling errors. (*Note:* Having the correct spelling written beside each error makes this very easy to do.) On the third-grade list, where James's power score was 75%, he misspelled three

Third grade (75%)		Fourth grade (50%)		Fifth grade (17%)	
1. ✓		1. poped	popped	1. exsplosin	explosion
2. ✓		2. plastick	plastic	2. justis	justice
3. ✓		3. ✓		3. copare	compare
4. ✓		4. ✓		4. sedlement	settlement
5. carful	careful	5. ✓		5. mesur	measure
6. chaseing	chasing	6. skiry	scurry	6. ✓	
7. ✓		7. ✓		7. neadle	needle
8. cought	caught	8. ✓		8. persurve	preserve
9. ✓		9. slamed	slammed	9. honnrble	honorable
10. ✓		10. cabbij	cabbage	10. lunner	lunar
11. ✓		11. ✓		11. oferd	offered
12. ✓		12. sunden	sudden	12. ✓	

FIGURE 2.6. James's performance on the third-, fourth-, and fifth-grade spelling lists.

words (see Figure 2.6). But notice that in each case, he misspelled the word by only one feature (CHASEING for *chasing*; CARFUL for *careful*; COUGHT for *caught*). On the fourth-grade list, where James's power score of 50% again fell within the instructional-level range, he made six errors. These, too, were generally off by only one feature (POPED for *popped*; PLASTICK for *plastic*; SLAMED for *slammed*), and, importantly, each of the six misspellings at fourth grade preserved the phonemic structure of the target word.

Now we come to the fifth-grade list, for which James spelled correctly only 2 of the 12 words, achieving a frustration-level score of 17%. At this frustration level, the nature of his spelling errors changed. Not only did he misspell some words by more than one feature (e.g., EXSPLOSIN for *explosion*; MESUR for *measure*; LUNNER for *lunar*), but he also began to omit letter sounds in his spellings (COPARE for *compare*; HONNRBLE for *honorable*)—something that he did not do on the previous four spelling lists. This tendency for quality of spelling errors to deteriorate when spelling power is low (in this case, 17%) has been documented in the research literature (Morris et al., 1986; Schlagal, 1989). For our purposes, this second "qualitative" look at James's spelling performance strengthens our confidence that he is instructional at fourth grade and frustrated at fifth grade.

This brings us to the end of a rather detailed description of how to administer and score the three assessment tasks: word recognition in isolation, contextual reading, and spelling. (*Note*: Appendix 2.3 provides a concise summary of this information that will be of considerable help to the novice diagnostician.) Before moving on, however, we need to consider briefly how the assessment battery can and should be adapted when working with beginning readers—that is, children who are unable, or are just beginning, to read independently.

ADAPTING THE ASSESSMENT
FOR BEGINNING READERS

A First-Grade Reading Battery

When assessing a child who reads at the first-grade level (preprimer to late first grade), we can use the same *word recognition* and *spelling* tests that were described earlier in this chapter. We begin the word recognition test with the preprimer list and the spelling test with the first-grade list. However, we should not expect a first-grade-level reader to progress very far on these assessments. For example, the child may be able to attain a 50% flash word recognition score on the preprimer list but not on the primer list. Similarly, he or she may spell correctly only 3 of the 12 words on the first-grade spelling list. But even if the examiner stops the word recognition test after two lists (preprimer and primer) and the spelling test after one list (first grade), the child will have had ample opportunity to demonstrate his or her knowledge of first-grade-level word patterns.

In assessing *contextual reading*, the situation is different. Most commercial IRIs include only two first-grade-level passages: primer and late first grade. Moreover, these passages are usually very short, uninteresting, and devoid of pictures. I, therefore, suggest using excerpts from real books to assess first-grade-level readers. In school-based intervention programs, we have successfully used passages from the four books shown in Figure 2.7 to establish where a child reads along a continuum of first-grade reading ability (e.g., emergent to late first grade). In interpreting the child's performance on these passages, minimal instructional-level scores are 90% for oral reading accuracy and 45 wpm for rate (rate applies only to the late-first-grade passage). The examiner can make up four comprehension questions for the primer and 1-2 passages (questions are not needed for the emergent and preprimer passages), or he or she can use the questions provided in *The Howard Street Tutoring Manual* (Morris, 2005a).

In administering the first-grade reading battery, the examiner discontinues the word recognition task when the child falls below 50% correct on the flash presentation of a given list. He or she discontinues the spelling task when the child misspells 8 or more words (out of 12) on a given list. And the examiner discontinues the passage reading when the child's oral reading accuracy falls below 90%. If a beginning reader does happen to read the late-first-grade passage with adequate accuracy and rate, then the examiner should administer the second-grade passage from the IRI (see p. 20).

Assessing the Emergent Reader

If a young child shows little or no reading ability (e.g., is unable to finger-point read even the emergent reading passage), the examiner can still obtain valuable information from the child's performance on the *word recognition* and *spelling* tasks. For example, on the preprimer word recognition list, did the child recognize any of the words? Did his or her word recognition attempts show attention to beginning and ending consonants (e.g., "my" for *me*; "p-" for *play*; "bag" for *big*)? On the first-

---

Emergent passage (42 words): Entire text of *Look at Me* (1996). Rigby's *PM Starters One*. (*Note*: On this passage only, the teacher and child echo-read the first page [page 2] before the child begins to finger-point read independently on page 4. The page 2 echo reading is not scored.)

Preprimer passage (82 words): Pages 3–13 from Beverly Randell's *Baby Bear Goes Fishing* (1996). Rigby's *New PM Story Books*.

Primer passage (100 words): Pages 18–23 from Arnold Lobel's *Mouse Tales* (1972). Harper Trophy.

Late-first-grade passage (100 words): Pages 30–33 from Arnold Lobel's *Frog and Toad All Year* (1976). Harper Trophy.

FIGURE 2.7. Suggested passages in a first-grade reading assessment battery.

grade spelling list, did the child represent beginning or ending consonants (e.g., B in *bed* or JP in *drop*)? Was there any sign of vowel awareness in his or her spellings (e.g., SESDR for *sister*; BOP for *bump*)?

With an emergent reader, the examiner should also check *alphabet knowledge* by having the child name the alphabet letters (upper- and lowercase) as the examiner points to them in random order. The child should also be asked to the write the alphabet letters as the examiner calls them out in random order.

A four-task assessment of early word knowledge (alphabet, concept of word in text, phoneme awareness, and word recognition) can be found in Chapter 2 of *Every Child Reading* (Morris & Slavin, 2003). However, the informal measures mentioned above provide the same type of diagnostic information.

In this chapter I have described how to administer and score a diagnostic battery that includes word recognition, contextual reading, and spelling tasks. I also showed how the battery could be adapted when working with beginning readers. In the next chapter we consider the interpretation of test scores and, importantly, their implications for reading instruction.

Word Recognition Test
(Preprimer through Eighth-Grade Lists)

Preprimer	Primer	First grade	Second grade
1. and	1. back	1. leg	1. able
2. cat	2. eat	2. black	2. break
3. me	3. sun	3. smile	3. pull
4. is	4. bird	4. hurt	4. week
5. go	5. pat	5. dark	5. gate
6. play	6. saw	6. white	6. felt
7. where	7. feet	7. couldn't	7. north
8. like	8. lake	8. seen	8. rush
9. thing	9. hid	9. until	9. wrote
10. old	10. cut	10. because	10. perfect
11. your	11. about	11. men	11. change
12. up	12. one	12. winter	12. basket
13. said	13. rain	13. shout	13. shoot
14. big	14. water	14. glass	14. hospital
15. for	15. two	15. paint	15. spill
16. by	16. how	16. children	16. dug
17. dog	17. window	17. table	17. crayon
18. not	18. need	18. stand	18. third
19. who	19. that's	19. head	19. taken
20. here	20. mother	20. drove	20. prize

Third grade	Fourth grade	Fifth grade	Sixth grade
1. accept	1. average	1. labor	1. elevate
2. favor	2. hamster	2. cripple	2. conservation
3. seal	3. select	3. hasten	3. tenderness
4. buffalo	4. tobacco	4. frontier	4. barrier
5. slipper	5. brilliant	5. riverbed	5. adulthood
6. receive	6. liberty	6. settlement	6. kennel
7. legend	7. prance	7. absent	7. humiliated
8. haircut	8. solemn	8. dissolve	8. nonfiction
9. dresser	9. disease	9. plea	9. revive
10. icy	10. impress	10. surrender	10. wallet
11. customer	11. miracle	11. organization	11. depression
12. thread	12. wrestle	12. evidence	12. carvings
13. plop	13. coward	13. width	13. similarity
14. bandage	14. explode	14. rampaging	14. unanswered
15. further	15. opinion	15. horseshoe	15. fingernail
16. moat	16. suffer	16. grammar	16. breed
17. closet	17. vast	17. assorted	17. marrow
18. unroll	18. relationship	18. soybean	18. starter
19. storyteller	19. furnace	19. troublesome	19. pedestrian
20. yarn	20. clan	20. circumstance	20. quantity

Seventh grade

1. civic
2. shirttail
3. nominated
4. gruesome
5. disadvantage
6. architecture
7. tonic
8. straightforward
9. warrant
10. unthinkable
11. ridicule
12. engulf
13. kindhearted
14. maturity
15. impassable
16. bolster
17. copyright
18. foliage
19. prune
20. persecution

Eighth grade

1. administration
2. federation
3. militia
4. shambles
5. bankrupt
6. goldenrod
7. perishable
8. toddler
9. cavernous
10. imperative
11. notorious
12. subconscious
13. corps
14. laborious
15. rivet
16. unimaginable
17. dizzily
18. irritability
19. puncture
20. wholehearted

Spelling Test
(First-Grade through Eighth-Grade Lists)

First grade	Second grade	Third grade	Fourth Grade
trap	train	scream	popped
bed	thick	noise	plastic
when	chase	stepping	cable
wish	trapped	count	gazed
sister	dress	careful	cozy
girl	queen	chasing	scurry
drop	cloud	batter	preparing
bump	short	caught	stared
drive	year	thirsty	slammed
plane	shopping	trust	cabbage
ship	cool	knock	gravel
bike	stuff	send	sudden

Fifth grade	Sixth grade	Seventh grade	Eighth grade
explosion	mental	succeed	permissible
justice	commotion	patience	assumption
compare	declaration	confident	warrant
settlement	musician	necessary	probable
measure	dredge	irresponsible	respiration
suffering	violence	aluminum	olympic
needle	wreckage	subscription	gaseous
preserve	decision	exhibition	subtle
honorable	impolite	regretted	overrate
lunar	acknowledge	correspond	insistent
offered	conceive	emphasize	snorkel
normal	introduction	flexible	prosperous

Abbreviated Instructions for Administering, Scoring, and Interpreting the Word Recognition, Passage Reading, and Spelling Tests

Word Recognition Test

1. *Start.* Start the test at the preprimer level.
2. *Administration.* Flash each word for approximately ¼ second. If student's response is correct, proceed to next word in the list. If the flash response is incorrect, expose the word for an untimed response. Then proceed to the next word.
3. *Recording responses.* Mark the score sheet *only when an error is made.* If the student misreads a word on the flash or untimed presentation, write his or her response in the appropriate column. If the student does not respond to a word, write *0* in the appropriate column. If the student hesitates ½ second or more in responding to a flashed word, write *h* in the flash column and put a ✓ in the untimed column. The following example shows three incorrect responses in the flash column and 2 incorrect responses in the untimed column.

	Flash	Untimed
1. accept	0	assēt
2. favor	flavor	0
3. seal		
4. buffalo	h	✓
5. slipper		

4. *Stop.* Stop the test when the student's *flash score* on a given list falls below 50%.
5. *Scoring.* In scoring the test, start with the flash column. Take off 5% for each error in the flash column and subtract the total from 100. For example, if the student makes 6 errors in the flash column, his flash score is 70% (6 × 5% = 30%; 100% − 30% = 70%).

   The untimed score is a cumulative score. Start with the flash score and add 5% for each correct response (✓) in the untimed column. In the preceding example, the student's flash score was 70%; if he read 3 additional words correctly in the untimed column (3 × 5% = 15%), his untimed score would be 85%.

6. *Interpretation.* A score of 70% or better in the flash column indicates that the student has sufficient sight vocabulary to read at that level.

Passage Reading Inventory

The oral reading passages are administered first, followed by the silent reading passages.

1. *Start.* Begin the oral reading passages at the highest level at which the student achieved an 80% (or better) score on flash word recognition. In the following example, oral reading would begin at the second-grade level.

	Flash		Oral reading
First grade	95%		
Second grade	80%	→	Start
Third grade	60%		

2. *Administration.* Before beginning, explain to the student that she will be reading aloud a few passages and answering some questions. Tell the child to read at her normal speed. Then turn on the tape recorder and leave it on throughout the oral reading testing. Remember to read to the child the brief introductory statements that precede each passage. Also, be sure to record (using a stopwatch) the number of seconds the child takes to read each passage.

3. *Recording responses.* As the student reads the oral passages, record her errors using the following marking system:

Type of error	Marking procedure	Example
Substitution	Write above	tree the train
Omission	Circle	in ⟨the⟩ water
Insertion	Use a caret and write in	little the puppy ^
Self-correction	Put a ✓ beside error	fin ✓ a fine day
Help from teacher	Write *H* above word	H impossible task

4. *Stop.* Stop the oral reading test when the child becomes frustrated. Signs of frustration include a marked increase in word recognition errors, an increase in meaning-change errors, a need for more teacher help, a significant decrease in rate or fluency, and behavioral signs of frustration.

5. *Scoring.* To obtain the *oral reading accuracy* score for a given passage, multiply the number of errors (e.g., 10) times the error quotient (e.g, .68) for an error percentage (6.8 or

7%). Then subtract this number from 100% to obtain the *oral reading score* (100% × 7% = 93%).

To obtain the *oral reading rate* (wpm), multiply 60 times the number of words in the passage and divide by the number of seconds the child took to read the passage (60 × No. of words ÷ No. of seconds).

To obtain the *oral reading comprehension* score, count the number of incorrect responses (e.g., 2) and multiply by 16.6%. Subtract this error percentage (33%) from 100% to obtain the comprehension score (67%). Because there are six questions at the end of most passages (third grade and above), the following chart of precalculated scores may be helpful:

No. of comprehension errors	Comprehension score
0.5	92%
1.0	83%
1.5	75%
2.0	67%
2.5	58%
3.0	50%
3.5	42%
4.0	33%
4.5	25%
5.0	17%
5.5	8%
6.0	0%

6. *Interpretation.* Oral reading yields three scores: word-reading accuracy, rate, and comprehension. In establishing an oral reading instructional level, all three scores must be considered (see performance criteria at the end of this appendix).

   The silent reading passages are administered following the oral reading passages. Start the silent reading *one level below* the highest level where the child was instructional (or comfortable) in oral reading. Proceed with the silent reading passages until the student scores below 50% on comprehension. Rate and comprehension scores for silent reading are computed in the same manner as was described for oral reading.

Spelling

1. *Start.* Start with the first-grade spelling list.
2. *Administration.* Pronounce each word clearly, use it in a sentence if appropriate, and then say the word again. After the child has spelled each 12-word list, pick up the paper and count the spelling errors. If the child misspells 8 or more of the 12 words, stop the test. If the child misspells 7 or fewer words, proceed to the next list.
3. *Scoring.* For each list, write the correct spelling beside each misspelled word (this will assist later qualitative analysis). Then multiply the number of errors (e.g., 3) times 8.3 and

subtract this error percentage (25%) from 100% to obtain the spelling score (75%). Again, the following chart may prove helpful.

No. of spelling errors	Spelling score
1	92%
2	83%
3	75%
4	67%
5	58%
6	50%
7	42%
8	33%
9	25%
10	17%
11	8%
12	0%

4. *Interpretation.* A score of at least 50% on a spelling list (e.g., fourth grade) indicates that the student has sufficient word knowledge to benefit from instruction at that level.

Performance Criteria

Word Recognition Test (%)

Independent: 90–100
Instructional: 70–89
Gray area: 50–69
Frustration: below 50

Passage Reading Test

	Oral reading accuracy (%)	Oral reading comprehension (%)*
Independent	98–100	90–100
Instructional	95–97	75–89
Gray area	90–94	50–74
Frustration	below 90	below 50

*Same performance criteria for silent reading comprehension.

Spelling Test (%)

Independent: 80–100
Instructional: 50–79
Gray area: 40–49
Frustration: below 40

Note: Gray area scores are borderline scores and require teacher judgment with regard to level setting.

Average End-of-Year Reading Rate Ranges (Grades 1 through 8)

Grade	Oral rates (wpm)	Silent rates (wpm)
First	45–85	50–90
Second	80–120	95–145
Third	95–135	120–170
Fourth	110–150	135–185
Fifth	125–155	150–200
Sixth	135–160	160–210
Seventh	145–160	170–220
Eighth	145–160	180–230

CHAPTER 3

Interpretation
of Reading Scores

In Chapter 2 we learned how to administer a diagnostic reading battery that included informal tests of word recognition, contextual reading, and spelling. In this chapter we learn how to interpret scores on these diagnostic tasks with the dual goal of establishing a reading instructional level for a student and identifying strengths and weaknesses in his or her reading performance. I begin with simple, straightforward cases to help the novice diagnostician "walk through" the interpretation process. As the chapter advances, I introduce more complex cases—ones that do not neatly fit a pattern and therefore require careful reasoning on the diagnostician's part. Finally, at the end of the chapter I briefly consider how to interpret the scores from the alternative reading assessment for first-grade-level readers (see pp. 37–38).

THE CASE SUMMARY SHEET

The case summary sheet (see Table 3.1; also Appendix 3.1) is a helpful tool that provides a record of the child's performance on the various diagnostic tasks—word recognition, contextual reading, and spelling. After the various tests have been administered (see Chapter 2), the examiner carefully transfers the child's scores to the appropriate cells of the summary sheet. With the scores from various tests on one chart, we are now in a position to examine the child's performance across grade or difficulty levels and thereby determine the level at which he or she should be instructed in reading (and spelling).

To make sense of the summary sheet scores, we need to apply performance criteria; for example, at third grade, what is an adequate or instructional-level score

TABLE 3.1. Case Summary Sheet 1 (*Thomas—Fourth Grade*)

Level	Word recognition		Oral reading			Silent reading		
	Flash	Untimed	Accuracy	Compre-hension	Rate (wpm)	Compre-hension	Rate (wpm)	Spelling
Preprimer	100	100						
Primer	95	100						
First grade	85	95						92
Second grade	80	90	98	100	105	100	115	67
Third grade	70	85	95	83	96	75	113	25
Fourth grade	30	65	87	67	81	50	87	

Note. Meaning-change errors: *third grade—2 of 7; fourth grade—7 of 19.*

for flash word recognition, for oral reading accuracy, for comprehension, and so on? These performance criteria, introduced in the previous chapter (see Appendix 2.3), are again summarized in Tables 3.2 and 3.3.

Before proceeding to an interpretation of the scores shown in Table 3.1, keep in mind that we can anticipate relationships among scores at a given grade or difficulty level. For example, a child's flash word recognition score at a given level should predict both his or her oral reading accuracy and reading rate at that level. A strong flash word recognition score at second grade (e.g., 80%) indicates a good sight vocabulary that should lead to accurate, fairly fluent reading of a second-grade passage. Conversely, a low flash word recognition score (e.g., 35%) would indicate that the child might struggle in reading a second-grade passage because of a deficit in sight vocabulary. Other anticipated relationships among the diagnostic measures include flash word recognition versus spelling (both are rigorous measures of orthographic knowledge), and reading rate versus comprehension (automatic print-processing allows the reader to focus attention on meaning). These hypothesized relationships between components of the reading process (word recognition, fluency, and comprehension) provide us with a starting point for interpreting or making sense of a child's performance on the diagnostic battery.

TABLE 3.2. Performance Criteria (Percentages) for Flash Word Recognition, Oral Reading Accuracy, Comprehension, and Spelling

	Word recognition (flash)	Oral reading accuracy	Comprehension	Spelling
Independent level	90–100%	98–100%	90–100%	90–100%
Instructional level	70–89%	95–97%	75–89%	50–89%
Frustration level	Below 50%	Below 90%	Below 50%	Below 40%

TABLE 3.3. Average End-of-Year Reading Rate Ganges (Grades 1–8)

Grade	Oral rates (wpm)	Silent rates (wpm)
First	45–85	50–90
Second	80–120	95–145
Third	95–135	120–170
Fourth	110–150	135–185
Fifth	125–155	150–200
Sixth	135–160	160–210
Seventh	145–160	170–220
Eighth	145–160	180–230

INTERPRETATION OF SCORES: SET 1 (EASY CASES)

Case 1 (Thomas—Fourth Grade)

I use Thomas's case (see Table 3.1) to introduce a *routine* for analyzing the scores on the case summary sheet. Beginning diagnosticians should find this routine helpful, although more experienced practitioners may find their own idiosyncratic routines to be more efficient. In other words, there is more than one way to approach the analytic task. Keep in mind that the main purpose of the summary sheet analysis is to determine the student's reading instructional level and, secondarily, to identify strengths and weaknesses in his or her reading profile.

Step 1: Establish a Tentative Reading Frustration Level

The analysis begins with the oral reading accuracy column. Moving down this column, we identify the first score *below* 90%—in this case, 87% at fourth grade. We hypothesize that Thomas is frustrated at fourth grade because his oral reading accuracy falls below 90% at this level. To check this hypothesis, we move next to the flash word recognition column, where we find that Thomas's fourth-grade flash score of 30% also falls in the frustration range. A deficient sight vocabulary is predictive of poor reading fluency. Therefore, we move next to the oral and silent rate columns, where the child's reading rates (81 and 87 wpm, respectively) are, in fact, well below the instructional-level rate minimums for fourth grade (110 wpm for oral and 135 wpm for silent). At this point, we have convergent evidence (oral reading accuracy, flash word recognition, and reading rate) that, in terms of print processing, Thomas is frustrated at the fourth-grade level.

Regarding comprehension, Thomas's fourth-grade scores (67% oral; 50% silent) reveal near-frustration-level performance. Moreover, 7 of his 19 oral reading errors on the fourth-grade passage changed the meaning of the text.

Step 2: Move Up the Chart to Establish a Reading Instructional Level

With fourth grade established as a frustration level, we move up to third grade to determine if this is Thomas's instructional level. (Note that conceivably third grade could also turn out to be a frustration level.) At third grade, we find an instructional-level oral reading accuracy score of 95% that is supported by instructional-level scores in flash word recognition (70%) and reading rate (96 wpm orally; 113 wpm silently). Third-grade oral and silent comprehension scores (83 and 75%, respectively) fall within the instructional range; in addition, the reader made only two meaning-change errors on the third-grade oral passage. Third grade is clearly Thomas's reading instructional level, with across-the-board scores supporting this determination. A quick glance at the second-grade scores reveals that second grade is Thomas's independent reading level (e.g., 98% oral reading accuracy, 100% comprehension, and high reading rates).

Step 3: Attempt to Confirm the Instructional- and Frustration-Level Settings by Looking for Performance Drop-Off between the Two Levels

Often a child will skillfully read a series of IRI passages before encountering a difficult passage that leads to distinctly poorer reading. In our present case, Thomas read well at the second- and third-grade levels but encountered considerable difficulty at fourth grade. Looking at the case summary sheet (Table 3.1), we find consistent "drop-off" between Thomas's third-grade (instructional-level) scores and his fourth-grade (frustration-level) scores; for example, flash word recognition (from 70 to 30%), oral reading accuracy (from 95 to 87%), oral reading rate (from 96 to 81 wpm), and silent reading comprehension (from 75 to 50%). These down-the-column differences—large and consistent, in this case—strongly support the designation of third grade as Thomas's instructional level and fourth grade as his frustration level.

Step 4: Establish Spelling Instructional and Frustration Levels

With the reading levels determined, it is now time to establish an instructional (and frustration) level for spelling—usually a fairly straightforward process. Thomas's spelling scores clearly show him to be independent at first grade (92%), instructional at second grade (67%), and frustrated at third grade (25%). An important point warrants mention here. We do *not* use spelling scores in determining reading levels. Although word recognition and spelling are strongly correlated in a normal population of schoolchildren, disabled readers often spell more poorly than they read. Note, in the present case, that Thomas's spelling (instructional at second) lags approximately 1 year behind his word recognition (instructional at third).

Before moving on, let us briefly review the four-step routine for analyzing the case summary-sheet scores:

- *Step 1.* Establish a reading frustration level. Locate the first score below 90% (frustration level) in the oral reading accuracy column. Look for further support, first in the flash word recognition column, then in the rate columns, and finally in the comprehension columns.
- *Step 2.* Establish a reading instructional level. Moving one level up from frustration level on the cover sheet, check for instructional-level scores in the following columns: oral reading accuracy, flash word recognition, oral and silent rates, oral and silent comprehension. If scores are not clearly instructional level, move up (or back) still another level.
- *Step 3.* Confirm reading level settings by looking down the columns for any drop-offs in performance (e.g., word recognition, rate, comprehension) between instructional level and frustration level.
- *Step 4.* Establish spelling instructional and frustration levels by applying performance criteria to the spelling scores.

Our application of the four-step process led to the following interpretation of Thomas's scores. A fourth grader, Thomas appears to have a third-grade reading instructional level. A deficit in automatic word recognition at fourth grade led to inaccurate, halting reading, which may have impeded his ability to comprehend at this level. Thomas spells at the second-grade level.

	Instructional level	Frustration level
Reading	3	4
Spelling	2	3

Case 2 (Jennie—Third Grade)

Jennie was tested midway through her third-grade year; her scores are shown in Table 3.4. Again, let us follow the four-step routine in analyzing her case summary sheet.

Step 1

In searching for a reading frustration level, we find that, at third grade, Jennie read with only 83% accuracy and made 12 meaning-change errors. Her flash word recognition is very low (30%), as is her oral reading rate (61 wpm). Finally, Jennie's oral comprehension is borderline (67%), and her silent comprehension is low (33%) at the third-grade level. In summary, weak print-processing scores clearly establish third grade as Jennie's reading frustration level

TABLE 3.4. Case Summary Sheet 2 (*Jennie—Third Grade*)

Level	Word recognition		Oral reading			Silent reading		Spelling
	Flash	Untimed	Accuracy	Compre-hension	Rate (wpm)	Compre-hension	Rate (wpm)	
Preprimer	100	100						
Primer	95	100						
First grade	85	95	99	100	74	100	77	92
Second grade	75	80	95	83	75	83	82	75
Third grade	30	60	83	67	61	33	97	33

Note. Meaning-change errors: *second grade*—1 of 6; *third grade*—12 of 23.

Step 2

Moving up to the second-grade row, we find instructional-level scores across the board, with the exception of slightly depressed second-grade reading rates. Oral reading accuracy (95%), flash word recognition (75%), and oral and silent comprehension (83%) are all strong at second grade. Only the oral and silent reading rates (75 and 82 wpm, respectively) are a little low. Second grade appears to be Jennie's instructional level, particularly given her strong independent-level scores at first grade.

Step 3

The designation of second grade as instructional level and third grade as frustration level is confirmed when we note the drop-off in print-processing performance between these two levels (e.g., flash word recognition, 75 to 30%; oral reading accuracy, from 95 to 83%; and oral reading rate, from 75 to 61 wpm). The surprisingly high silent reading rate at third grade can be attributed to Jennie's skimming through, as opposed to carefully reading, the passage (note her low silent comprehension score at third grade).

Step 4

Regarding spelling, Jennie's instructional level is second grade and her frustration level is third grade.

Overall, Jennie, a third-grade child, is approximately 1 year behind in reading. She has word knowledge at the second grade level (flash word recognition, 75%; spelling, 75%) that should support a faster reading rate. She needs to work at a second-grade level, improving both her reading fluency (oral and silent) and word recognition before making the big jump to third grade.

	Instructional level	Frustration level
Reading	2	3
Spelling	2	3

Case 3 (Gregory–Sixth Grade)

Our final case study in this section is Gregory, a sixth-grade boy who is functioning far below grade level in reading. Gregory's scores on the diagnostic battery are displayed in Table 3.5. In the oral reading accuracy column, there is no score below 90%; therefore, we begin our analysis at the fourth-grade level where Gregory read with 91% accuracy.

His flash word recognition score at fourth grade (25%) is very low, as are his reading rates (oral, 61 wpm; silent, 65 wpm). Gregory's oral and silent comprehension scores are also weak at fourth grade, and he made five meaning-change errors on the fourth-grade oral passage.

Moving up to third grade, we find that Gregory's oral reading accuracy score of 94% is just below the instructional range (95–97%). All other reading scores at third grade are adequate, except for Gregory's rates (oral, 82 wpm; silent, 93 wpm) which are low. Third grade appears to be the instructional level, whereas second grade is a clear independent reading level.

The performance gaps between third and fourth grade confirm these levels as instructional and frustration, respectively. Specifically, the steep drop-offs in flash word recognition (from 70 to 25%) and reading rate (oral, from 82 to 61 wpm; silent, from 93 to 65 wpm) indicate that Gregory lacks the automatic print-processing skill necessary to read successfully at the fourth-grade level.

As is the case with many disabled readers, Gregory's spelling ability lags 1 year behind his reading ability. His spelling instructional level is second grade (see 58% score at this level).

TABLE 3.5. Case Summary Sheet 3 (*Gregory—Sixth Grade*)

Level	Word recognition		Oral reading			Silent reading		Spelling
	Flash	Untimed	Accuracy	Comprehension	Rate (wpm)	Comprehension	Rate (wpm)	
Preprimer	100	100						
Primer	100	100						
First	95	100						100
Second grade	80	90	99	100	90	100	105	58
Third grade	70	75	94	83	82	100	93	33
Fourth grade	25	30	91	75	61	50	65	

Note. Meaning-change errors: *third grade*—1 of 8; *fourth grade*—5 of 13.

To some, it is alarming to think of a sixth-grade child reading at a third-grade level. These educators fear—with some justification—that such a reader will never "catch up" with his or her peers. Could not Gregory, they may argue, be taught at least at the fourth-grade level; after all, he could read 91% of the words correctly at fourth grade, and his oral reading comprehension was acceptable (75%). Unfortunately, Gregory's overall diagnostic profile does not support such a position. His print-processing ability (word reading accuracy and speed)—the "engine" that drives reading—is *inadequate* at fourth grade. Gregory will experience only failure and frustration if he is forced to read consistently at the fourth-grade level or higher. However, he does have the capacity to read at the third-grade level, and, if he receives instruction in interesting third-grade material, he will begin to make progress.

	Instructional level	*Frustration level*
Reading	3	4
Spelling	2	3

INTERPRETATION OF SCORES:
SET 2 (MORE DIFFICULT CASES)

In determining a child's reading instructional level, not all case summary sheets are as clear-cut as the ones that we considered in the previous section. In some cases, individual scores "straddle" the instructional–frustration ranges; for example, a flash word recognition score of 60% (instructional level minimum = 70%), or a fourth-grade oral rate of 100 wpm (instructional level minimum = 110 wpm). In other cases, a reader's scores at a given grade level are inconsistent, fluctuating across the areas assessed. For example, a third-grader reading a third-grade passage may demonstrate adequate word recognition, oral reading accuracy, and comprehension but fall well below the norm in reading rate or fluency. Or a fifth grader reading a fifth-grade passage may show good print-processing skills but do poorly on comprehension questions. Interestingly, although these scoring anomalies sometimes make it more difficult to determine a student's instructional level, they clearly reveal specific problem areas in the reading profile. In this section, we interpret case summary sheets that feature such inconsistency and therefore provide a bit more challenge to the diagnostician.

Case 4 (Nathan—Seventh Grade)

Nathan is a seventh-grade student who presents a profile common to struggling middle school readers. His scores in the oral reading accuracy column (see Table 3.6) are instructional though sixth grade, with little variation. Therefore, we have to look to other columns on the summary sheet to establish Nathan's functional reading levels and to identify his particular weaknesses and strengths.

TABLE 3.6. Case Summary Sheet 4 (*Nathan—Seventh Grade*)

Level	Word recognition		Oral reading			Silent reading		
	Flash	Untimed	Accuracy	Compre-hension	Rate (wpm)	Compre-hension	Rate (wpm)	Spelling
Preprimer	100	100						
Primer	100	100						
First grade	100	100						100
Second grade	90	100						92
Third grade	85	95	98	100	107	100	103	67
Fourth grade	70	90	95	83	105	75	111	58
Fifth grade	40	85	94	92	81	83	88	25
Sixth grade	30	80	95	83	65	50	71	

Note. Meaning-change errors: *fourth grade*—1 of 8; *fifth grade*—2 of 10.

Nathan's flash word recognition performance is fine through fourth grade but plummets at fifth grade to 40%. There is a corresponding drop in his reading rate from fourth to fifth grade (oral, from 105 to 81 wpm; silent, from 111 to 88 wpm). But notice that despite the drop-off in reading rate, Nathan's comprehension scores at fifth grade remain strong (92 and 83%) and that even his sixth-grade oral comprehension score (83%) is within the instructional range.

What we have here is a youngster who can read words in context and can comprehend what he reads through sixth grade. However, from fifth grade on, he reads at a torturously slow rate that resembles translating an unfamiliar code (*Note*: Some readers of this book may recall their attempts to "read" Latin in high school.) At fifth grade, Nathan reads silently (88 wpm) at about the half the speed (175 wpm) of his average-achieving classmates—a crippling academic handicap for a 12-year-old boy.

The rate or fluency dimension is the key to setting Nathan's reading frustration level at fifth grade and his instructional level at fourth grade. Note that even at fourth grade, Nathan's silent reading rate is below the norm (111 vs. 135 wpm). However, this is a difference with which we can live, especially given the strength of his other reading scores at fourth grade.

Nathan's spelling scores also present a problem in interpretation. Whereas he is clearly independent at second grade (92%) and frustrated at fifth grade (25%), Nathan's third- and fourth-grade spelling scores (67 and 58%, respectively) both fall within the instructional-level range. Which is the true instructional level—third or fourth grade? Because Nathan is a seventh grader, we should probably teach him to spell at the higher level (i.e., fourth grade), keeping in mind that there are gaps in his knowledge of third-grade spelling patterns.

Taking a final look at the scores on Nathan's case summary sheet in Table 3.6, we find little variation, from third to fifth grade, in untimed word recognition (from 85 to 95%), oral reading accuracy (from 94 to 98%), and oral reading comprehension (from 83 to 100%). This lack of variation raises an important point: the need for measures of automaticity in a reading diagnosis. Notice that if we only considered Nathan's untimed word recognition, oral reading accuracy, and comprehension scores, he could be classified as a fifth-grade-, even sixth-grade-level reader. It is only when we factor in flash word recognition and reading rate (measures of reading automaticity) that we get a true picture of this student's reading instructional level: that is, fourth grade.

	Instructional level	Frustration level
Reading	4	5
Spelling	4	5

Case 5 (Amanda—Fourth Grade)

Amanda, a fourth grader, was referred for testing because of a possible reading comprehension problem. In examining Amanda's case summary sheet (see Table 3.7), fifth grade appears to her frustration level. At this level, her oral reading accuracy score (92%) is in the gray area, and 4 of her 13 errors are meaning changes. Amanda's fifth-grade flash word recognition score (50%) is low, as are her oral and silent reading rates (95 and 90 wpm, respectively). Finally, she had difficulty answering comprehension questions at the fifth-grade level (oral, 50%; silent, 42%).

At fourth grade, Amanda has instructional-level scores in oral reading accuracy (95%), flash word recognition (75%), and oral reading rate (115 wpm). She can read with adequate fluency at this level, but her comprehension scores are low (oral, 58%; silent, 50%). In fact, even at third grade, where Amanda has strong print-processing skill, she still has some difficulty with comprehension.

TABLE 3.7. Case Summary Sheet 5 (*Amanda—Fourth Grade*)

Level	Word recognition — Flash	Word recognition — Untimed	Oral reading — Accuracy	Oral reading — Comprehension	Oral reading — Rate (wpm)	Silent reading — Comprehension	Silent reading — Rate (wpm)	Spelling
Preprimer	100	100						
Primer	100	100						
First	95	100						100
Second grade	90	95						83
Third grade	90	100	97	67	121	58	117	83
Fourth grade	75	100	95	58	115	50	109	75
Fifth grade	50	90	92	50	95	42	90	33

Note. Meaning-change errors: *fourth grade*—2 of 8; *fifth grade*—4 of 13.

Amanda's profile is typical of a child with a reading comprehension problem. In setting an instructional level for her, we must keep in mind that she *can* process text fairly fluently at the fourth-grade level. And if a child can "read" the text, a teacher can help with comprehension by preteaching vocabulary, building background knowledge, and guiding the reading with relevant questions. Therefore, it is possible to teach Amanda at the fourth-grade level despite her weakness in comprehension. (Note that if she could not read fluently at fourth grade, teacher support with comprehension would not solve the underlying print-processing problem.)

Setting functional spelling levels is no problem in Amanda's case. Her spelling instructional level is clearly fourth grade (75%) and her frustration level is fifth grade (33%).

Two smaller points warrant mention. First, note that Amanda's flash word recognition and spelling scores are equally strong through fourth grade. These scores indicate her sound knowledge of grade-level spelling patterns. Second, notice that her silent reading rates are lower than her oral rates—opposite from the pattern we would expect. It could be that Amanda just needs more practice with silent reading. Or it could be that she slows down when reading silently because of difficulties with comprehension. In any case, a good instructional program would focus on improving her silent reading comprehension and her silent reading rate.

	Instructional level	Frustration level
Reading	4	5
Spelling	4	5

Case 6 (Dion—Fifth Grade)

Dion, a fifth grader and our final case in this section, has difficulty reading at the fifth-grade level (see Table 3.8). His oral reading accuracy score (92%) is in the gray area, but his other scores at fifth grade are low: flash word recognition—30%; oral and silent comprehension—33 and 67%, respectively; and oral and silent rates—94 and 91 wpm, respectively. Because of a lack of automatic word recognition, the reading process for Dion breaks down at fifth grade. This is his frustration level.

Moving up to fourth grade, we find instructional-level scores across the board, with the exception of flash word recognition, which borders on frustration level. Notice that Dion maintained an acceptable oral reading rate at fourth grade (109 wpm), in spite of a low flash word recognition score (50%). When this happens—when these two measures of automaticity clash—we generally give more weight to reading rate—a contextual as opposed to an isolated measure of word processing. Thus, we can declare fourth grade as Dion's instructional level. Still, the examiner should look warily upon Dion's fourth-grade flash score of 50% because it may indicate an underlying problem with automatic word recognition. Third grade is clearly Dion's independent reading level, although, again, note his borderline flash word recognition score (55%) at this level.

TABLE 3.8. Case Summary Sheet 6 (*Dion—Fifth Grade*)

Level	Word recognition		Oral reading			Silent reading		Spelling
	Flash	Untimed	Accuracy	Compre-hension	Rate (wpm)	Compre-hension	Rate (wpm)	
Preprimer	100	100						
Primer	95	100						
First grade	95	100						83
Second grade	90	100	96	80	113	100	129	58
Third grade	55	90	97	100	110	92	127	33
Fourth grade	50	80	95	75	109	83	119	
Fifth grade	30	75	92	33	94	67	91	

Note. Meaning-change errors: *fourth grade*—1 of 8; *fifth grade*—5 of 13.

Dion's performance on the spelling task is alarming. A fifth grader, he appears to spell at the second-grade level (58%), a full 3 years below his grade level and 2 years below his reading level. Dion desperately needs help with spelling.

A pattern emerges as we take into account all of Dion's scores. Here is a fifth-grade student whose orthographic (or spelling pattern) knowledge drops significantly at third grade (i.e., flash word recognition score of 55% and spelling score of 33%). In contextual reading, Dion is able to compensate and reads adequately through fourth grade. At fifth grade, however, his dearth of word knowledge (30%) catches up with him, resulting in borderline oral reading accuracy, poor comprehension, and low reading rates. Because of his contextual reading skill, Dion can be instructed in fourth-grade reading material. However, his deficit in word knowledge must be addressed or it will stall future reading progress. A knowledgeable teacher would take Dion back to second- and third-grade word patterns and teach him to internalize these patterns through a combination of word categorization and spelling activities.

	Instructional level	Frustration level
Reading	4	5
Spelling	2	3

Dion's case brings to an end our initial discussion of how to interpret a set of diagnostic reading scores. Because diagnosis and instruction go hand in hand, we will have the opportunity to examine several more case summary sheets in Chapters 5 and 7, which address instructional issues. To conclude the present chapter, however, I want to take up the interpretation of scores from the first-grade reading battery that was briefly mentioned at the end of Chapter 2.

INTERPRETING SCORES FROM A FIRST-GRADE READING BATTERY

First-grade-level readers present a diagnostic problem in that they tend to become frustrated early on traditional reading inventories, thereby providing little information other than that they are novice readers. We learned in Chapter 2 that the early word recognition and spelling lists in our diagnostic battery can be used successfully with first-grade readers. However, we need to use a different passage reading inventory—one that includes multiple difficulty levels *within* first grade—if we are to pinpoint a beginning reader's instructional level. The alternative first-grade reading inventory recommended in Chapter 2 includes four levels (emergent, preprimer, primer, and late first). These are shown in Table 3.9.

Case 1 (Rebecca—First Grade)

Rebecca, a child nearing the end of her first-grade year, has gotten off to a slow start in reading. Her scores in Table 3.9 show that she could read a preprimer (or early first-grade) passage with adequate accuracy (94%), but experienced difficulty reading the primer (or mid-first-grade) passage (82%). (*Note:* In this first-grade battery, 90% is the instructional-level minimum for oral reading accuracy.) Rebecca's word recognition scores are consistent with her passage reading efforts. She shows some sight vocabulary at the preprimer level (55%), but her flash word recognition score drops off at the primer level (30%). She was able to decode a good percentage of the preprimer (90%) and primer words (70%) when given additional time.

The instructional implications of these scores are clear. A teacher should start Rebecca in preprimer reading material. The child needs to build her sight vocabulary through reading and rereading appropriately leveled books, and she needs to strengthen her decoding skills through a systematic word study program. As Rebecca gains skill and confidence as a reader, she can move up to the primer level.

TABLE 3.9. First-Grade Case Summary Sheet 1 (*Rebecca—First Grade*)

	Word recognition		Oral reading			
	Flash	Untimed	Accuracy	Compre-hension	Rate	Spelling
Emergent			100			
Preprimer	55	90	94			
Primer	30	70	82	75		
Late first						17
Second[a]						

[a]If necessary, the second-grade passage from the regular IRI is used.

Before leaving this case, let us address Rebecca's spelling performance. The solitary percentage-correct score (17%) at first grade actually tells us very little. However, if we look closely at Rebecca's 10 spelling errors on the first-grade list (see Figure 3.1), we can gain insight into her underlying word knowledge. First, Rebecca can "hear" the sequence of sounds in one-syllable words. In each of her misspellings, except *JRP*, Rebecca included both beginning and ending consonants and the medial vowel. Second, Rebecca has not learned the conventional spellings of short-vowel sounds; for example, she substituted *e* for *i* in her spellings of *wish*, *sister*, and *ship*, and *o* for *u* in her spelling of *bump*. These vowel substitutions, though phonetically appropriate (see Templeton & Morris, 1999; Read, 1971), indicate her lack of short-vowel pattern knowledge.

Third, Rebecca shows some knowledge of consonant digraphs (e.g., WESH for *wish*; SHEP for *ship*), but confusion regarding consonant blends, specifically *-r* blends (e.g., CHAP for *trap*; JRIV for *drive*). Again, these consonant-blend substitutions do make sense phonetically. Fourth, Rebecca is inconsistent in marking long-vowel words with an extra vowel letter. She spelled *bike* correctly, but failed to mark the long vowels in JRIV for *drive* and PLAN for *plane*.

This qualitative look at Rebecca's spelling errors directly informs instruction. That is, phonics instruction should aim at helping the child learn the short-vowel patterns, consonant blends, and high-frequency long-vowel patterns, in that order.

Case 2 (Jose—Second Grade)

Jose is in the low reading group in his second-grade class. Because his teacher says that Jose still reads at a first-grade level, we decide to use the first-grade reading battery with this second-grade child.

Spelling word	Rebecca's spelling
trap	CHAP
bed	bed (c)
when	WEN
wish	WESH
sister	SESDR
girl	GRLL
drop	JRP
bump	BOP
drive	JRIV
plane	PLAN
ship	SHEP
bike	bike (c)

FIGURE 3.1. Rebecca's performance on the first-grade spelling list.

TABLE 3.10. First-Grade Case Summary Sheet 2 (*Jose—Second Grade*)

	Word recognition		Oral reading			Spelling
	Flash	Untimed	Accuracy	Compre-hension	Rate	
Emergent			—			
Preprimer	80	100	98			
Primer	65	85	97	100		
Late first grade	35	75	88	100	38	50

Jose's scores, shown in Table 3.10, indicate that he can read successfully up to the primer or mid-first-grade level. His oral reading accuracy and flash word recognition scores (97 and 65%, respectively) fall within or near the instructional-level range at primer. At late first grade, Jose's automatic word recognition (35%) drops off, leading to a low oral reading accuracy score (88%) and a very slow reading rate (38 wpm). Late first grade is his frustration level.

Jose was able to spell 50% of the first-grade word list correctly (remember that Rebecca [Case 1] could spell only 2 of the 12 first-grade words correctly). Moreover, a close look at the quality of Jose's spellings (see Figure 3.2) reveals that his orthographic knowledge is more advanced than Rebecca's. Jose knows the short-vowel patterns (e.g., *trap*, *bed*, *wish*, and SISTR) and is consistent in spelling consonant blends and digraphs (e.g., *trap*, *wish*, DRIV, and PLAEN). However, he needs to master the CVCe long-vowel pattern; note that he spelled *bike* correctly but misplaced the *e* marker in PLAEN and omitted it in DRIV.

Spelling word	*Jose's spelling*
trap	trap (c)
bed	bed (c)
when	WIN
wish	wish (c)
sister	SISSTR
girl	GRIL
drop	drop (c)
bump	BUPE
drive	DRIV
plane	PLAEN
ship	ship (c)
bike	bike (c)

FIGURE 3.2. Jose's performance on the first-grade spelling list

Overall, Jose (primer) is reading a level higher than Rebecca (preprimer). The reading scores in our test battery (particularly oral reading accuracy and flash word recognition) helped us to identify a precise instructional level (within first grade) for each child. The qualitative analysis of their spelling errors yielded important information about the developmental level of each child's word knowledge.

In this chapter we have considered the interpretation of scores from informal tests of reading and spelling. In the next chapter we consider other areas of reading diagnosis, including diagnosis through teaching, standardized assessments, and parent interviews.

Reading Diagnosis Summary Sheet

Name _____ Date _____

Grade _____ Examiner _____

| | Word Recognition Test | | Informal Reading Inventory | | | | | |
| | | | Oral | | | Silent | | |
	Flash	Untimed	Reading accuracy	Comp.	Rate	Comp.	Rate	Spelling
PP								
P								
1st								
2nd								
3rd								
4th								
5th								
6th								
7th								
8th								

Independent Level _____

Instructional Level _____

Frustration Level _____

Level	Total errors	Meaning change	Comments on established levels:

CHAPTER 4

Beyond the Initial Reading Diagnosis

The initial reading diagnosis (word recognition, passage reading, and spelling) provides a good first estimate of a child's reading ability and a baseline against which future growth in reading can be compared. Nonetheless, there are additional ways to gain information about the child's reading. A short parent interview can provide needed insight into the child's developmental and educational history. Observations made in the first few teaching lessons can confirm or sometimes challenge the results of the initial reading diagnosis (e.g., an observant teacher may see that the child can actually be taught in early-second-grade material when the initial test results point to a late-first-grade reading level). Further down the road (perhaps after 8–12 months of instruction) the teacher will want to assess the child's reading progress by re-administering the initial diagnostic battery or, if requested, by administering a standardized reading test. It is these topics—the parent interview, diagnosis through teaching, pre- and posttesting with an informal test battery, and standardized reading assessment—that we consider in this chapter.

THE PARENT INTERVIEW

Generally, a child's parents are the best source of information about his or her reading problem. A mother (or primary caretaker) knows her child's developmental history (e.g., when he or she began to walk and talk), personality (e.g., likes and dislikes, strengths and fears), and position within the family (e.g., number of siblings, birth order, rivalries). The parent also knows the child's educational history. Having worried about the child's reading problem over a considerable period of time, the parent can usually recount, with some specificity, when the problem surfaced (kindergarten, first grade, or second grade?), who identified it (the parent or a teacher), and how the school and the family have addressed the problem (psychological testing, Title I or special education placement, tutoring in or outside the school).

In the past, the parent interview was an integral part of the diagnostic process in university-based reading clinics. I know that at the University of Virginia in the late 1970s, we interviewed the parents of *each* child who was tutored in the reading clinic (60 or more per year). However, over the past 25 years, the world has speeded up, time and resources have become scarce, and the clinical tradition in reading has declined. Today, I doubt that face-to-face parent interviews are conducted for most children who are tutored in university-based practicum courses. I know that in my own reading clinic we are guilty of omitting the initial parent interview, and we pay a price for doing so.

Let me cite two examples. First was John, a sixth-grade boy from a working-class family who read at the second-grade level. John surely had a serious reading problem, but what caused more trouble during the tutoring lessons was his behavior. When he met even the slightest obstacle in reading, he became angry and oppositional toward his tutor. Because the tantrums were definitely interfering with his learning, I decided to interview John's mother to learn something of his background. The interview was progressing normally when, in passing, the mother mentioned that John was a twin whose brother had died in a car accident 2 years ago. Moreover, both twins were in the car when the accident happened, and their father was the driver. To add to the tragedy, the guilt-ridden father left the family shortly after, breaking off ties with the remaining twin . . . John. Given this information, my remaining interview questions paled in significance. I did not have to be a licensed psychologist to appreciate the impact this tragic event must have had on the child. And I can certainly say that, from that day forward, we showed a great deal more patience in dealing with John's occasional outbursts of emotion. We continued to teach him to read, but we did so with a better understanding of his life context.

A second case comes to mind. Jason had completed first grade and was attending our 4-week summer reading clinic. One day, his tutor (an experienced kindergarten teacher) asked if I would come by and take a look at Jason. "He's trying hard," she said, "but nothing seems to stick. He is getting frustrated and so am I." I visited Jason's room the next day and observed him being tutored. Although his tutor was supporting him in reading the simplest of first-grade books (one line of text and a picture), Jason was visibly upset by the activity. I had, in fact, never seen a first-grade child bang his head against the table in frustration. Something was wrong.

I interviewed Jason's parents, a college professor and a nurse, a few days later in my office. They told me that Jason, after 2 years of kindergarten, had experienced a very difficult first-grade year. Not only did he have trouble learning to read and write, but he was regularly sent to the principal's office for acting up in the classroom. In fact, the father spent many mornings in the back of the first-grade classroom in an attempt to control Jason's behavior. The parents further stated that Jason was taking separate medications for attention-deficit disorder and anger management, and still the school principal was not sure if the child belonged in a regular classroom setting.

I learned a few other things in the 45-minute interview. First, Jason was doing passing work in math but, after 3 years in school, this 7-year-old had not yet mastered the alphabet. Second, Jason's father had experienced difficulty learning to read and was an underachieving student through his high school years. Third, despite his struggles with reading, Jason loved books and being read to. And fourth, it was quite apparent that Jason's parents were totally committed to his development as a student and as a happy, well-adjusted human being.

From this parent interview and my brief observation of Jason in the summer reading clinic, I deduced that (1) the child probably had a severe disability in the area of reading (the lack of alphabet knowledge after 3 years of school); (2) he may have inherited the reading problem from his father (severe reading disability runs in families); (3) he might benefit from an alternative, highly structured reading approach that focused on learning the alphabet, letter sounds, and regular spelling patterns (e.g., Orton–Gillingham); and (4) learning to read, even if he progressed slowly, might take some emotional pressure off this anxious, confused young boy and thereby allow him to function in school.

I decided to tutor Jason myself and have continued to do so, two times per week, for the past 5 years. It turned out that Jason did have a severe reading disability and, even with one-to-one help, he has struggled mightily with the process. However, learning to read has helped to calm Jason's "inner demons," and he now functions quite successfully in the classroom. Entering sixth grade this fall, he reads at the second-grade level but has the oral vocabulary of a 15-year-old. He is also a much happier child with a strong sense of self.

I have presented the cases of John and Jason as a cautionary note. Of course, not all parents of disabled readers will have such dramatic stories to tell, but . . . you never know. The parents' perspective on a reading problem is always informative; to ignore it in the diagnostic process is short-sighted and, on occasion, dangerous.

A Parent Interview Schedule

Many possible questions could be posed to parents in a 1-hour interview. The interview schedule shown in Appendix 4.1 is provided only as an example. Actually, the questions on this form represent my attempt to reduce in size the much longer interview schedule we used at the McGuffey Reading Center back in my graduate student days. I have good reasons for including each question, and the validity of most will be readily apparent to the reader. However, I do want to comment briefly on some of the questions.

Note that the interview schedule is divided into two parts: *Developmental and*

Family Data and *Educational History*. Under Developmental and Family Data, questions 1 and 2 probe for the possibility of brain trauma that may have affected reading development. Question 3 regarding general health is an important one. Children who are absent from school an unusually large number of days (particularly in grades K–2) may experience reading problems simply because they missed foundational instruction at a critical point in development. Regarding question 4, children who are 6 or more months late in developing oral language are often late in learning to read. In question 7 we are trying to identify school or nonschool activities (e.g., sports, clubs, hobbies, types of play) that bring the child enjoyment and a feeling of success. Questions 8–10 address the child's position in the family and its possible influence on academic achievement. Many a struggling reader turns away from the activity with discouragement when an older (or younger) sibling is perceived to be an expert reader. And finally, question 11 gets at the potential heritability of the reading problem. The evidence is clear that reading disability can be inherited (Gayán & Olson, 1999; Olson, 2006), although sometimes the trait may skip a generation. For example, the parent interview may reveal that though the child's father and mother are adequate readers, both grandfather and great uncle Tom (on father's side) struggled with reading in school.

The second part of the interview attempts to trace the child's educational history. Question 1 establishes when the parent became aware of the reading problem. Question 2, extremely important, asks the parent to recapitulate, grade by grade, the child's progress in school. As stated previously, parents often have detailed memories of their child's struggles with reading during the first few years of school. They can remember the teacher who identified the reading problem and also the one(s) who did not. They can remember the specific grade in which the child became frustrated and "turned off" to reading. And, finally, they can recall the grade in which the child was referred for extra reading assistance, the type of assistance provided (e.g., Title I or learning disabilities; one-to-one tutoring or small group), and the effects of the extra help. Obviously this type of information is extremely helpful to the diagnostician. There is a huge difference between two third-grade children with reading problems: one who has experienced extreme difficulty with reading from first grade on, and the other whose reading problem was first identified at the end of the third grade by a low score on a statewide reading test.

Question 3 addresses the child's present functioning in school, specifically how the reading problem might affect performance in different subject areas (e.g., literature, social studies, science, math). Question 4 concerns the handling of homework, often a thorny problem for the disabled reader and his or her family. If assigned homework is too difficult (in terms of reading level) for the child, parents adapt in different ways. Some parents spend an inordinate amount of time—up to 2 or 3 hours—helping the poor reader complete the homework assignments. Others read the material to the child, and still others tend to ignore homework because of the frustration involved. Question 6 (Do you read to the child at home?) usually produces a *no* response, especially from the parents of older children. In fact, most mothers and fathers quit reading aloud to their children on a regular basis once the children enter school. This omission is very unfortunate, particularly for a youngster with a reading problem, because being read to builds vocabulary, knowledge of the world, and a feel for the rhythm of written language, while at the same time developing a love for books in the child.

The face-to-face parent interview takes time—45–60 minutes on the part of a busy parent and clinician. This time requirement is undoubtedly why, today, the interview is omitted in many university-based teaching practicums. Nonetheless, such an interview can provide a much fuller picture of the child than we can gain through teaching alone. Parents know their children, and we, as reading educators, should make every effort to tap this important resource.

DIAGNOSIS THROUGH TEACHING

The effective teaching of reading involves ongoing diagnosis and decision making on the tutor's part. This begins in the first teaching lesson. For example, based on initial diagnostic results, a tutor may start a third-grade child off reading a late-first-grade story and working with three short-vowel patterns (e.g., *hat, fit, job*). To the tutor's surprise, the child has no difficulty reading the story and breezes through the short-vowel activity. Therefore, the tutor decides that, in the next lesson, she will try an early-second-grade story and introduce a new short-vowel pattern (e.g., *net*). This scenario raises two points. First, initial diagnostic results provide a first *estimate* of reading ability that may need to be modified slightly once instruction begins. Second, effective teaching involves observing the reader's behavior (e.g., accuracy, fluency, comprehension) and deciding whether he or she should continue at the present difficulty level, be moved forward, or, on occasion, moved backward. This process is called *instructional pacing*, an important concept that we meet again and again in this book.

A clear example of diagnosis through teaching occurs when working with a beginning reader. In a typical lesson, the child reads and rereads simple texts, trying to learn new words and apply emerging phonics skills (e.g., the beginning consonant letter–sound). The tutor understands that the beginner's acquisition of new sight words is the key to reading progress. Therefore, after a story has been read several times, the tutor points randomly to individual words in the text to see if the child can identify them. If he or she can read the word immediately, it is printed on an index card and entered into a "word bank" or stack of known words. These known words are reviewed each lesson, and the rate at which the child's word bank grows is an important diagnostic indicator.

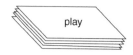

One hopes for rapid growth, but the slow, steady accrual of words in memory is fine. On the other hand, extreme difficulty in establishing an initial sight vocabulary can be a sign of a serious reading problem.

A good tutor is always making informal judgments as the child reads: Is there sufficient accuracy or are there too many errors? Is fluency rhythmic or choppy? Is comprehension detailed or sketchy? On occasion the tutor may want a more formal assessment of the child's reading ability. Fortunately, the diagnostic procedures described in Chapter 2 can be used to obtain and analyze samples of reading behavior.

Let us say a tutor is thinking about advancing a child from late-second-grade to third-grade reading material. But the tutor wants to be sure that the child has a solid foundation at late second grade before moving forward. Therefore, in the next lesson's second-grade story, the tutor selects a 150-word passage (approximately a page) for diagnosis. The teaching routine does not change; the tutor introduces the story, the child reads, and at selected stopping points tutor and child discuss the plot. The only difference is that when the child starts to read the 150-word passage, the tutor clicks on the tape recorder. After the lesson is over, the tutor goes back and listens to the tape-recorded words, scoring the reading for *accuracy* (error quotient = 100 ÷ 150 = .67) and *rate* (60 × 150 ÷ No. of seconds). If the child reads with 98% accuracy at a rate of 93 wpm, then the tutor feels confident that the move up to third-grade material is warranted. Of course, another reading sample, perhaps taken the next lesson and showing similar results, would increase the tutor's confidence in making this instructional move.

Another example of diagnosis within a teaching context is an oral–silent rate comparison. A tutor may have been working with a girl who reads at the fourth-grade level, trying to improve her oral reading accuracy and rate. Improvement has been made and now the tutor wants to check the child's silent reading rate. Within a fourth-grade story or book chapter, the tutor chooses two passages, each 150 words in length, for a rate check. When the child reaches these preselected passages during the reading lesson, she reads one orally and one silently. The tutor times her reading with a stopwatch so that later he can go back and calculate reading rates (remember that rate equals 60 × No. of words read ÷ No. of seconds). In this case, we would hope that the child's silent rate is at least as high as her oral rate, and possibly a little higher. Again, a second oral–silent rate comparison would be helpful.

Comprehension is still another area that can be diagnosed in a teaching situation. In guiding the child's reading of a story, the tutor will want to stop at various points and pose questions. The child's responses to these questions will reveal much about his or her comprehension abilities. For example:

- The ability to recall basic plot-related information (e.g., Where does this story take place? What problem does Mary face? How did she solve the problem?).
- The ability to make connections between events or character motivations in a

story (e.g., Why do you think Tom didn't tell his father about the bully at school? Why was Anna suspicious of the salesman?).
- The ability to interpret or analyze the story from one's own perspective (e.g., Did John do the right thing? Why or why not? What do you think the author was trying to say about loyalty in this story?).

Often, children's comprehension of a story is governed by the amount of text they have to read. That is, whereas they are perfectly capable of reading and understanding a single page, three pages of text may overwhelm their memory and lead to poor comprehension. Therefore, the skillful tutor will manipulate the amount of text to be read, searching for the optimal length that provides the child with challenge but success. Gradually, as the reader gains skill, stamina, and confidence, the tutor can lengthen the amount the child reads between stopping (or questioning) points. Comprehension success over longer sections of text is a clear sign that the child is making progress.

PRE- AND POSTTESTING WITH AN INFORMAL DIAGNOSTIC BATTERY

We administer the diagnostic reading battery (see Chapters 2 and 3) as a *pretest* to determine where to begin instruction. After a long period of instruction (preferably a school year), we can readminister the same battery as a *posttest* to determine how much the child has improved as a reader. In a sense, the pretest establishes the child's starting rung on a ladder, and the posttest shows how many rungs he or she has been able to climb up.

Remember that the diagnostic battery measures performance in three areas: word recognition, contextual reading (oral and silent), and spelling. Regarding administration, the same word recognition and spelling lists can be used for pretesting and posttesting; however, the reading passages should be changed. That is, if passages A and B were used for testing oral and silent reading on the pretest, then passages C and D should be used on the posttest. Many commercial IRIs include four passages (forms A–D) at each grade level, but unfortunately not all four passages are equally interesting. One way around the "passage interest" problem is to create a hybrid IRI (four forms) by selecting the best passages from two or more commercial IRIs.

Table 4.1 shows the pretest–posttest results of Brett, a student whom we first evaluated at the end of his sixth-grade year. The pretest scores showed Brett to be reading, at best, at the second-grade level, and even there his oral reading was inaccurate (90%) and very slow (55 wpm). In the parent interview, Brett's mother stated that he got off to a very slow start in reading in first grade and was referred for special education services in second grade. Over the next 5 school years, Brett received a variety of reading help, in and outside of school, but his reading skill did not im-

TABLE 4.1. Pretest–Posttest Results for Brett over a 2-Year Period

Level	Word recognition		Oral reading			Silent reading		Spelling
	Flash	Untimed	Accuracy	Compre-hension	Rate (wpm)	Compre-hension	Rate (wpm)	
Pretest scores (end of sixth grade)								
Preprimer	100	100						
Primer	90	100						
First grade	70	90	94	80	69	80	72	67
Second grade	70	85	90	80	55	60	63	42
Third grade	30	60	84	58	51	50	65	17
Posttest scores (end of eighth grade)								
Preprimer	100	100						
Primer	100	100						
First grade	90	100						92
Second grade	90	95						75
Third grade	55	100	98	100	110	92	116	67
Fourth grade	30	70	99	92	104	100	112	50
Fifth grade			94	100	55	100	89	—

prove appreciably. The mother was particularly concerned that special education services for Brett in seventh grade would not include direct reading instruction, but instead would focus on his "accommodation" to the middle school curriculum.

I assigned an experienced first-grade teacher, Mrs. Ervin, to tutor Brett in our 4-week summer reading clinic. She did an outstanding job, and it was apparent, after just 14 lessons, that the child had made progress. At the mother's request, Mrs. Ervin continued to tutor Brett twice weekly during the following school year (seventh grade). His lessons included guided reading in second- and third-grade material, word study, and fluency drills. At home, he practiced reading stories that his tutor put on audiotape (see Morris, Ervin, & Conrad, 1996, for a fuller description of this case). Brett returned to our reading clinic the next summer and then was tutored once per week during his eighth-grade year. Thus, over 2 school years and two summers, he received 78 hours of one-to-one tutoring from well-trained reading teachers.

The posttest results in Table 4.1 show the reading improvement made by Brett over the 2-year period. He started off reading at a low-second-grade level; 2 years later, he read at a solid fourth-grade level. Notice that at fourth grade, Brett read with near-perfect accuracy (99%) and good comprehension. His oral and silent rates were a bit low but vastly improved from the pretest. Brett's lone low reading score at the fourth-grade level was flash word recognition (30%), indicating a continuing problem with word-level automaticity. It is true that leaving eighth grade, Brett still read at only the fourth-grade level. However, there is another way to think about this student's progress. At the end of sixth grade, Brett read, at best, at the second-grade level; at the end of eighth grade, he read at the fourth-grade level. In other words, Brett, with a tutor's help, made as much reading progress in seventh and eighth grades as he had made in his previous 6 years in school. We cannot turn back the clock, but . . . if Brett had received adequate reading instruction earlier in his schooling, it seems unlikely that he would have fallen so far behind in reading.

Let us now look at an at-risk reader who *did* receive effective intervention instruction in the early grades. At the beginning of second grade, Mariah was referred to the Title I reading program in her school. The reading teacher administered the first-grade reading battery (see pp. 37–38) and found that Mariah was reading not quite at the primer or mid-first-grade level. The pretest scores (see Table 4.2) showed that Mariah had some sight vocabulary (80% on the flash presentation of the preprimer list) and some decoding skill (70% on the untimed presentation of the primer list); however, she had fallen at least a half year behind her classmates in reading achievement.

In second grade, Mariah's year-long Title I reading instruction was intensive. On Mondays and Wednesdays, she worked with the reading teacher in a small group of four children, each of whom had a similar reading level. On Tuesdays and

TABLE 4.2. Pretest–Posttest Results for Mariah over a 1-Year Period

| | Word recognition | | Oral reading | | | |
	Flash	Untimed	Accuracy	Compre-hension	Rate	Spelling
Pretest scores (beginning of second grade)						
Emergent						
Preprimer	80	95	97			
Primer	40	70	88	75		
Late first grade			81	50		42
Posttest scores (end of second grade)						
Emergent						
Preprimer	100	100				
Primer	95	100	99	100		
Late first grade	90	95	98	100	92	92
Second grade[a]	70	90	95	83	84	50
Third grade[a]	45	75	87	58	71	33

[a]Passage is from the regular IRI.

Thursdays, she was tutored (one-to-one) by a Title I assistant working under the close supervision of the reading teacher (see Morris, 2005b). Mariah's Title I reading lessons were 30 minutes in length, and she also received 20 minutes of daily small-group reading instruction in her regular classroom. Mariah responded well to this regimen. As her reading skill progressed during the year, she was moved from primer to late-first-grade to second-grade reading material—in the Title I room and in the classroom. In fact, in January, the reading teacher persuaded the classroom teacher to move Mariah from the low to the middle reading group in the class.

Posttest results at the end of second grade (see Table 4.2) showed Mariah to be at or near grade level in reading. All of her scores at the second-grade level (word recognition, oral reading accuracy, comprehension, and rate) met instructional-level criteria. Mariah still has work to do (keep in mind that she will be entering third grade in the fall). However, having benefited from an effective reading intervention in second grade, this child made up distance on her average-achieving peers and is now ready to move forward academically.

INFORMAL VERSUS STANDARDIZED TESTS

This book focuses on the *informal assessment* of individual students' reading. In informal testing, we are interested in how well a student's performance on a given task (e.g., oral reading accuracy) at a given level (e.g., third grade) matches an agreed-upon criterion (e.g., 95%). The ultimate goal of such testing is to inform instruction. Thus, if John can read a third-grade passage with 95% accuracy (along with adequate comprehension and rate), then he can be instructed at this level. Similarly, if he can spell 50% of the words on a third-grade spelling list, he can be instructed in a third-grade spelling book.

Stauffer et al. (1978) listed the following characteristics of informal or criterion reference tests:

- There must be a clear definition of the task or skill to be measured.
- The items in such a test are used to determine mastery, rather than to obtain a normal distribution.
- The items should represent skills that are essential to learning to read.
- The test items should appear in an established sequence or hierarchy.
- The tasks should be accomplished in a normal reading situation.

Note that each of these five characteristics is found in the oral and silent reading tasks of our informal test battery. Moreover, four of the five characteristics (all except the last one) are found in the word recognition and spelling tasks. In these instances, it makes sense to assess orthographic knowledge in isolation rather than in context.

The first step in providing effective reading instruction is to identify the student's instructional level, along with relative areas of strength and weakness. Thus, the teacher needs diagnostic tasks that are graded in difficulty, afford agreed-upon levels of mastery (e.g., independent, instructional, frustration), and measure important components of the reading process. If administered and scored carefully, the informal diagnostic tasks (word recognition, passage reading, and spelling), described in the previous two chapters, will go a long way toward addressing this need.

Although not the focus of this book, there is another form of assessment, *standardized tests*, with which reading teachers should be familiar. Standardized, or norm-reference tests, allow us to compare the performance of an individual student to that of a larger group. A standardized reading test has several characteristics:

- *The test contains norms.* In the development process, the test is administered to a large sample of children, perhaps nationwide, and this group's performance is used to derive a set of *norms*. In the future, the performance of an individual who takes the test is compared to the performance of the norm group.
- *The test should be reliable and valid. Reliability* refers to the extent that the test instrument is consistent in producing results. For example, we expect a thermometer to yield a correct temperature reading time after time. We should also expect measurement consistency from a reading test. *Validity* simply means that the test measures what it says it measures. Validity relates to content, and a reading test should measure things that are important to reading. (Note that a carefully developed IRI could be both reliable and valid.)
- *The standardized test includes clear directions for administration and scoring.* The test must be administered and scored the same way each and every time or else performance comparisons to the norm group will be inaccurate and unmeaningful.

Standardized tests yield four types of scores, and teachers should be familiar with each type. The *raw score* is the number of items that the child got correct on a given test. The raw score is then transformed into a normed score so that comparisons can be made across different tests or subtests. The most common normed scores are stanines, percentiles, and grade-equivalent scores.

- *Stanines* provide performance bands (1-low to 9-high) by dividing the normal curve into nine equal parts. Stanines 4–6 represent average performance on the test; stanines 1–3, below-average performance; and stanines 7–9, above-average performance.
- *Percentiles* indicate a student's relative position in the norm group—from the 1st percentile to the 99th percentile. For example, if a child scores at the 58th percentile, this means that he or she scored better than 58 percent of the other students who took the test.
- *Grade-equivalent (GE) scores* indicate level of achievement in terms of years and months in school. Thus, a GE score of 4.3 indicates average performance for a

student who is in the third month of fourth grade. Although GE scores reflect the popular tendency to measure reading achievement by a grade-level metric (e.g., first-grade reading level, second-grade reading level, and so on), care should be taking in interpreting these scores. The GE scores are not derived from careful testing of students at monthly intervals, but rather from mathematical extrapolation (see Barr et al., 2002).

There are three major types of standardized reading tests: individually administered tests, group-administered tests, and new, state reading tests that have characteristics of both standardized and criterion-referenced assessment.

Individually administered standardized tests include, among others, the Gray Oral Reading Test (Wiederholt & Bryant, 2001), the Woodcock–Johnson Reading Test (Woodcock, Mather, & Schrank, 2006), and the Peabody Individual Achievement Test (Markwardt, 1998). Each of these tests measures at least two components of reading (e.g, word recognition, vocabulary, comprehension, rate) and provides standardized scores that can be compared to a norm-reference group. This makes them especially attractive to special education teachers and school psychologists who must, by law, use standardized achievement instruments. However, reading teachers, who are not under such legal constraints, usually opt for informal assessments when testing students individually. They believe that such performance-based measures of word recognition, comprehension, and rate (see Chapters 2 and 3) allow for more accurate placement in the instructional program.

Group-administered standardized reading tests, which have a long history in our country, include, among others, the Gates–MacGinitie Reading Test (MacGinitie, MacGinitie, Maria, Dreyer, & Hughes, 1999), the Stanford Achievement Test (Harcourt Assessment, 2002) and the Iowa Test of Basic Skills (Hoover, Dunbar, & Frisbie, 2001). In these tests the student reads silently a series of short passages, answering multiple-choice comprehension questions after each passage. Again, the student's performance is compared to a large norm-reference group. Critics have complained that the short, unrelated, often bland reading passages do not provide a good measure of comprehension. This may be true. However, these tests, by including a *series* of passages graded in difficulty, do allow the struggling reader a chance to read at least one or two "easy" passages before taking on a frustrating grade-level passage.

In response to criticism of traditional group-administered reading tests, many states have recently developed what are called "end-of-grade" reading tests. These are, technically, standardized tests, with all the accompanying psychometric properties (e.g., standardized administration, reliability and validity, multiple-choice answer format, norm-reference group). What distinguishes these state tests from the traditional group-administered reading tests (e.g., Gates–MacGinitie) is the nature of the reading passages. In the state tests, the student is asked to read two to six long reading passages, *each of which is of grade-level difficulty* (i.e., fourth graders read fourth-grade-level passages; fifth graders read fifth-grade-level passages). The length and quality of the passages are supposed to provide a more ecologically valid measure of reading comprehension. And this may be the case for the majority of students who take the state tests. However, consider the plight of a fourth-grade boy who reads or processes text at the second-grade level. On the end-of-grade reading test, this youngster is asked to read four long passages, each of which is two grades above his reading level. The child may (or may not) have a good day slowly "translating" the text, or he may (or may not) have a good day guessing at the multiple-choice questions. But in any case, we should question whether this is a proper test of his true reading ability.

Policymakers, newspapers, and much of the citizenry continue to evaluate schools by standardized test scores. For this reason, alone, teachers need to understand these tests: how they are developed, what they can do, and what they cannot do. Standardized reading tests have their uses; however, in the areas of reading diagnosis and corrective instruction, these uses are limited. On the other hand, thoughtfully constructed informal assessments offer many advantages to the reading teacher, a point that Emmett Betts (1946) made forcefully almost 60 years ago.

This brings to a close our three-chapter discussion of reading diagnosis. However, as we move to the topic of corrective instruction in Part II of the book, we will find that diagnosis is inextricably involved in the teaching process from start to finish.

A Parent Interview Schedule for a Reading Clinic

Date _____

Student's name _____   Interviewer _____

Age _____ Grade _____

School _____

Parent's name _____

Address _____

Phone (H) _____ (W) _____

Occupation _____

Developmental and Family Data

1. Were there any complications at birth?

2. Were there any serious childhood injuries or medical conditions?

3. How would you describe your child's general health? (*Probe* for school attendance)

4. When did language develop? (When did the child begin to talk?)

5. How would you describe your child's personality? (*Probe*: cheerful, moody)

6. Does your child have any anxiety or worry about school? (*Probe*: about reading?)

7. What are his or her favorite hobbies or things to do?

8. How many siblings? _____

Names	Ages
_____	_____
_____	_____
_____	_____

9. How are the other children doing in reading?

10. Is there any sibling rivalry or resentment regarding achievement?

11. Has any other member of the family (parent, grandparent, uncle, aunt) had difficulty learning to read? Please elaborate.

Educational History

1. When did you first become aware of your child's reading problem?

2. Now we are going to trace your child's school history. (*Note*: The interviewer should proceed grade level by grade level, starting with kindergarten. Check on referrals for psychological testing, Title I placement, or learning disabilities placement.)

   Kindergarten:

   First grade:

   Second grade:

   Third grade:

   Fourth grade:

   Fifth grade:

3. How is your child doing in school this year? (*Probe*: What are his or her favorite subjects, least favorite subjects? How does he or she do in math?)

4. How is homework handled? (*Probe*: Is there time set aside each night for homework? How long does it take to complete homework? Does your child work independently or do you provide help?)

5. Does your child do *any* reading at home other than school-assigned work? (*Probe*: comic books, computer game magazines, mysteries, etc.)

6. Do you read to your child at home? (*Probe*: How often? If you have stopped, when did you stop?)

7. Have any other professionals been consulted regarding your child's reading problem?

8. Is there anything else you would like us to know about your child—that is, anything we have overlooked?

PART II

CORRECTING READING PROBLEMS

CHAPTER 5

Preventing
Reading Problems
in the Early Grades

This chapter and the two that follow deal with reading instruction. In Chapter 5, I take up the teaching of beginning readers, and in Chapters 6 and 7, the teaching (or remediation) of older readers. I approach this task uneasily, with the words of my mentor in the back of my mind: "When a teacher writes about teaching, the principal problem for the reader is the fear that he will never stop" (Henderson, 1981, p. 124). Given the purpose of this book—that is, to provide perspective on a *particular* clinical approach—I will try hard not to overwhelm the reader with pedagogical detail. On the other hand, the teaching of reading is a craft and a degree of explicit explanation is necessary if I am to avoid recycling unhelpful generalities.

In the present chapter I describe a set of tutoring techniques or strategies that can be used with beginning readers. I go on to show how the various techniques can be combined and adjusted to meet the needs of beginning readers functioning at different developmental levels. Finally, I note briefly how the tutoring strategies can be adapted for small-group reading instruction in the primary-grade classroom. Before proceeding, however, let us consider a few preliminary concepts that will, I hope, lend structure and coherence to the discussion.

LESSON PLANS AND TEACHING TOOLS

The major task facing the teacher of a struggling, beginning reader is to pace the child efficiently through a set of graded reading materials, ensuring that he or she acquires sufficient word or orthographic knowledge along the way. However, the preceding statement begs the question of how the teacher is to accomplish the goal. For example, what instructional activities (e.g., guided reading, phonics, fluency drills, writing) are called for? How much time should be spent on each activity? And how does one know when to advance the learner to a higher (or more difficult) level?

Figure 5.1 depicts one way to think about these questions. Looking at the "learner" side of the figure, we see that instructional level and interest are key considerations. The *reading instructional level* is the difficulty level where the reader is challenged but not overwhelmed (see Chapters 2 and 3). *Reading interests* pertain to subjects preferred by an individual child (e.g., animals, outer space, mysteries, sports). Interest cannot be ignored because it spurs the effort that leads to learning.

Turning now to the "tutor" side of the figure, we find the concept of teaching tools. A skilled reading teacher is like a craftsperson with a toolbox. The craftsperson knows how to build, the teacher knows how to teach; still, each requires a good set of tools with which to work. The first component in the reading tutor's toolbox is a set of quality *reading materials*. These books should be interesting and well-written, carefully leveled in difficulty (early-first through sixth grade), and should represent a variety of genres and subject areas. The second component in the tutor's toolbox is a set of *teaching techniques* that address various aspects of reading. For example, the tutor needs a few effective ways to teach word recognition, another set of techniques to teach reading fluency, and still another to teach comprehension.

The lesson plan, in the middle of Figure 5.1, is the "blueprint" or plan of action—the place where learner characteristics and tutor decision making come together. In devising a lesson plan, the tutor must choose activities that address the learner's specific needs and also decide how much time to allot to each activity. For example, a 50-minute lesson plan for a young child might include guided oral reading (20 minutes), phonics (10 minutes), fluency drill (10 minutes), and being read to (10 minutes). For an older student, the 50 minutes might be allotted differently: silent reading comprehension (30 minutes), fluency drill (10 minutes), and writing (10 minutes). And it should go without saying that, in planning each lesson, the tutor must take into consideration the reader's instructional level and interests.

The learner →	Lesson plan ←	The tutor
Reading instructional level	1. Activity (____ minutes)	Teaching tools
Reading interests	2. Activity (____ minutes)	• Reading materials
	3. Activity (____ minutes)	• Teaching techniques
	4. Activity (____ minutes)	

FIGURE 5.1. The mediation of teaching and learning through a lesson plan.

The lesson plan is important for several reasons: (1) It affords the tutor an ongoing opportunity for reflection (e.g., whether to maintain or change a course of action); (2) it evolves over time, thereby providing a concrete record of the student's progress; and (3) as we will see in Chapter 8, it can serve as an important vehicle for communication between a tutor-in-training and his or her supervising clinician.

A TOOLBOX FOR TUTORING BEGINNING READERS

As noted, this chapter focuses on teaching beginning readers. Some of these children may know only a few printed words, others may be able to read simple preprimer texts, and a few may even read haltingly at the mid-first-grade level. Still, they are all beginners in need of support, and, for our purposes, there is a finite set of teaching tools (materials and techniques) from which a tutor can select in providing this support.

Reading Materials

The careful leveling of reading materials is crucially important in first grade, a nascent, tentative period of development. In our reading clinic, we have divided first-grade reading books into 10 difficulty levels. Book difficulty is determined by predictability of the text, amount of print on each page, and number of new vocabulary words. Table 5.1 shows how the 10 book levels correspond to traditional basal reader levels.

Book Characteristics by Level

Books in levels 1 and 2 are characterized by predictable or repeating sentence patterns that provide needed support to the beginning reader (e.g., Wright Group's *Story Box* or Rigby's *PM Starters*). These books contain a good percentage of high-frequency words (e.g., *is, the, run, dog, can*), but they also contain lower-frequency

TABLE 5.1. A Comparison of the 10 First-Grade Book Levels with Traditional Basal Reader Levels

Book levels	Basal levels
Levels 1–2	Preprimer 1
Levels 3–4	Preprimer 2[a]
Levels 5–6	Preprimer 3
Levels 7–8	Primer[a]
Levels 9–10	Late first grade[a]

[a]Levels that are assessed on the First-Grade Reading Battery.

words (e.g., *truck, grandpa, paddled, nose*) that are often accompanied by a picture
cue. Books in levels 3–6 are of two types: predictable texts and texts that tend to re-
peat a set of high-frequency words (e.g., Rigby's *PM Story Books*). As a group, the
books in levels 1–6 have enough vocabulary control and repetition to help the child
develop an initial sight vocabulary (75 or more known words). At the same time,
the language patterns in these books are sufficiently "natural" to enable the reader
to anticipate upcoming words in the text—to "read beyond the word" (Cunningham, Koppenhaver, Erickson, & Spadorcia, 2004, p. 28). By level 7, or primer level,
the child has acquired a bit of reading independence. Books in levels 7–10 feature
the natural language patterns and engaging story lines that are found in good first-
grade basal readers or trade books (e.g., books by Syd Hoff, Arnold Lobel, or Ed-
ward Marshall).

Over the years, we have developed a book sequence that helps children progress
through the first-grade reading levels (see Table 5.2). Of course, this is only one of
many possible first-grade book sequences, and experienced reading teachers will
have their own. Nonetheless, it is a sequence that we have used successfully with
many struggling first- and second-grade readers. Before leaving this topic, notice in
Table 5.2 the inclusion of pre-1990 basal readers at the primer and late-first-grade
(1–2) levels. We have found that these older basals (e.g., Holt, 1980; Houghton
Mifflin, 1986; Laidlaw, 1980) contain some good stories written in acceptable language. Moreover, they feature systematic word control (or repetition) that is not
found in basal readers published since 1990.

Placing the Reader at the Correct Level

Remember that in our first-grade reading battery (see pp. 37–38), we administered
reading passages at four levels: emergent, preprimer 2, primer, and late first grade.
A child's performance on these passages directly informs instructional placement
(see Table 5.1). For example, suppose Danny is able to read the emergent passage
but not the preprimer 2 passage. Our instructional decision is to start him off at
level 1 (or possibly level 2). A second child, Emily, reads the preprimer 2 passage
easily but just misses instructional level (87% accuracy) on the primer passage. She
is placed at level 6 for instruction. Finally, Curt reads the primer passage with 95%
accuracy, but is frustrated on the late-first-grade passage. We start him off reading
at level 8. Thus, we see how initial passage-reading performance can be used to
place a child at the appropriate first-grade reading level (1–10).

Teaching Techniques

Techniques or strategies for working with a beginning reader (emergent through
mid-first-grade) fall within four areas: support reading, sight vocabulary, word
study, and writing (see Table 5.3).

TABLE 5.2. A Sequence of First-Grade Reading Materials

Levels 1–2 (preprimer 1)	Levels 3–6 (preprimer 2–3)	Levels 7–8 (primer)	Levels 9–10 (late first grade)
Wright Group's *Story Box* books *Sunshine* books	Rigby's *PM Story Books*	Rigby's *PM Story Books*	Random House's *Step into Reading*
Rigby's *PM Starters*	Wright Group's *Story Box* books	Scott Foresman's *Reading Unlimited*	Books by Arnold Lobel and Edward Marshall
	Scott Foresman's *Reading Unlimited*	Random House's *Step into Reading*	Pre-1990 basal readers (1–2 level)
		Books by Mercer Mayer and Syd Hoff	
		Pre-1990 basal readers (primer level)	

Note. See Appendix 5.1 for examples of individual book titles.

Support Reading

The tutor can support the beginning reader in several ways: (1) by helping the child anticipate what is going to happen in the story; (2) by actually doing some of the reading, thereby modeling the process for the child; and (3) by providing difficult words quickly when the child is about to stumble. A tutor learns to provide such support through practice–but, make no mistake, its expert provision can make a huge difference to a child learning to read.

TABLE 5.3. Teaching Techniques for Working with a Beginning Reader

Support reading	Sight vocabulary	Word study	Writing
Preview	Word bank	Beginning consonants	Sentence writing
Prediction questions		Word families (short vowels)	Partner writing
Plot-related questions		Short-vowel patterns	Independent writing
Echo reading			
Partner reading			
Independent reading			
Language experience			

Comprehension Support

The tutor promotes comprehension of a story by previewing, eliciting predictions, and asking questions. Before reading, the tutor and child preview the first six to eight pages of the selection, discussing the pictures on each page and making guesses about the story line. This phase is sometimes referred to as a *picture walk* ("What do you think is happening in this picture, Beth? [*turning to the next page*] Now what do you think is happening?") During the preview, the tutor may also point to and identify a few difficult words in the text. Then, tutor and child return to page 1 and begin to read. Done appropriately, a preview can provide important support. As the child reads, he or she can begin to "fill in" a mental outline, confirming or modifying expectations that were developed during the preview. This process reduces anxiety and makes the reading purposeful (see Clay, 1991b).

During the reading, the tutor may stop at certain points and ask the child for a prediction (e.g, "What do you think is going to happen next?"). The child's response provides a check on comprehension (i.e., we can infer understanding from a good prediction), but it also serves another function. Making a prediction tends to increase the reader's mental investment in the story; he or she wants to find out what happens ("Was I right?"). This investment often produces a more careful reading of the next few pages, which aids both comprehension *and* word recognition.

The picture walk and one or two prediction questions may suffice in reading short selections. However, with longer selections (e.g., mid-first grade), the tutor may need to intersperse a few additional questions. These plot-related questions, posed during the reading of the story, can address characters, setting, the problem facing the characters, and how it is resolved. The idea is to help the child follow the story line from beginning to end.

Text-Processing Support

The beginning reader faces a dilemma. He or she needs to read text in order to learn new words, but how does he or she read even simple texts when knowing very few words? Fortunately, there are time-honored ways to support children's initial reading efforts, several of which use what Holdaway (1979) termed "memory support." In this section I describe a three-stage support strategy—a "scaffold," if you will—that allows even a nonreader (i.e., a child with very few sight words) to read simple texts.

Let us assume that Darren, a true beginning reader, is attempting to read a 12-page book with two lines of text per page. After previewing the book, the tutor and child return to page 1 and begin to *echo-read*. That is, the tutor reads aloud the first page, pointing to each word; then Darren echo reads the same page, again finger-pointing to the words. Pages 2 and 3 are read in the same echoic manner. On page 4, the child and tutor begin to *partner-read*, taking turns reading the next four pages (4–7). On reaching page 8, the tutor asks Darren to predict how the story will end. Then she says, "You know, I think you can read the rest of the story by your-self. If you run into trouble, I'll help." Darren proceeds to *read independently* the last five pages (8–12), with the tutor providing assistance on two words.

In the preceding example, echo reading of the first few pages served to intro-duce character names and the book's distinctive sentence patterning. In truth, the child would not have been able to read these initial pages without the full memory support offered by echo reading. The partner reading or turn taking on the middle pages continued to provide the child with support until he was ready to take over and read the last five pages by himself. And even then, he needed the tutor's help on two words. In this guided reading strategy, the tutor's job is to skillfully move from full support (echo) to partial support (partner) to limited support (independent), en-suring that the child is challenged, but not over-challenged, as he reads.

Echo, partner, and independent reading can be used together to support a reader with limited sight vocabulary. They can also be used separately or in differ-ent combinations. For example, in working with a primer-level reader (level 7 in our scheme), the tutor may use echo reading only to introduce the story. After echo-reading the first two pages, the tutor stops and asks the child to predict what is go-ing to happen next. From page 3 onward, the child reads independently, with the tutor providing assistance as needed. Stops are made every second page or so to check on comprehension and make further predictions. The echo or memory-supported reading on the first two pages is important because it gets the child "into the story," providing him or her with character names, setting, and preliminary in-formation about the plot.

The tutor can also use partner reading for different purposes. It can be used to ease the child into a story; for example, the tutor reads the first page, the child reads the second page, and then a prediction is made. Or, partner reading can be used to provide the child with a respite if he or she tires after reading several pages inde-pendently. The tutor's reading of alternate pages keeps the flow of the story going and, importantly, provides the child with a fluent model of oral reading.

A final word about "independent" reading is warranted. Beginners do not re-ally read independently; they need help. They omit words, insert words, misread words, and sometimes stop abruptly when they meet a difficult word in the text. Knowing how to respond to their difficulties is at the center of the tutoring art. Un-fortunately, no set of fixed rules or recommendations will work, because the read-ing situation changes from line to line, page to page, book to book. The basic idea is for the tutor to anticipate upcoming problems the child may face and provide help quickly when it is needed (see Morris, 2005a, pp. 121–125, for a fuller discussion).

Language Experience

Thus far we have considered how to support a child in reading leveled books. However, there is another time-honored way to introduce reading to beginners—the language-experience or dictated-story method (see Huey, 1968; Stauffer, 1970;

Morris, 2003a). In this method the child dictates a short story (or personal experience) to the tutor, who writes down the sentences. Then, with the tutor's support, the child practices reading the dictated account until he or she can do so with some facility. The tutor's skill in using the language-experience method involves:

- Knowing the child's interests.
- Eliciting talk about one of these interests.
- Helping the child construct a coherent verbal account (beginning, middle, and end).
- Providing the appropriate amount of support that will allow the child to read back his of her dictation.

At this point, let us follow a child through a 3-day experience-story cycle. On *day 1*, Beth dictates a short account about losing a tooth. The tutor writes down the story and then reads it aloud, pointing to each word (see Figure 5.2). Next, Beth and the tutor choral-read the story, with the tutor again doing the finger pointing. Finally, armed with a "memory for the text," Beth reads the story by herself, requiring help on only one word (*when* in line 3). On *day 2*, Beth finger-point reads the story by herself after only one choral reading. And on *day 3*, she reads "My Tooth Fairy" independently with no support from the tutor. At the end of the day 3 reading, the tutor points randomly to a few words in the story to see if Beth can read them (e.g., *not* in line 2, *my* in line 4). If she can, these words go into a sight word bank (see next section).

Once the child has dictated, read, and illustrated three or four experience stories according to the plan above, a *First Book* of dictations can be made. The tutor simply staples the four pages into a manila file folder (9" × 12") and has the child provide an illustration for the cover. Such a book, which provides concrete evidence of progress, can be reread at home or in future tutoring lessons.

My Tooth Fairy

My tooth was loose. Then I kept loosening it till

I pulled it. I put it under my pillow but it did not

work. Then when I had another tooth loosened,

I put it under my pillow. This time it worked. I got

a dime and I spent it on candy.

FIGURE 5.2. Example of a language-experience story.

Sight Vocabulary

The *word bank* is a collection of known words culled from stories (leveled books or dictations) that the child has read. The word bank works in the following manner. After a story has been read several times, the tutor and child go back through the text, two pages at a time, "hunting" for sight words. The tutor randomly points to a few words and checks the quality of the child's word recognition. That is, if the child identifies the word immediately, the word is recorded on a 2" × 3" sight-word card. If he or she has to use context to identify the word or attempts to sound it out, then the word is not recorded as a sight word. In checking for sight words, the tutor generally focuses on two word types: frequently occurring words (e.g., *to, is, and, went*) and pattern words (e.g., *ran, make, sit, like*).

Over several weeks of tutoring, the number of words in the word bank increases—from 2 to 6 to 10 to 15. These sight words are flashed to the beginning reader at the start of each lesson. If a given word is identified, it remains in the bank; if the child fails to read the word, it is removed from the bank. When there are 30 words in the bank, 20 of these known words are sent home, and the child starts working toward a new goal of 30 words.

Regular review of the word bank enables the child to practice a newly learned set of words and eventually store them in automatic memory. The child needs about 25 sight words to read comfortably at level 3 and 40 sight words to read comfortably at level 4. The word bank is usually discontinued at level 6 (late preprimer) when the child possesses a sight vocabulary of 70 or more words.

The word bank is both an instructional and diagnostic tool. The steady accumulation of words in the bank is a reliable sign of reading progress; conversely, unusual difficulty in establishing a core sight vocabulary is cause for concern.

Word Study

Written English is an alphabetic language in which a limited set of letters (26) map, in various combinations, to a limited set of sounds or phonemes (44). There is a letter–sound or orthographic system to be learned. Whereas a beginning reader may initially commit a few whole words to memory, to progress he or she must learn how to decode words, that is, attend to their letter–sound properties (e.g., *bat* = /b/-/ă/-/t/; *ship* = /sh/-/ĭ/-/p/) . Many children learn to decode words in an effortless fashion, requiring minimal instruction. Others struggle mightily with this aspect of reading. In fact, a deficit in decoding or word recognition skill is at the heart of most serious reading problems.

Teaching a child how to decode words (word study) requires knowledge and skill. First, the tutor must understand the content or developmental continuum of word study (e.g., beginning consonants, short vowels, consonant clusters, long-vowel patterns, multisyllable words). Second, he or she must determine where the child needs to be taught along this continuum. And third, the tutor must have a method or procedure for teaching the various letter–sound relationships and spelling patterns.

There is agreement on what constitutes the basic *content* of a word study program (see Calfee, 1982; Henderson, 1990; Wilson, 1996). Table 5.4 shows a typical sequence of instruction. In the table, think of each element in a given column as representing a particular word pattern. For example, *-at* in the word-family column might stand for *cat, bat, sat,* and *flat*; *big* (short *i*) in the short-vowel column might stand for *big, hit, pin,* and *trip*; and *lake* in the vowel-pattern column might stand for *lake, made, name,* and *place*. The sequence of instruction depicted in the table moves from left to right. In fact, a child's learning of concepts further along the continuum (e.g., long-vowel patterns) will depend, in large part, on his or her mastery of concepts introduced earlier (e.g., word families, short vowels). In this chapter on beginning readers, our discussion of word study focuses on the first three columns: beginning consonants, word families, and short vowels.

In *placing a student* along the word study continuum, we must keep in mind that aiming instruction too low (e.g., teaching beginning consonants when a child already knows these letter–sounds) wastes time and effort. On the other hand, aiming too high (e.g., teaching long-vowel patterns to a child who does not understand the basic short-vowel CVC [consonant–vowel–consonant] patterns) can produce frustration and, worse, confusion. Fortunately, it is not difficult to diagnose a child's word recognition level, particularly if we think in terms of broad conceptual levels (see Table 5.4) instead of discrete skills. We consider the placement issue in three case studies at the end of this chapter.

Regarding instructional *method*, we will use a word categorization or "word sorting" approach that was developed at the University of Virginia in the late 1970s and popularized in the textbook *Words Their Way* (Bear, Invernizzi, Templeton, & Johnston, 2003; also see Henderson, 1990; Morris, 2005a). Word sorts, along with accompanying reinforcement games, can be used to teach the spectrum of word recognition concepts, from beginning consonants to multisyllable words.

At this point, some readers may be wondering why I have not yet mentioned phoneme or sound awareness, a prominent issue in beginning reading circles (see Snow, Burns, & Griffin, 1998; Blachman, 2000; National Reading Panel Report, 2000). Researchers have argued that a child needs to be aware that a spoken word (e.g., /băg/) is

TABLE 5.4. Sequence of Word Study Instruction

Beginning consonants	Word families[a]	Short vowels[a]	One-syllable vowel patterns	
b	-at	a hat	(a)	mat
c	-an			lake
d	-ap			park
f	-ack			tail
g				
h	-it	i big	(i)	kid
j	-in			ride
k	-ig			bird
(etc.)	-ick			light
ch	-ot	o top	(o)	job
sh	-op			rope
th	-ock			coat
wh				born
	-ed	e pet	(e)	leg
	-et			seed
	-ell			meat
	-ut	u rub	(u)	bug
	-ug			mule
	-ub			burn
	-uck			suit

[a]Consonant blends (*bl, dr, st,* etc.) are introduced at the word-family and short-vowel levels.

comprised of a sequence of sounds (/b/ /ă/ /g/) *before* he or she can be expected to match letters (*bag*) to sounds (/b/ /ă/ /g/) in the act of reading. I have no quarrel with this logic. However, I do believe the following: (1) phoneme awareness emerges not all of a piece but in stages; (2) it need not be taught in isolation from print; and (3) there are a variety of ways to facilitate its development. In fact, as we will see in the following sections, systematic word study or phonics instruction—attuned to the learner's developmental level—is one very effective way to teach phoneme awareness.

Beginning Consonants

The beginning consonant letter–sound is a very useful word recognition cue for the emergent reader, as in the following example:

Me and my uncle use night crawlers to catch f_____.

Saturday, we c_____ nine fish.

They were little. W__ threw them back.

In this dictation example, it is easy to see how the beginning consonant letters, *f*, *c*, and *W*, could aid the child's contextual recognition of the words, *fish*, *caught*, and *We*. In fact, the use of beginning consonants along with sentence context has long been considered an effective word recognition strategy (Clay, 1991a).

An excellent activity for teaching beginning consonant discrimination is to have the child sort picture cards (spoken words) into categories by beginning consonant sounds. First, the tutor and child take turns sorting a dozen or so words (pictures) into three columns by beginning sound alone. It may take several lessons for the child to grasp the concept of segmenting off the beginning sound in a word (e.g, /b/ in /bīk/; /m/ in /măp/).

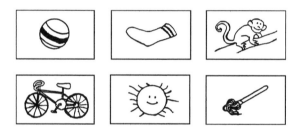

Once the child can reliably sort the words by beginning consonant sound, letter cards are brought out. Now the child sorts the words according to beginning consonant sound–letter match. The picture of a mouse is placed under the letter *m*, because its first sound is /m/. Similarly, a picture of a ball is placed under *b* and a picture of a sock under *s*. A final step has the child write the consonant letters to dictation. The tutor dictates six sounds (e.g., /b/, /m/, /s/) or six words (e.g, *bear*, *sock*, *moon*), and the child writes the corresponding letter for each.

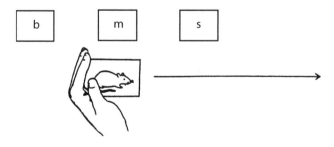

Once the child has learned the first set of consonants (*b*, *m*, and *s*), a second set (*c*, *f*, and *l*) is introduced. The same task sequence applies:

- Column sorting by beginning consonant sound
- Column sorting by sound–letter match
- Writing letters to dictation

The child's learning rate will usually be faster on this second set of consonants. Nonetheless, there is no need to rush, and the tutor should ensure that the child is making fluent, accurate responses before moving on. A possible order for introducing the remaining consonants is:

b, m, s
c, f, l
t, g, r
j, p, v
k, n, d
w, z, h

Awareness of the beginning consonant in isolated words is an important starting point; however, it is the application of this knowledge in contextual reading that is the ultimate goal. Thus, if the child hesitates or misreads a word in context, *the tutor should point to the beginning consonant letter in the misread word, signaling the child to use this cue as he or she attempts to read the word.* The beginning reader's eventual internalization of this word recognition strategy (sentence context plus beginning consonant cue) is an important step forward.

The above discussion of beginning consonant instruction has ushered in the topic of phoneme awareness. Certainly beginning readers must be able to attend to individual sounds (phonemes) in words before they can match letters to these sounds (*Note*: This is why sound matching preceded sound–letter matching in the instructional sequence described above.) Nonetheless, many reading educators wrongly equate phoneme awareness with full segmentation ability—that is, the child's ability to attend to each sound in a spoken word (e.g., /bĭt/ = /b/-/ĭ/-/t/). Instead, phoneme awareness is a complex, multilayered understanding that develops slowly over time. First, children become aware of the initial consonant sound in words (the /b/ in /bĭt/), later, the initial and ending sounds (/b/—/t/), and, finally, the consonants and the medial vowel (/b/ /ĭ/ /t/) (Ehri, 1998; Lewkowicz, 1980; Morris, Bloodgood, Lomax, & Perney, 2003). At the outset, then, it makes good sense to prioritize beginning consonant discrimination and to teach this foundational skill carefully.

Word Families

After the child has mastered beginning consonants, the tutor introduces the next phase of word study: word families. Word families or short-vowel rhyming words are used because they provide an easy entry into word analysis. Knowing the word *man*, the child can decode a new word (e.g., *pan*) by simply changing the beginning consonant (/m/ to /p/) and then blending the consonant (/p/) with the vowel–consonant ending (/ăn/). Most beginning readers find this to be a doable task and, through word-family column sorts, games, and spell checks, they steadily develop sight vocabulary and decoding skill. That is, they learn to read many short-vowel words at sight (e.g., *cat*, *fan*, *sit*, *top*) and to decode or "sound out" others (e.g., *clap*, *tip*, *fed*, *shop*) that are not sight words.

To begin the initial word-family sort, the tutor places two word cards (*cat* and *man*) on the table and a deck of six more cards below (e.g., *sat*, *ran*, *pan*, *bat*, *fan*, *mat*).

cat   man

DECK

If the child can read both *cat* and *man*, the sort can begin; if he or she can read only *cat*, the tutor must teach *man* before proceeding. (Drawing a small stick figure in the upper-right-hand corner of the *man* card is often helpful.)

After explaining that the words in the deck can be sorted under *cat* or *man*, the tutor picks up the top word in the deck (*ran*), places it under *man*, and reads the two words aloud—"man," "ran."

cat   man

ran

The child picks up the next word in the deck, *sat*, and places it incorrectly in the *-an* column. The tutor pauses for a moment and then says, "No, that one doesn't go there." She moves *sat* into the *-at* column and reads the words aloud, "cat," "sat."

cat   man

ran

 sat

The tutor and child each take two more turns before the activity ends. (*Note*: Each time a word is sorted, the entire column is read from top to bottom.)

cat   man

sat   ran

bat   pan

mat   fan

What is being learned in this simple word-family sort? To what features is the child learning to attend? In sorting word families containing the same short-vowel sound, it is the *ending consonant* that actually cues the child as to which words belong in a given column.

cat   man

sat

bat

Bat goes under *cat* and *sat* because the words share the same final consonant letter–sound. Thus, the word-family sort leads the child to attend consistently to the end of the word–a first-time experience for many beginning readers. Note also that this attention to the ending consonant is the next step forward in phoneme awareness development.

After several lessons of sorting the same eight -*at* and -*an* words, the tutor introduces the *memory game*. Following a column sort, the tutor shuffles the eight cards and arrays them face down on the table, as shown below. The game begins with the child turning over two cards, reading them aloud, and checking for a word-family match (e.g., *cat* and *hat*). If there is a match, he or she can remove the two words from the table and take another turn. If there is no match, the child turns the cards back over, and the tutor takes a turn. The game is over when all the words have been removed from the table.

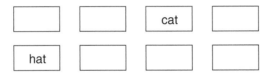

The *memory game* is a perfect reinforcement activity. The format not only randomizes the words, requiring the student to read them out of column context, but also encourages the child to hold the short *a* patterns in visual memory as he or she searches for matches on the table.

Spell checks are a second way to review and reinforce the short *a* word families. The procedure is simple. After completing a column sort or game, the tutor scoops up the cards, leaving only two exemplars on the table.

<u>cat</u>   <u>man</u>

The tutor then proceeds to dictate four or five spelling words. As the child writes the words, he or she can use the exemplars on the table as a pattern reminder. On completion of the test, the tutor and child review the spellings and correct any mistakes.

mat

ran

sat

~~pat~~ pan

The spell check is an integral part of the word study lessons because it provides an alternative route or process for securing target patterns (in this case, short *a* word families) in memory.

Once the student is comfortable with sorting, reading, and spelling the *-at* and -*an* families, a third family, *-ap*, is added.

hat	man	cap
rat	fan	lap
sat		
	clap	

On completion of the short *a* word families (this may take several weeks), the tutor introduces short *i* word families (see below), followed by short *o*, short *e*, and short *u* families, in that order. Beginning consonant blends (e.g., *bl-*, *dr-*, and *st-*) and digraphs (e.g., *ch-*, *sh-*, and *th-*) are introduced early (with short *a* and *i*) and practiced throughout the word-family phase of instruction.

hit	pin	big
fit	win	pig
sit	tin	wig
bit	spin	twig

Now and again, a given child may have trouble progressing through the word-family lessons. He or she may have difficulty attending to the individual letter–sounds within the short-vowel words or have difficulty committing the pattern words to sight memory. In either case, a drop-back teaching strategy ("make-a-word") is to have the child build and take apart short-vowel words using individual letter chips. After arraying eight consonants and two vowels on the table (see Figure 5.3), the tutor says to the child, "Make the word *mat*; now make *mad*; now *bad*; now *bag*; now *big*."

Or better still, the tutor might move the letters around and have the child read a sequence of tutor-constructed words. This format more closely approximates the decoding process. Keep in mind that "make-a-word" always takes place in the context of the specific short vowels being studied, for example, *a* and *i*. In this way, the tutor can provide the child with both an analytic (column sorting) and synthetic (making words) route to improving his or her recognition of short-vowel words.

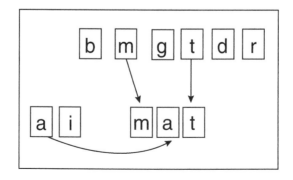

FIGURE 5.3. "Making words" with individual letters: a short-vowel lesson.

In conclusion, word-family instruction serves as a bridge between beginning consonants and short-vowel patterns (see Table 5.4). By carefully teaching the short-vowel word families (*a, i, o, e,* and *u*), the tutor helps the student (1) increase his or her phoneme awareness, (2) learn about beginning consonant blends, and (3) acquire a small sight vocabulary of short-vowel words. This knowledge readies the learner for the next stage in word study—short-vowel patterns.

(*Note*: A more detailed description of short-vowel word-family instruction can be found in Chapters 3 and 4 of *The Howard Street Tutoring Manual* [Morris, 2005a]. Also see Appendix 5.2 at the end of this chapter for a comprehensive list of short-vowel word families along with a suggested sequence of word sorts.)

Short-Vowel Patterns

Short-vowel words can be categorized in *families* or in *patterns*:

Word family (-at)	Vowel pattern (short a)
cat	cat
mat	bad
hat	tap
flat	plan

In short-vowel word families, the vowel and ending consonant (-at) remain constant, as does the rhyme. In short-vowel patterns, only the vowel sound (/ă/) and the spelling pattern (CVC, CCVC) remain constant, thus presenting the child with a more difficult or abstract concept to learn.

To begin short-vowel pattern instruction, the child must be able to read at least three words in each vowel category (*a, i, o, e,* and *u*). To identify known words, the tutor can flash a set of short-vowel words that were introduced in the previous word-family stage.

Known words	New words
cat	wag
tap	cab
flag	slap
big	hid
win	tip
hit	chin
job	dot
pot	log
mom	drop

The sort begins with the tutor placing three known words on the table to serve as exemplars. He or she also places three additional known words at the top of the sorting deck.

<u>cat</u>   <u>big</u>   <u>job</u>

DECK

The tutor explains that the words in the deck can be sorted under *cat*, *big*, or *job*. The idea is to find words that have the same vowel sound.

The child picks up the first word in the deck, *tap*, pronounces it, and places it in the short *a* column under *cat*. The tutor follows by sorting *hit* under *big*; then the child again, sorting *pot* under *job*. After each sort, the tutor points out that words in the same column have the same vowel sound (/ă/, /ĭ/, or /ŏ/). Thus far, no problem; six words have been sorted, and *these were six that the child could already read*.

<u>cat</u>   <u>big</u>   <u>job</u>
tap   hit   pot

DECK

Now we come to the critical transfer phase of the task. Among the remaining 12 unsorted words in the deck are some *new* words; that is, the child has either misread them in the past or the tutor suspects that the words may not be in the child's sight vocabulary. As the child picks up the first "new" word (*tip*), the following scenario might unfold:

CHILD: I don't know this one.

TUTOR: See if you can put it in the right column.

CHILD: (Places *tip* under *big*, cueing visually on the *i* in the middle of the word.)

<u>cat</u>   <u>big</u>   <u>job</u>
tap   hit   pot
             (tip)

TUTOR: (pointing to *big*) Read down the column and see if that helps you with the new word.

CHILD: "Big" . . . "hit" . . . "t-i-p" . . . "tip."

TUTOR: "Tip"—like the "tip" of your nose. Good!

CHILD: (Picks up *log* from the top of the deck and quickly places it in the short *o* column.) "Job" . . . "pot" . . . "l-og" . . . "log."

TUTOR: Nice going.

Note that the first two words in each column are *known words*. This strategy sets up a situation where each time the child is faced with decoding a new short-vowel word (e.g., *tip*), he or she can compare the new word to two known words that have the same visual pattern and vowel sound.

The sort continues, with the child and the tutor taking turns. Each time a word is sorted, all the words in that column are read aloud. This process consistently draws the child's attention to the spelling–pronunciation relationship, the *raison d'être* for sorting word cards.

<u>cat</u>	<u>big</u>	<u>job</u>
tap	hit	pot
wag	tip	log
cab	hid	drop
flag	chin	mom

After a few lessons, ending consonant blends and digraphs (e.g., *fast, lamp, rich, sock*) are introduced in the sort. Also, the tutor and child begin to play the memory game, which is particularly useful at this point. After turning over a word card (see *tip*, below), the child must search his or her visual memory for matching short *i* words that were turned over earlier in the game. This requires true concentration on short-vowel patterns, albeit within a game-like activity.

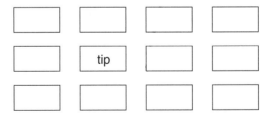

Short *spell checks* provide the child with auditory–visual–kinesthetic practice of the various short-vowel patterns. After a completed sort, the tutor scoops up the word cards and dictates five or six spelling words. Initially, an exemplar for each pattern (e.g., *cat, big, job*) is left on the table to aid the child's spelling. After a few lessons, the exemplars are removed, forcing the child to spell the short-vowel patterns from memory. Each spell check concludes with the tutor and child correcting any misspellings and then graphing the results (e.g., five out of six correct).

Over a few weeks' time, the child will show some mastery of the *a, i,* and *o* short-vowel patterns, and a fourth pattern (*e*) can be introduced. A good way to do this is to contrast the new pattern with two of the old patterns:

hit	top	pet
hid	rob	red
rich	mom	beg
miss	lock	men
swim	drop	less

The introduction of only one new pattern focuses attention on the short *e* words and at the same time allows for important review of the old *i* and *o* patterns.

Finally, it will be time to introduce the last short-vowel pattern (*u*). Again, the overlapping of old with new is appropriate:

job	red	bug
fog	met	sun
mop	hen	bus
spot	bell	rush
lock	mess	club

Timed trials are usually the last activity that is introduced. After shuffling 30–40 word cards (three to five patterns) into a deck, the tutor flashes the words to the child one at a time, stopping after 1 minute. The number of correct and incorrect responses is tallied, and a second trial is administered. Timed trials are motivating for the learner. They also provide useful information to the tutor because the number of short-vowel words read in 1 minute can be a sensitive indicator of progress.

It can be a long march from the initial two-column word-family sort (see p. 96) to the final timed trial on short-vowel words. Nonetheless, the short-vowel patterns (CVC, CCVC, CVCC), consistent and frequently occurring, need to be taught carefully. In fact, the child's mastery of these patterns is an important benchmark that sets the stage for future learning. Henderson (1990, p. 123) stated: "Success in learning [long-vowel patterns] will depend very much on the foundation that is built during the letter-name [short-vowel] stage of word knowledge."

Writing

The linguist Carol Chomsky (1971) once remarked that children should "write first, read later." She had observed that preschoolers who know the alphabet often construct or spell words by attending to their sequential sounds. Thus, a young child might write KR for *car*, RID for *ride*, and YET for *went* (the letter name "y" being a sensible representation of the initial /w/ sound). Chomsky reasoned that early writing might play an important role in reading acquisition because it provides children with purposeful experience in analyzing the sequence of sounds in spoken words and in matching appropriate letters to these sounds (see Clay, 1991b; Ehri, 1989; Richgels, 2001).

The work of Henderson and his students (Henderson & Beers, 1980; Templeton & Bear, 1992; Invernizzi & Hayes, 2004) added to Chomsky's insight by describing a developmental path that is taken by beginning spellers. As shown in Table 5.5, once children can write the alphabet letters, their early *semiphonetic (1)* spellings often include only the beginning consonant (B for *back*, S for *seat*). Later in this stage, *semiphonetic (2)*, they represent the beginning and ending consonants of one-syllable words (BK for *back*; ST for *seat*). In the next stage, *letter–name* (or *phonetic*), young spellers begin to represent vowels. They "sound their way" through the word to be spelled, making one-to-one sound–letter matches as they write. Long vowels are represented with the corresponding letter name (PLAT for *plate*, DRIV for *drive*). Short vowels are also represented with letter names, but, curiously, with those letter names that bear a phonetic similarity to the specific short-vowel sound. For example, the short *i* and long *e* sound are articulated in a similar manner (the tongue is in a similar position in the vocal tract). When the child attempts to represent the short *i* in *fill*, he or she lacks a letter–name referent (there is no alphabet letter "ih"). Therefore, he or she tacitly chooses the nearest long-vowel letter name, *e*, and spells *fill*, FEL. Other phonetically appropriate short vowel–letter name pairings are: *a* for short *e*; *i* for short *o*; and *o* for short *u* (see Read, 1971).

During the second half of first grade—that is, after extended opportunities to read and write—many children move into the *within-word pattern* stage. Here, they begin to spell short vowels correctly (FIL for *fill*; DRES for *dress*) and to mark long vowels (PLAET for *plate*; FLOTE for *float*), even though the vowel markers are often misplaced. Within-word pattern spellings, though still incorrect in the conventional sense, are a clear step forward developmentally. They indicate that children

TABLE 5.5. Developmental Spelling Stages

Word	Semiphonetic (1)	Semiphonetic (2)	Letter-name	Within-word pattern
back	B	BK	BAK	BAKC
seat	S	ST	SET	SETE
plate	P	PT	PLAT	PLAET
drive	J	JRV	DRIV	DRIAV
fill	F	FL	FEL	FIL
dress	J	JS	DRAS	DRES
float	F	FT	FLOT	FLOTE

are abandoning their earlier conception of spelling as a one-to-one code (i.e., one sound = one letter), and instead are searching actively for the legitimate *patterns* of letters (CVC [*mat*]; CVCe [*lake*]; CVVC [*tail*]) that actually map the sounds of the spoken language to the spelling system.

Early writing obviously serves a communicative function. However, from a reading teacher's perspective, it does more. First, writing with invented spellings provides the child with a meaningful context for developing phoneme awareness and exploring sound–letter relationships. Second, writing samples can provide the teacher with valuable diagnostic information. Because early writing—or at least its spelling component—tends to advance in stages, a student's developmental level can be identified and instruction crafted to meet his or her needs. In the sections that follow, I describe three tutoring strategies that do just that.

Sentence Writing

Sentence writing is a basic support-writing strategy that can be used with children who can read few words and have limited phoneme awareness (see Clay, 1993). It does help, however, if the child has some alphabet knowledge.

The child's task is to come up with a sentence and, with the tutor's help, write it down on paper. Topic possibilities are unlimited—friends, pets, hobbies, family activities, school activities, and so on. In the example below, Ben, a first grader, chooses to write about the school bus.

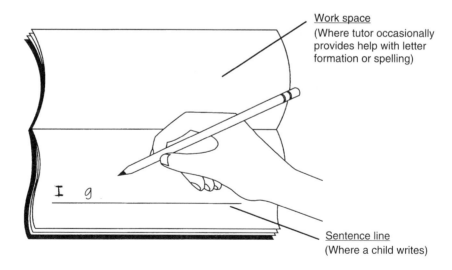

Work space
(Where tutor occasionally provides help with letter formation or spelling)

Sentence line
(Where a child writes)

As Ben begins to write, he pronounces each word slowly, trying to attend to its beginning sound. *It is critical that the child (not the tutor) say each word*; the child needs to feel his or her own articulatory movements, hear his or her own pronunciation, and search independently for the initial sound. In the first weeks of tutoring, Ben can represent only beginning consonants in his sentence writing:

I	G	N	the*	B	T	S.
(I	go	on	the	bus	to	school.)

In the preceding example, the tutor probes for the initial consonant sound on most of the words ("What sound do you hear at the beginning, Ben?"). Ben is hesitant but is able to "hear" and write the beginning consonants in most cases. When he hesitates on *the* (a high-frequency word), the tutor writes the word in the work space and lets the child copy it into his sentence ("This word comes up a lot, Ben; we need to learn it; 'the'—T-H-E.").

Three weeks later, Ben has become familiar with the sentence-writing routine. He has no trouble coming up with a sentence, segmenting the spoken sentence into word units, or writing down the beginning consonant for each word. At this point, the tutor decides to probe for additional letter–sounds in the writing. For example, "Ben, you heard the first sound in *dog* and wrote a *d*. Say *dog* slowly. What comes after the *d*?" (*Child says /daw-g/—/g/.*) "Good! What letter should we put down?" (*Ben writes a g.*) The same probe is used successfully with *can* and *flies*; the tutor provides the tricky -*ch* in *catch*. Notice in these examples that the act of writing led the child naturally to attend to individual sounds within words. Notice also that when the tutor probed for additional sounds, she was actively teaching phoneme awareness.

M	D(G)	C(N)	CCH*	F(S).
(My	dog	can	catch	flies.)

Another month goes by. Ben's sentence-writing ability is progressing nicely. He now knows several high-frequency spellings (e.g., *the, is, and, like, my*) and consistently writes the beginning and ending consonants in words. The tutor decides it is time to probe for medial vowels.

BUCK	F( )L	OF	HZ	B( )K	AND	GT	HRT.
(Buck	fell	off	his	bike	and	got	hurt.)

In Ben's sentence about his older brother Buck, the tutor probes for the long-vowel sound in *bike* and the short-vowel sound in *fell*. First, she sketches a "sound box" in the work space above the child's writing.

---

*Throughout, an asterisk indicates that the tutor assists the child in spelling the word.

TUTOR: (*pointing to the sound box*) Ben, you got the beginning and ending letters in *bike*. Say the word slowly and try to hear another sound in the middle.

BENJAMIN: /b — ī — k/; /b — ī — /. It's an *i*.

TUTOR: Good! Why don't you change your spelling? (*Ben changes the spelling BK to BIK.*)

Ben is led through a similar routine with *fell*. He is able to "hear" the medial /ĕ/ sound but says the letter should be *a*. The tutor, at this point, accepts Ben's response; after all, the short *e* sound does bear a phonetic resemblance to the letter name, *a*.

The sound box provides a visual representation of the spoken word, in effect freezing the word's sequential speech sounds for analysis (Clay, 1993; Elkonin, 1973). The success of this teaching strategy depends on the child's developmental readiness to perceive the medial vowel sounds. The issue cannot be forced. If the strategy does not work the first time it is tried, patience is required. More reading, writing, and word study will eventually ready the child for vowel awareness, a crucial step forward in reading acquisition.

Sentence writing is an important part of an emergent reader's tutoring program. It helps the child to develop sound awareness and letter–sound knowledge in the context of purposeful writing. Sentence writing at this stage is not uncomplicated, requiring concentrated effort from the child and thoughtful, moment-to-moment support from the tutor. Still, it is worth the effort. Over time, the daily writing notebook (unedited) will provide the clearest and most persuasive evidence of the emergent reader's growth in word knowledge. Note Ben's development in the few examples cited above:

September

I   G   N   the*   B   T   S.

October

M   DG   CN   CCH*   FS.

November

BUCK   FAL   OF   HZ   BIK   AND   GT   HRT.

Partner Writing

Partner writing is a bridge between supported sentence writing and the independent writing of stories. It is generally used with preprimer-level readers who can spell phonetically but lack the fluency or stamina to write stories independently.

In partner writing, as in partner reading, the child and tutor take turns. After a

Lupe: I HAV A PET HAMSTR.

Tutor: I like to take him out of the cage.

Lupe: WON DAY HE BET ME ON THE FEGR.

Tutor: He is fuzzy and sweet, but if you make him mad he can bite you.

FIGURE 5.4. Example of partner writing.

short, prewriting discussion, Lupe proceeds to write her first sentence (see Figure 5.4). Then she dictates the next sentence to the tutor who writes it down. Lupe writes sentence 3 and the tutor serves as scribe on sentence 4. Note that all four sentences are composed by the child although she writes only the first and third.

After all four sentences have been written, Lupe reads the story back. Next, the tutor may have her focus on certain words that have been misspelled. These are usually high frequency words (e.g., HAV for *have*; WON for *one*) or short-vowel patterns (e.g., BET for *bit*) that have been covered in previous word study lessons.

Partner writing is obviously an extension of sentence writing. The child takes responsibility for writing two sentences instead of one; in addition, his or her selection and sequencing of all four sentences is good preparation for the next stage—independent writing of stories.

Independent Writing

Beginning readers will differ as to when they are able and willing to write independently. A child struggling to hear the individual sounds in words does not usually find story writing to be an appealing task. Nonetheless, when the child achieves a late-preprimer or primer reading level (i.e., has a core sight vocabulary and can spell phonetically) then he or she should be encouraged to write independently.

An independent writing activity has three phases: prewriting, writing, and postwriting. In the *prewriting* phase, the child self-selects a topic and, with the tutor's assistance, brainstorms ideas about this topic. Dalton, a second-grade child reading at the primer level, is very interested in snakes. He chooses to write about anacondas. As Dalton eagerly recounts some characteristics of this tree-dwelling snake, the tutor fills in a story map (see below). Notice that, in filling in the map, the tutor writes down only one or two words for each idea mentioned by Dalton.

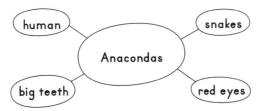

With the brainstorming completed, the tutor effects a transition into the *writing* phase.

> TUTOR: Okay, Dalton, how are we going to start your story about anacondas? What's your first sentence going to be?
>
> DALTON: Anacondas are big and have red eyes.
>
> TUTOR: That's good! But shouldn't we start off by telling the reader of your story that anacondas are snakes. Some people might not know.
>
> DALTON: Yeah.

Dalton proceeds to write the first sentence and then, referring to the story map, writes several more sentences about anacondas. As he writes (see Figure 5.5), the tutor writes her own story about a long ago encounter with a black snake.

Dalton begins the *postwriting* phase by going back and reading his story aloud. In doing so, he spontaneously inserts a period after MONKYS in line 2 and corrects the spelling of LIV in line 3. Aside from these changes, he seems quite satisfied with his piece. The tutor has two objectives in this postwriting phase: (1) to help the child improve or clarify the content of the writing sample, and (2) to help him correct mechanical errors such as punctuation and spelling. Nonetheless, the tutor proceeds very cautiously in providing feedback. In fact, she starts off by telling Dalton how much she likes his story, particularly his vivid descriptions of the anaconda (e.g., "eyes as red as a monkey's; "live in water and will eat anything they see moving").

Regarding revision of content, the tutor might ask Dalton where anacondas live—North Carolina, the United States, another continent? Or she might ask him how the snake kills its prey? If the child is unsure about the answers to these questions, a quick visit to the encyclopedia might be helpful (in fact, anacondas live in tropical South America and suffocate their prey). If Dalton chooses to add information to his account, he can write a new sentence at the bottom of the page and use an arrow to show where the sentence should be inserted in his story.

Regarding editing, the tutor might call Dalton's attention to a missing period on line 3. She might also have him focus on his misspellings of *water* and *anything*, because these are frequently occurring words that he needs to learn to spell. With revi-

Anacondas are big snakes. They are
very long and have eyes as red as a MONKYS
anacondas LIV in WATR they will eat ENETHING
they see MOOVING. They have big TETH and
they will eat a human.

FIGURE 5.5. Example of independent writing.

sion and editing completed, the tutor types up the story (correcting spelling and punctuation), has Dalton illustrate it, and sends the finished product home with the child.

This brings to an end our discussion of a toolbox of materials and methods that can be used in working with beginning readers. In the case studies that follow, we will see how these tools can be adapted or combined in various ways to meet the needs of beginners functioning at different levels of reading proficiency.

CASE STUDIES

In this section, we encounter three cases representing different levels of beginning readers: emergent, preprimer, and primer. Each case includes (1) characteristics of the reading level, (2) initial diagnostic information, (3) a lesson plan that draws selectively from the toolbox of materials and teaching techniques, and (4) a description of the initial tutoring lesson along with brief commentary on later lessons.

The Emergent Reader

Characteristics

The emergent reader, or true beginner, knows most of the alphabet letters but may be unable to attend to even the beginning consonant sound in spoken words. Such a beginner possesses few sight words (3–10) and may have difficulty finger-point reading (i.e., matching spoken words to printed words in the act of reading). This is obviously a fragile stage in reading development—one that calls for careful tutor support. The emergent reader needs to read and reread simple texts in order to firm up finger-point reading skill and establish an initial sight vocabulary. He or she also needs to engage in word study and sentence writing to develop rudimentary decoding skills (e.g., the beginning consonant letter–sound) that can be applied in reading text. In our materials scheme, the emergent reader starts off reading level 1 books.

Initial Diagnostic Results

After 2 months in first grade, Antonio had made little reading progress. Tested by the school-based reading teacher, he achieved the following scores on the first-grade reading battery (see Table 5.6). Antonio could read only 3 of the 20 words (15%) on the preprimer word recognition list (*cat*, *me*, and *go*). He was able to finger-point read the emergent passage, but only after the tutor provided a finger-point reading model on each of the first four pages (no score for oral reading accuracy was recorded). On the first-grade spelling task, Antonio was able to represent the beginning consonant on 7 of the 12 words. (*Note*: J or /j/ is an acceptable phonetic substitution for the first part of the /dr/ blend in *drop* and *drive*.)

TABLE 5.6. Case Summary Sheet of an Emergent Reader (*Antonio—First Grade*)

	Word recognition		Oral reading			
	Flash	Untimed	Accuracy	Compre-hension	Rate	Spelling
Emergent			—			
Preprimer	—	15				
Primer						
Late first grade						0

bed	B	drop	J
trap		bump	B
wish		drive	J
sister	S	plane	P
let	T	ship	
girl		bike	B

As a precaution, the tutor assessed Antonio's alphabet knowledge; he was able to name 24 of the 26 lowercase letters.

Overall, the diagnostic results show a child at the very beginning stages of learning to read. Alphabet knowledge is a relative strength, but in terms of sight vocabulary, contextual reading ability, and phoneme awareness, Antonio is at the starting gate.

Lesson Plan

The lesson plan for the emergent reader draws from each of the areas in the tutor's instructional toolbox.

- *Reading materials*: level 1 and 2 books
- *Support reading*: echo- and partner-reading of leveled books; also independent rereading of these books
- *Sight vocabulary*: establishment of a word bank
- *Word study*: review of beginning consonant letter–sounds before moving to short-vowel word families
- *Writing*: sentence writing with tutor support

These materials and teaching activities are combined into a set lesson plan (35 minutes) that includes four parts:

1. Rereading 3 leveled books
2. Word study
3. Sentence writing
4. Introduce new book

The four parts of Antonio's lesson plan are interrelated. The knowledge gained through finger-point reading the simple texts (e.g., attention to the spoken word–written word match, use of beginning consonant cues, sight vocabulary) is applied in the sentence-writing activity. Conversely, the letter–sound knowledge that is exercised in the sentence writing is applied in the book reading. Even the seemingly isolated phonics work in Part 2 of the lesson is immediately put into practice each time the student finger-point reads a book or invents spellings in the sentence writing. The result is an integrated tutorial lesson that melds whole-to-part and part-to-whole learning in a meaningful way. (*Note:* Parts 1, 3, and 4 of the lesson were first introduced by Clay, 1993, in her Reading Recovery program. The word study activity in the second part can be traced back to the work of Henderson, 1990.)

The First Tutoring Lesson

1. *Rereading books* (12 minutes). (Actually, this is the second lesson because there could be no rereading of books in the very first lesson.) Antonio does a nice job rereading three level 1 books (see example in Figure 5.6). The tutor provides help on a few words, sometimes having Antonio use the picture as a word recognition cue (e.g., see picture of *toes* in the figure). Antonio's finger-point reading is erratic. However, when he occasionally mismatches spoken word to printed word, he is able to self-correct by going back and rereading the line. After the child finishes reading each eight-page book, the tutor goes back and points to individual words on several pages. Antonio cannot identify the words immediately, but he is able to return to the beginning of the line and finger-point over to the target word. (*Note:* These contextually identified words are not counted as sight words.)

2. *Word study* (8 minutes). Antonio sorts spoken words (picture cards) into columns by beginning consonant sound (e.g., /b/, /m/, and /s/). (See pp. 93–94 for a description of beginning consonant sorts.) He sorts the words tentatively but accurately. Antonio seems able to attend to the beginning consonant sound in a word. As his speed and confidence improve in this activity, sound–letter matching will be added.

3. *Sentence writing* (8 minutes). In response to the tutor's query, "What did you do over the weekend," Antonio produces the following sentence:

We*   P   K   aNd*   R.

(We   played   cops   and   robbers.)

See my fingers,   see my toes,

FIGURE 5.6. Two pages from *In the Mirror* (Cowley, 1986a). Reprinted by permission of McGraw Hill Education.

With concentration, he is able to write the beginning consonant letter for each word. The tutor probes for an ending sound in *played*, but to no avail. After Antonio reads his sentence aloud, the tutor helps him complete the correct spellings of the high-frequency words, *We* and *and*.

4. *Introduce a new book* (7 minutes). Antonio and the tutor preview the first six pages of a new book (*Yuk Soup*; Cowley, 1986b), naming the pictures on each page. Next, they return to the beginning and echo-read the first two pages (i.e., tutor reads, then child reads). With the sentence pattern established ("In go some snails/ In go some feathers/ In go . . ."), Antonio attempts to finger-point read the remaining six pages. Relying on the sentence pattern and the picture cues, he does a good job, coming "off the track" on only one page. (*Note*: This new book will be one of the three books reread at the beginning of the next lesson.)

The Next Lesson

The next lesson builds directly on the one just described. Antonio rereads three books, sorts the same three beginning consonant sounds, writes a new sentence, and, with the tutor's help, reads a new level 1 book.

Two Months Later

After 2 months or 18 tutoring lessons, Antonio has progressed nicely. He now has a sight vocabulary of 25 words, which are reviewed at the start of each lesson. He reads level 3 books independently, skillfully using beginning consonant and picture cues as word recognition aids. In word study, Antonio has progressed to the next stage—short-vowel word families (see pp. 95–99). He is fairly fluent in sorting short *a* word families (*-at*, *-an*, and *-ap*) into columns, and he has committed a half dozen of these words to sight memory. In sentence writing, Antonio has become consistent in representing the ending consonant sound in his spellings; however, he still has difficulty attending to medial vowel sounds in words he wants to write.

I	WT	TO	BNS	HS	YSDRDAY*
(I	went	to	Ben's	house	yesterday.)

Overall, we can say that this emergent reader has made important steps forward. Antonio's sight vocabulary, phoneme awareness, and contextual reading skill have advanced significantly, as has his confidence in himself as a reader. What he needs is additional reading practice and word study in the presence of a knowledgeable, supportive tutor.

The Preprimer Reader

Characteristics

The preprimer (or early-first-grade) reader has a small sight vocabulary of 25–40 words, reads in a halting, word-by-word fashion, and spells phonetically, representing beginning and ending consonants and sometimes the medial vowel. Although more skillful and independent than the emergent reader, the preprimer reader still requires systematic instruction in contextual reading and word study. Immediate goals are to increase sight vocabulary and phoneme awareness, learn the short-vowel spelling patterns, and improve contextual reading fluency.

Initial Diagnostic Results

Tested in January of first grade, Barbara achieved the following scores on the First-Grade Reading Battery (see Table 5.7). Her flash score on the preprimer word list was 50%, but she could read only 3 of the 20 words (15%) on the primer list. Barbara's contextual reading followed the same pattern. She was able to read the preprimer passage with 92% accuracy, but was frustrated when reading the primer passage (78%).

Barbara's spelling score (0% correct) is a bit misleading because it fails to reflect the quality of her misspellings (note that the previous case study, Antonio, also achieved a 0% score on the spelling task).

bed	BAD	drop	JP
trap	TP	bump	BP
wish	W	drive	JIV

TABLE 5.7. Case Summary Sheet of a Preprimer Reader (*Barbara—First Grade*)

	Word recognition		Oral reading			
	Flash	Untimed	Accuracy	Compre-hension	Rate	Spelling
Emergent						
Preprimer	50	70	92			
Primer	15	30	78			
Late first grade						0

sister	SDR	plane	PAN
let	LAT	ship	CHP
girl	GRL	bike	BIK

These spellings reveal considerable phoneme awareness, as Barbara consistently represents beginning and ending consonant sounds and a few medial vowels. She represents several long vowels with the corresponding letter name (e.g., JIV for *drive*; PAN for *plane*) and makes a sensible letter–name substitution for the short *e* sound (e.g., BAD for *bed*; LAT for *let*). She obviously lacks knowledge of consonant clusters (e.g, *sh*, *tr*, *pl*). Barbara needs to improve her awareness of medial vowel sounds and eventually learn the conventional spellings of short vowels. The more abstract long-vowel patterns can wait.

Although this child has fallen a bit behind her peers at the midpoint in first grade, she is ready to "take off" in reading. For the tutor, placing Barbara at the correct reading level (4) and word study level (short vowels) is the first order of business.

Lesson Plan

The lesson plan for the preprimer reader draws from the instructional toolbox in the following manner:

- *Reading materials*: level 4 books
- *Support reading*: mostly independent reading of these books, with the tutor providing assistance when needed
- *Sight vocabulary*: acquisition and review of sight words
- *Word study*: short-vowel word families (*a*, *i*, *o*, *e*, and *u*, in that order)
- *Sentence writing*: writing a sentence with tutor support, eventually evolving into partner writing of four-sentence accounts

In structure, Barbara's lesson plan is identical to that used with Antonio, the emergent reader. The four parts of her lesson (rereading three books, word study, sentence writing, and reading a new book) are described in the section that follows.

The First Tutoring Lesson

1. *Rereading books* (14 minutes). (Again, this is the second lesson because there would be no books to reread in Lesson 1.) Barbara finger-point reads the first two level 4 books with ease. On the third book, *Seagull Is Clever* (Randell, 1996c; see Figure 5.7), she has trouble getting started, and the tutor decides to echo-read the first two pages. Given this support, Barbara is able to read the remaining eight pages independently, requiring help on only two words (*waves, shellfish*).

Barbara's finger-point reading is accurate, and she skillfully uses the beginning consonant letter–sound as a word recognition cue. After each book is read, the tutor goes back and points to individual words on several pages. Barbara is able to read several of the words immediately (e.g., *is, fish, not, up*). The tutor jots down these words and later places them in Barbara's word bank, which is reviewed at the start of each lesson.

2. *Word study* (8 minutes). The tutor and child begin by sorting short *a* rhyming words into three families.

hat	man	cap
pat	can	lap
sat	ran	tap
bat	fan	nap

Barbara has no trouble sorting the words into columns, and she can read down the columns, slowly but accurately (e.g., "hat—pat—sat—bat"). The tutor decides to play a memory game (see p. 97) in which the child has to visually remember pattern matches (e.g., *man—ran*). Barbara has some difficulty reading the word cards

Seagull is a big bird.
He is hungry.
He is looking for fish.

FIGURE 5.7. Two pages from *Seagull Is Clever* (Randell, 1996c). Reprinted by permission of Thomson Learning Australia.

that she turns over, leading the tutor to think that they should spend more time on column sorting before playing the memory game.

3. *Sentence writing* (8 minutes). Barbara chooses to write a sentence about her dog, Barney. Initially, she spells with beginning and ending consonants only, leaving out the medial vowel in words (e.g., DG for *dog*; CN for *can*). The tutor decides to go back and probe for medial vowels:

MY   DG   C( )N   CH   A   B(O)N.

(My   dog   can   catch   a   bone.)

TUTOR: Barbara, let's look at your spelling of *bone*. You got the beginning and ending sounds. I want you to say *bone* slowly and see if you can hear a sound right after the B. Say *bone* slowly.

CHILD: /b — ō — n/. I hear o.

TUTOR: Good! Let's put an *o* in your spelling of *bone*.

The tutor tries the same strategy with the word, *can*, but this time Barbara is unable to attend to the /ă/ sound in the middle of the word.

4. *Introduce a new book* (5 minutes). Barbara and the tutor preview the first six pages of a new level 4 book (*Father Bear Goes Fishing*; Randell, 1996a), using the pictures to help predict the story line. After echo-reading the first two pages of the book, Barbara reads the remaining pages by herself. Her reading is halting, but she requires the tutor's help on only two words (*here* and *shouted*). Level 4 books provide appropriate challenge for this child.

The Next Lesson

Barbara rereads three books, the third being *Father Bear Goes Fishing*, which she reads with more confidence today. She sorts the same three short *a* word families, writes a new sentence (the tutor again probes for medial vowels), and reads a new level 4 book.

Two Months Later

After 17 lessons, Barbara has made significant progress. She now has 50 words in her word bank (30 mastered words were sent home, and she is now working on her second set of 30). With the larger sight vocabulary and a new-found ability to "sound through" words (e.g., /d/-/ĭ/-/sh/), she is a more independent reader. Barbara is comfortable reading level 5 books and, in week or so, should move up to level 6.

In word study, Barbara has worked through the short *a, i,* and *o* word families and is ready to begin work on short *e*. Through the word-family sorts and games, she has increased her phoneme awareness (attention to the medial vowel), learned some consonant clusters, and committed a good number of short-vowel words to sight memory.

pet	red	tell
let	bed	sell
wet	led	fell
jet	sled	bell
get	shed	shell

In sentence writing, Barbara is now consistent in including the medial vowel in her spellings. However, she does not always use the correct letter to represent short vowels (e.g., SLAD for *sled*), and she seldom marks long vowels with an extra letter (e.g., CON for *cone*). Although long-vowel patterns have not yet been introduced in the tutoring lessons, short-vowel patterns have, and the tutor holds Barbara responsible for spelling short vowels conventionally. For example, in the sentence below, the tutor goes back and has the child attend to the misspelled vowel in *chicks* and the omitted consonant in *Friday*. In each case, she is able to correct the spelling.

I	GOT	FIV	CHEKS	ON	FIDAY.
I	got	five	chicks	on	Friday.

Given Barbara's progress, the tutor is considering a move to *partner writing*, where the child and tutor combine to write a four-sentence story (see p. 106). Such a change seems warranted although it will necessitate adding five minutes to the writing portion of the lesson.

To sum up, Barbara is moving forward in reading. Her steadily increasing sight vocabulary and emerging knowledge of consonant blends and short-vowel patterns are very positive signs. Moreover, the child feels her growing skill as a reader and is investing herself fully in the tutoring lessons. Given time and continued work, she will learn to read.

The Primer Reader

Characteristics

The primer (or mid-first-grade) reader is qualitatively different from the preprimer reader. The primer reader possesses a large sight vocabulary (100+ words), well-developed phoneme awareness, and some knowledge of short-vowel spelling patterns. He or she uses context skillfully and has more reading stamina (i.e., can read longer stretches of text before tiring). The primer reader requires occasional word recognition assistance, but the most helpful tutor support is that which allows the child to anticipate meaning as he or she reads.

Initial Diagnostic Results

Tested in the second month of second grade, Curtis achieved the following scores on the First-Grade Reading Battery (see Table 5.8). His flash word recognition score was strong on the preprimer list (90%) and borderline instructional on the primer list (60%). Similarly, he was able to read the preprimer passage with ease (98% accuracy) and attained an instructional-level score (93% accuracy) on the primer passage. Curtis was clearly frustrated at the late-first-grade level, scoring 35% on flash word recognition and 85% on oral reading accuracy.

Curtis spelled almost half (42%) of the 12 first-grade spelling words correctly, demonstrating some knowledge of short-vowel patterns and consonant blends (e.g., BED, TRAP, DROP). However, his seven misspellings revealed gaps in short-vowel knowledge (e.g., WESH for *wish*; BOP for *bump*) and little awareness of long-vowel patterns (e.g., DRIV for *drive*; PLAN for *plane*; and BIK for *bike*).

bed	BED (c)	drop	DROP (c)
trap	TRAP (c)	bump	BOP
wish	WESH	drive	DRIV
sister	SISTR	plane	PLAN
let	LET (c)	ship	SHIP (c)
girl	GRIL	bike	BIK

Overall, these test results reveal a child who has fallen a half year behind. At the start of second grade, Curtis is reading and spelling at a primer or mid-first-grade level.

TABLE 5.8. Case Summary Sheet of a Primer Reader (*Curtis—Second Grade*)

	Word recognition		Oral reading			
	Flash	Untimed	Accuracy	Compre-hension	Rate	Spelling
Emergent						
Preprimer	90	95	98			
Primer	60	80	93	100		
Late first grade	35	60	85	75	37	42

Lesson Plan

The lesson plan for the primer reader draws from the instructional toolbox in a slightly different manner.

- *Reading materials*: level 7 books (trade books or basal readers written at the primer level)
- *Support reading*: guided oral reading of these books, with an emphasis on comprehension; also, reading of easier, level 6 stories to develop fluency
- *Word study*: review of short-vowel patterns and introduction of long-vowel and *r*-controlled patterns
- *Writing*: partner writing of four-sentence accounts evolving into independent story writing by the child

The structure of the lesson plan changes when a child reaches the primer reading level.

Preprimer lesson plan (35 minutes)	Primer lesson plan (45 minutes)
1. Rereading books (14)	1. Guided reading of new story (18)
2. Word study (8)	2. Word study (10)
3. Sentence writing (8)	3. Easy reading *or* story writing (10)
4. Introduce new book (5)	4. Tutor reads to child (7)

Whereas the preprimer lesson begins with the rereading of three short books, the primer lesson begins with the guided reading of a new, primer-level story each day. Rereading of a book can occur in Part 3 of the primer lesson, but "easy reading" usually means that the child reads a new, less challenging text (e.g., level 6) to help develop fluency and confidence. It can be difficult to fit both easy reading and story writing into Part 3 of the lesson. Some tutors, therefore, alternate these activities on a weekly basis—that is, easy reading one week, story writing the next. To sum up, there is less rereading of books in the primer lesson plan and a bit more emphasis on comprehension. Writing is still an important lesson component, but it does not occur each day.

The First Tutoring Lesson

1. *Guided reading* (18 minutes). Curtis and the tutor begin by previewing the first 10 pages of *Pepper's Adventure* (Randell, 1996b), a level 7 book. (*Note*: There are 15 pages in the book, with full-page pictures aside full pages of text; see Figure 5.8.) During the preview, Curtis uses the pictures to predict what is going to happen in the story; he says, "The little mouse is gonna get loose, but the kids will find him."

Returning to the beginning of the story, the tutor and Curtis echo-read the first

Dad made a big new cage
for Pepper and Salt.
It had a wheel and a ladder
and a room upstairs.
Sarah played with the mice a lot,
and so did Nicky from next door.
"Don't take them outside,"
said Mom.

FIGURE 5.8. Two pages from *Pepper's Adventure* (Randell, 1996b). Reprinted by permission of Thomson Learning Australia.

page of text. This step serves to introduce the names of the mice (Pepper and Salt) and the lead character (Sarah). From this point on, Curtis reads the story by himself. He needs help with a few words (e.g., *upstairs, sorry, hiding*), but overall his oral reading is accurate and includes stretches of appropriate phrasing. At three points in the story, the tutor stops and asks Curtis what has happened thus far and what will happen next (e.g., "How did Pepper get free?" "What might happen to him in yard?"). The child's answers are appropriate, and his predictions lead him to read the following pages with interest and concentration. Level 7 is the correct reading level for Curtis: not too easy, not to hard.

2. *Word study* (10 minutes). The tutor decides to review short-vowel patterns with Curtis to assess his mastery of consonant clusters and short vowels. She begins by flashing 20 short-vowel words to Curtis, one at a time. He reads 17 of the words correctly (e.g., *lap, flag, bit, trip, job, shot*), misreading only 3 words ("hide" for *hid*; "gin" for *grin*; "cloak" for *clock*).

The tutor shuffles the 20 word cards, placing the 3 words Curtis missed (*hid, grin,* and *clock*) on the bottom of the deck. Then, she and Curtis proceed to sort the words into three short-vowel categories:

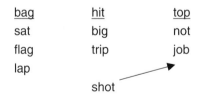

<u>bag</u>	<u>hit</u>	<u>top</u>
sat	big	not
flag	trip	job
lap		
	shot	

Curtis reads and sorts the words correctly, even the three words he originally missed on the flash assessment. The tutor and child follow up with a short memory game, and again Curtis shows good knowledge of these short-vowel patterns. If he continues to perform in this manner, the review of the five short-vowel patterns should take only a few weeks.

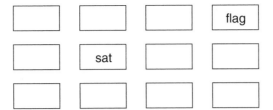

3. *Easy reading* (10 minutes). The tutor brings out a level 6 book. After a short preview, Curtis reads the book independently. The tutor stops the reading at two points to ask the child to make a prediction. Curtis actually guesses the outcome of the story and is quite pleased with himself on seeing his prediction born out.

There is time left over, so the tutor asks Curtis to think of topics he would be willing to write about next week. He decides on three: baseball, dirt-track car races, and his pet rabbit.

4. *Read to Curtis* (7 minutes). The tutor reads aloud the first half of Molly Bang's *Wiley and the Hairy Man*. Curtis listens attentively, commenting on the story at several points. This read-aloud time serves as an apt reward for Curtis's diligent effort; it is also a pleasant way to end the lesson.

The Next Lesson

Curtis reads a new level 7 book and sorts the same three short-vowel patterns (/ă/, /ĭ/, and /ŏ/). A game of memory and a spell check follow the sorting. Curtis then reads two level 6 books, the tutor reading half of the second one, so that there is time for the read-aloud (*Wiley*) at the end of the lesson. Next week (lesson 3), a new short-vowel pattern (/ŭ/) will be introduced, and, in Part 3 of the lesson, Curtis will write a story about his rabbit.

Two Months Later

Eighteen lessons later, Curtis is reading late-first-grade material. In fact, he has completed five stories in a 1–2 basal reader (see Figure 5.9). Curtis is reading more fluently, benefiting from the word control in this pre-1990s basal reader. His comprehension is excellent, and he seems to enjoy the stories that the tutor selects. (*Note:* Only the most interesting stories from the basal are read.)

In word study, Curtis has begun work on high-frequency vowel patterns: short, long, and *r*-controlled (see pp. 134–141). After reviewing short vowels for several weeks, he worked with the *a* vowel patterns (*cap*, *take*, *card*, *day*) and is now beginning to study the *i* patterns:

<u>hit</u>	<u>ride</u>	<u>bird</u>	<u>night</u>
dig	bike	girl	light
kick	drive	shirt	might
chin			bright

dime

All at once a car came to a stop.
A man and a boy got out.

"Oh, no!" said the man
when he looked at the tire.
"Now we will be here for a while."

Little Pocket Mouse was not far
from the light.
But no one could see him.
He just sat.

"This is not a good place to stop,"
said the man.
"But we have to fix that tire."

The boy looked up and down the highway.
"We were here once before," he said.
"This is where we saw a mouse.
Not far from that red rock.
I would like to see another mouse."

"Don't look for it now," said his father.
"Not while I'm fixing this tire.
Come and help me."

The boy put his coat down so he could help.

FIGURE 5.9. Two pages from *Toothless Dragon* (Eller & Hester, 1980). Reprinted by permission of McGraw Hill Education.

Column sorting is supplemented by reinforcement games (e.g., Memory, Bingo) and daily spelling checks.

Curtis now does his "easy" reading at the primer level, where there are many interesting book choices. The tutor uses selections from Rigby's *PM Story Books*, Random House's *Step into Reading*, and Scott Foresman's *Reading Unlimited*, as well as books written by Mercer Mayer and Syd Hoff.

Writing has become an important part of Curtis's tutoring program. He started out partner-writing four-sentence stories, but as his word knowledge and self-confidence increased, he began to write independently. His most recent story, in edited form, is shown below.

Baseball

By Curtis Smith

In baseball there are four bases, first, second, third, and home. The pitcher stands on the pitcher's mound. The batter only gets three strikes. Sometimes, the umpire yells at you. My favorite player is Chipper Jones. He plays for the Atlanta Braves.

Curtis has improved in all areas—contextual reading, word study, and writing. In the second half of the year, he will read a mixture of basal stories and trade books and continue to sort, read, and spell one-syllable vowel patterns (*a, i, o, e,* and *u*). With hard work and a little luck, Curtis has a chance to "catch up"—to be a grade-level (2–2) reader by the end of the school year.

CLASSROOM APPLICATIONS

The tutoring strategies described in this chapter can be adapted for use in first- and second-grade classrooms. Let us consider such adaptations across a set of issues that confront all primary-grade teachers of reading: assessment, individual differences, reading materials, and instructional procedures.

Assessment

The first-grade reading battery—described in Chapter 2 (pp. 37–38) and applied in the case studies in the present chapter—can be used effectively in the classroom. Depending on the purpose, classroom teachers can administer one, two, or all three assessments that comprise the battery (i.e., word recognition, oral reading, and spelling). For example, a first-grade teacher, wanting to place her students into reading groups at the beginning of the school year, might administer the spelling task (first six words) to the whole class. Based on the spelling results, the teacher could follow up by administering the preprimer word recognition list (untimed) to selected students. Performance on the spelling and word recognition tasks would provide the teacher with a good estimate of the range of printed word knowledge among students in the class.

A second-grade teacher may want to check mastery of basic sight words in his low reading group. He could do so by administering the preprimer word recognition list (flash presentation) to each child in the group (administration time is only about 3 minutes per student). On occasion, a teacher might require a more complete reading assessment; for example, on a new student who enters the class at midyear, or on a student who seems to be lagging behind (or speeding ahead) of his or her reading group. In such cases, keep in mind that the entire battery takes less than 20 minutes to administer.

Addressing Individual Differences

Most first- and second-grade teachers group students by ability for reading. Small groups (high, middle, low) allow instruction to be provided at the appropriate difficulty level. They also afford beginning readers more opportunities to interact with the teacher and the teacher more chances to observe the performance of individual children.

Figure 5.10 illustrates the rotation of three reading groups in a primary-grade classroom, from (1) teacher-guided instruction in the reading circle to (2) learning centers to (3) seat work. The tutoring strategies described in this chapter, particularly support reading and word study, pertain to the teacher-guided instruction in the reading circle. That is, the classroom teacher can adapt the tutoring techniques to fit the small-group context (see upcoming section, Instructional Procedures), and then use the learning center and seat-work contexts to reinforce skills taught in the small group. It is important to keep the low-ability reading group small in number (four to six children, if possible) to provide struggling readers with more learning opportunities—more chances to read aloud and sort word patterns under the teacher's watchful eye.

Reading Materials

The teacher of struggling readers needs a set of interesting reading materials that are carefully leveled in difficulty. Ideally, first-grade reading materials should include sufficient repetition of high-frequency words (e.g., *to, are, your*) and decodable words (e.g., *ran, sit, drop*), along with sentence patterns that allow beginning readers to anticipate upcoming words in text (see Cunningham et al., 2004). Unfortunately, and for many reasons, this is an ideal that is seldom realized, particularly in the basal reader programs that predominate in first- and second-grade classrooms.

The classroom teacher of struggling readers has two choices. First, he or she can use the imperfect sequence of stories found in a first-grade basal reader and try to compensate for materials deficiencies through expert teaching (e.g., echo reading, rereading, slow pacing). Second, the teacher can search for and, over time, develop a carefully leveled set of interesting stories that contain the characteristics previously mentioned: sight-word repetition, phonics pattern repetition, and natural (as opposed to stilted) sentence patterns. I strongly favor the second alternative, though I realize it poses problems for new teachers or teachers in schools with limited re-

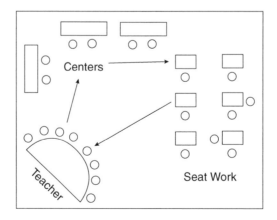

FIGURE 5.10. Rotation of reading groups in a first-grade classroom

sources. (See Table 5.2 for a possible sequence of first-grade reading materials. See Morris, 2003a, pp. 39–41, for a fuller discussion of the reading materials issue.)

Instructional Procedures

The tutoring techniques described in this chapter transfer directly into a small-group instructional setting. To illustrate this point, let us consider readers at three developmental levels: emergent, preprimer, and primer.

For *emergent* or true beginning readers, language experience is an effective small-group activity. The group of five or six children discuss an experience (e.g., playing in the leaf pile), dictate a few sentences to be written down, and then choral read the completed story with the teacher. In the 3-day language-experience cycle (see pp. 89–90), there is much teacher modeling, and individual children have a chance to finger-point read, identify individual words in the story, and use beginning consonants as a word recognition aid. Regarding word study in the small group, the emergent readers take turns sorting picture cards by beginning consonant sound until they eventually master this first stage of phoneme awareness.

For *preprimer* readers, who have small sight vocabularies and limited phoneme awareness, rereading leveled texts and sorting words into short-vowel families is easily accomplished in a small-group setting. The lesson might begin by the children ($N = 6$) rereading, in pairs, two preprimer stories introduced earlier in the week. The teacher monitors this rereading, providing word recognition support as needed. Next, the teacher leads the group in a short-vowel word sort:

The children take turns sorting words and then reading down the column to make sure the word belongs in that column. The teacher might follow up with a make-a-word activity, or she may have the children pair up to play Memory or Bingo with the short-vowel words. In the final 7 minutes of the small-group lesson, the teacher introduces a new book. She and the children preview the story by commenting on the illustrations; then they go back and echo-read the first four pages. At this point, the teacher elicits a prediction about what is going to happen in the story. The children respond and then proceed to take turns reading one or two pages aloud until the story is completed. (*Note*: This book will be one of the two stories to be reread at the beginning of the next day's lesson.)

For *primer* or mid-first-grade readers, the small-group lesson has a slightly different format. A new story is introduced each day at the beginning of the lesson. A picture walk may be used, or the teacher may have the children echo-read the first two pages before making a prediction. At this point, the teacher calls on individual children to read aloud, stopping the reading every now and then to ask questions and elicit further predictions. With four pages to go and the story's outcome at stake, the teacher asks the children to finish reading the story silently (or as silently as they can, for beginners often mumble the words when asked to read silently). With the guided reading completed, the teacher leads the children in a word study activity, usually involving short- or long-vowel patterns. Finally, if time allows, the children, working in pairs, might reread favorite stories introduced in earlier lessons. The goal here is to increase reading fluency.

In summary, if low-ability readers are taught in small groups at the appropriate difficulty level, then the tutoring techniques described in this chapter can be used effectively in the classroom.

In this chapter I have described a toolbox of reading materials and teaching techniques that is appropriate for use with beginning readers. The emphasis was on balanced instruction that includes reading for meaning, word study, and writing. In addition, we considered case studies of beginning readers at three levels of development: emergent, preprimer, and primer. Although the period covered may seem short (i.e., early to late first grade), keep in mind that the *first* year of learning to read is a difficult, fragile time for the child who struggles. Moreover, the knowledge developed in the first year—including phoneme awareness, sight vocabulary, decoding skill, and emergent fluency—lays the foundation for future growth.

In Chapters 6 and 7 we take up the broader—and more complex—terrain of reading difficulties from the second-grade to sixth-grade level. What will remain constant as we move from the beginning reader to the more advanced remedial reader are the notions of (1) teaching the child at the correct instructional level, and (2) providing balanced instruction that includes reading for meaning, word study, and fluency building.

First-Grade Reading Material: Representative Book Titles for Levels 1 through 10

The following book list includes titles used in *Early Steps*, a first-grade reading intervention program (Morris et al., 2000; Santa & Hoien, 1999). The 10 book levels correspond to traditional basal reader levels in the following manner:

Book level	Basal level
1, 2	Preprimer 1
3, 4	Preprimer 2
5, 6	Preprimer 3
7, 8	Primer
9, 10	Late first grade (1–2)

Title	Level	Author/Series	Publisher
Chocolate Cake, The	1	Story Box	Wright Group
Ghost, The	1	Story Box	Wright Group
If You Meet a Dragon	1	Story Box	Wright Group
In the Mirror	1	Story Box	Wright Group
In the Shopping Cart	1	PM Starters	Rigby
Look at Me	1	PM Starters	Rigby
Painting	1	Story Box	Wright Group
Pets	1	PM Starters	Rigby
Playing	1	PM Starters	Rigby
Yuk Soup	1	Story Box	Wright Group
Ball Games	2	PM Starters	Rigby
Little Brother	2	Story Box	Wright Group
Little Pig	2	Story Box	Wright Group
Lost	2	Story Box	Wright Group
Monster Sandwich, A	2	Story Box	Wright Group
My Accident	2	PM Starters	Rigby
Nighttime	2	Story Box	Wright Group
Stop	2	Story Box	Wright Group
We Can Run	2	PM Starters	Rigby
Where Are the Babies?	2	PM Starters	Rigby

Title	Level	Author/Series	Publisher
Big and Little	3	Sunshine	Wright Group
Big Kick, The	3	PM Story Books	Rigby
Cat and Mouse	3	PM Starters	Rigby
Copy-Cat	3	Story Box	Wright Group
Dan, the Flying Man	3	Read-togethers	Wright Group
Fishing	3	PM Starters	Rigby
Sally and the Daisy	3	PM Story Books	Rigby
Shark in a Sack	3	Sunshine	Wright Group
Silly Old Possum	3	Story Box	Wright Group
Two Little Dogs	3	Story Box	Wright Group
Baby Bear Goes Fishing	4	PM Story Books	Rigby
Ben's Teddy Bear	4	PM Story Books	Rigby
Father Bear Goes Fishing	4	PM Story Books	Rigby
Friend for Little White Rabbit, A	4	PM Story Books	Rigby
Goodbye Lucy	4	Sunshine	Wright Group
Hungry Kitten, The	4	PM Story Books	Rigby
In a Dark, Dark Wood	4	Read-togethers	Wright Group
Mrs. Wishy Washy	4	Story Box	Wright Group
Seagull Is Clever	4	PM Story Books	Rigby
Too Big for Me	4	Story Box	Wright Group
Big Toe, The	5	Read-togethers	Wright Group
Blackberries	5	PM Story Books	Rigby
Duck with a Broken Wing, The	5	PM Story Books	Rigby
Hairy Bear	5	Read-togethers	Wright Group
Jane's Car	5	PM Story Books	Rigby
Lion and the Rabbit, The	5	PM Story Books	Rigby
Little Bulldozer	5	PM Story Books	Rigby
Lucky Goes to Dog School	5	PM Story Books	Rigby
Red Rose, The	5	Read-togethers	Wright Group
Woosh!	5	Story Box	Wright Group
Brave Tricerotops	6	PM Story Books	Rigby
Clever Penguins, The	6	PM Story Books	Rigby
Come On, Tim	6	PM Story Books	Rigby
Honey for Baby Bear	6	PM Story Books	Rigby
Late for Soccer	6	PM Story Books	Rigby
Lion and the Mouse, The	6	PM Story Books	Rigby
Little Bulldozer Helps Again	6	PM Story Books	Rigby
Morris the Moose	6	Wiseman, B.	Harper Trophy
Rescue, The	6	PM Story Books	Rigby
Tiny and the Wave	6	PM Story Books	Rigby

Title	Level	Author/Series	Publisher
Chug the Tractor	7	PM Story Books	Rigby
Deer and the Crocodile, The	7	PM Story Books	Rigby
Fox Who Was Foxed, The	7	PM Story Books	Rigby
Hungry Giant, The	7	Story Box	Wright Group
Just for You	7	Mayer, M.	Donovan
Just Me and My Little Sister	7	Mayer, M.	Donovan
My New Boy	7	Step Into Reading	Random House
Tabby in the Tree	7	PM Story Books	Rigby
Three Little Pigs, The	7	Reading Unlimited	Scott, Foresman
Tiger Is a Scaredy Cat	7	Step into Reading	Random House
Cave Boy	8	Step into Reading	Random House
Cross-Country Race, The	8	PM Story Books	Rigby
Island Picnic, The	8	PM Story Books	Rigby
Just Me and My Little Brother	8	Mayer, M.	Donovan
Just Me and My Puppy	8	Mayer, M.	Donovan
Mrs. Spider's Beautiful Web	8	PM Story Books	Rigby
Nina, Nina, Ballerina	8	Step into Reading	Random House
Pepper's Adventure	8	PM Story Books	Rigby
Pot of Gold, The	8	Reading Unlimited	Scott, Foresman
Waving Sheep, The	8	PM Story Books	Rigby
All Stuck Up	9	Step into Reading	Random House
Chester	9	Hoff, S.	Harper Trophy
Danny and the Dinosaur	9	Hoff, S.	Scholastic
Good Hunting, Blue Sky	9	Parish, P.	Harper Trophy
How Turtle Raced Beaver	9	Literacy 2000	Rigby
Kiss for Little Bear, A	9	Minarik, E.	Harper & Row
Little Knight, The	9	Reading Unlimited	Scott, Foresman
Sammy and the Seal	9	Hoff, S.	Harper Trophy
Slim, Shorty, and the Mules	9	Reading Unlimited	Scott, Foresman
Stanley	9	Hoff, S.	Harper
Bike Lesson, The	10	Berenstain, S. and J.	Random House
Days with Frog and Toad	10	Lobel, A.	Harper Trophy
Fox All Week	10	Marshall, E.	Puffin
Fox and His Friends	10	Marshall, E.	Puffin
Frog and Toad Are Friends	10	Lobel, A.	Harper & Row
Frog and Toad Together	10	Lobel, A.	HarperCollins
Little Bear	10	Minarik, E.	HarperCollins
Little Bear's Visit	10	Minarik, E.	Harper Trophy
Mouse Tales	10	Lobel, A.	HarperCollins
Owl at Home	10	Lobel, A.	HarperCollins

Short-Vowel Word Families and a Possible Sequence of Word-Family Sorts

Short-Vowel Word Families

cat	man	cap	bag	back
mat	can	lap	rag	tack
sat	van	nap	tag	rack
pat	ran	tap	wag	sack
rat	fan	map	drag	pack
that	pan	sap	flag	black
flat	plan	clap		track

hit	big	win	tip	sick
sit	wig	tin	lip	kick
fit	pig	pin	hip	lick
pit	fig	fin	rip	pick
kit	dig	grin	sip	tick
bit	twig	chin	ship	trick
knit		spin	slip	brick

hot	top	log	job	sock
pot	pop	jog	rob	rock
lot	hop	hog	cob	lock
not	mop	frog	mob	block
got	cop		sob	clock
shot	stop		knob	knock
spot	drop			

pet	red	tell	hen
met	bed	sell	pen
wet	fed	fell	men
let	led	well	ten
jet	sled	bell	then
get	shed	shell	when
set		smell	

cut	bug	run	tub	luck
nut	hug	gun	rub	duck
but	dug	fun	cub	suck
hut	rug	sun	club	stuck
shut	jug	bun	truck	

Possible Sequence of Word–Family Sorts

cat	man	lap		
sat	fan	map	←——————— (Sample word-family sort)	
fat	pan	tap		
mat	ran	cap		
flat	can	clap		

cat	man	lap	back	←——— (Column headers for next sort)*
hit	big	win		
hit	big	win	kick	

Review:

cat	man	hit	
cat	man	hit	big

hot	top	job	
hot	top	job	sock

Review:

hit	win	hot	
hit	win	hot	top

pet	red	hen	
pet	red	hen	tell

Review:

hot	sock	pet	
hot	sock	pet	red

cut	bug	run	
cut	bug	run	luck

Review:

pet	tell	cut	
pet	tell	cut	run

---

*Every underlined word on the page (e.g., back) represents a column header for a potential sort. Under back might be sorted *sack, pack, tack, black*, etc.; under lap might be sorted *map, tap, cap, clap*, as shown in the first example sort.

CHAPTER 6

Correcting Reading Problems in the Later Grades

I. BASIC TEACHING STRATEGIES

Having considered instruction for beginning readers in Chapter 5, we now turn to instruction for more advanced remedial readers (e.g., second- to sixth-grade reading levels). This group presents an assortment of reading difficulties, including those related to word recognition, comprehension, and fluency. Severe reading disability or dyslexia is also to be found, although in a relatively small number of children. In approaching the complex topic of corrective reading instruction, I use the format introduced in the previous chapter. That is, in this chapter, I describe a "toolbox" containing a limited set of teaching techniques or strategies. Then, in the next chapter, I show how these teaching techniques, alone or in combination, can be applied to cases representing different types of reading problems.

A TOOLBOX FOR TUTORING STRUGGLING READERS

Reading Materials

An interesting, varied set of reading materials is a must for any reading teacher. Engaging stories and informational texts spur motivation and help struggling readers muster the concentrated effort that is needed if they are to improve. Nonetheless, there is an inherent problem in locating interesting books for low-achieving readers because talented authors usually aim their work at a particular age range; for example, Jerry Spinelli's *Maniac McGee* and Christopher Paul Curtis's *The Watsons Go to Birmingham* appeal to middle school students who read at a fifth- to sixth-grade level. Unfortunately, these wonderful books are not accessible to sixth-grade students who read at a third-grade level; these children simply do not possess enough print-processing skill to read the text. (*Note*: This does not preclude the teacher reading aloud *Maniac McGee* and *The Watsons Go to Birmingham* to the children.)

The tutor's task, then, is to find interesting material that his or her student can actually read. This might involve finding a third-grade-level book that appeals to a sixth-grade boy or a second-grade-level book that appeals to a fourth-grade girl. The idea is to identify the student's reading instructional level (the level where he or she can make progress) and then locate interesting, age-appropriate texts that are written at this level. Fortunately, over the past 15 years in the United States, many trade books (narrative, biography, and information) have been published that appeal to students who read below grade level. Appendix 6.1 includes a sampling of these texts at grade levels 2–5.

Teaching Techniques

Techniques or strategies for working with remedial readers (second through sixth grade) fall within four areas: word study, comprehension, fluency, and writing (see Table 6.1). The specific combination of techniques to be used with a given student is dictated by his or her strengths and weaknesses as a reader.

Word Study

Most children who can read at the second-grade level or higher understand the alphabetic nature of our written language. That is, they can attend to individual sounds in words and match letters to these sounds. What many low readers still need to learn, however, are the basic one-syllable spelling patterns in the language (e.g., CV, CVC, CVCe, CVVC, CV-r) and how these syllables conjoin or go together in longer multisyllable words (e.g., V/CV, VC/CV, VC/V, /Cle).

TABLE 6.1. Teaching Techniques for Working with a Remedial Reader (Reading Levels 2–6)

Word study	Comprehension	Fluency	Writing
One-syllable patterns	Guided reading	Easy reading	Independent writing
Two-syllable patterns	• Narrative text	Repeated readings	
	• Informational text	Taped readings	
		(Word work)	

One-Syllable Spelling Patterns

The most basic one-syllable pattern is the *short-vowel pattern*, in which a single vowel is bounded by consonants. For example:

CVC	CCVC	CVCC
mat	plan	last
tip	drip	rich
job	shot	sock
red	step	bell
bug	drum	rush

Many poor readers do not internalize the foundational short-vowel patterns in first and second grade, which can later lead to serious problems with word recognition.

One way to quickly assess a child's knowledge of short-vowel patterns is to accumulate a deck of 50 short-vowel words—10 word cards per vowel (see Appendix 6.2). Shuffle the deck of word cards and then flash them to the child, one at a time. Correctly identified words are placed in one pile, incorrectly identified words in a second pile. If the child reads 47 of the 50 words correctly—and if his or her responses are, for the most part, *immediate*—the tutor can assume short-vowel knowledge and move to the next stage of word study. However, if the child misreads more than three short-vowel words, or if his or her responses are slow, the tutor may decide to spend some time reviewing short-vowel patterns. This will be time well spent. (See pp. 99–102 for a description of how to teach short-vowel patterns.)

Once a child has mastered the short-vowel patterns, he or she is ready to study the other one-syllable patterns, namely *long-vowel patterns, r-controlled patterns*, and a few others. Because some of these patterns occur frequently in written English, it makes sense to study them first (see Figure 6.1, middle column). In the one-syllable-pattern column, think of each element as representing a particular word pattern. For example, *lake* in the *a* patterns might stand for *lake, race, made, name*, and *plate*. Similarly, *bird* in the *i* patterns might stand for *bird, girl, dirt, first*, and *shirt*. *Coat*, in the *o* patterns, might represent *coat, road, soap, float*, and *coach*. It is the teaching and learning of such patterns that concerns us in this section.

Getting Started: Sorting Patterns of the Vowel A

It is helpful, at the outset, to view vowel-pattern work as proceeding in five phases: sorting word patterns across the vowel *a*, sorting patterns across the vowel *i*, sorting patterns across the vowel *o*, and so on. Therefore, let us begin with the vowel *a*.

The first three *a* patterns to be sorted are CVC (short *a* words), CVCe (long *a* words), and CV-r (*r*-controlled *a* words). Six to eight words per pattern are needed, and the student should be able to read 75% of these words before the sort begins. The examination (or sorting) of known words (e.g., *jar, park, card, barn*) allows the

Short vowels	One-syllable patterns		Two-syllable patterns	
a hat	(a)	mat	VC/CV	happen
		lake		rabbit
		car		discuss
		tail		
i big	(i)	kid	V/CV	razor
		ride		predict
		bird		student
		light		
o top	(o)	job	VC/V	robin
		rope		gravel
		coat		lizard
		told		
		go		
e pet	(e)	leg	/Cle	table
		seed		noble
		meat		single
		he		mumble
u rub	(u)	bug		
		rule		
		burn		
		suit		

FIGURE 6.1. Sequence of word study for remedial readers.

child to induce an invariant sound–letter pattern (*-ar*). He or she can then use this knowledge to read new words containing the same pattern (e.g., *harm, start*). (See Appendix 6.2 for vowel-pattern word lists.)

The tutor begins the sort by putting three word cards on the table in a horizontal array:

<u>mat</u>   <u>rake</u>   <u>car</u>

Next, she produces a deck of 15 word cards and explains to Thomas, a third grader, that each of the 15 words goes in one of the three categories (under *mat*, under *rake*, or under *car*). The tutor models the sorting of the first word in the deck, *sad*, by placing it under *mat* and reading both words aloud. She then sorts the second word, *name*, in a similar manner.

mat	rake	car
sad	name	

Thomas picks up the next word in the deck, *hard*, reads it aloud, and places it under *rake* and *name*. The tutor corrects him by simply moving *hard* over to the *-ar* column (under *car*), and again reads the two words aloud. She tells Thomas that in sorting the words into columns, he must attend both to the way the word "looks" and to the sound that the letter, *a*, makes in the word.

mat	rake	car
sad	name	
	(hard) ⟶	

It's the tutor's turn again. She sorts *page* under *rake* and *name* in a deliberate fashion, with Thomas watching closely now, trying to figure out the rules of this new game.

mat	rake	car
sad	name	hard
	page	

Thomas's following play is interesting. Picking up the next word, *cap*, he puts it in the *-ar* column briefly. Then he changes his mind, places *cap* gingerly under *mat* and *sad*, and removes his hand uncertainly. When the tutor says, "Good, Thomas!", a smile crosses the child's face. He reads aloud the three short *a* words and then eagerly looks to see where the tutor will place the next card.

mat	rake	car
sad	name	hard
cap	page	

The tutor and child continue to take turns sorting the 15 words, with the tutor modeling correct responses and also giving Thomas immediate feedback as to the correctness of his sorting attempts. By the end of this 5-minute task, Thomas is still tentative and inconsistent when sorting the words, but he does seem to be actively involved in the activity.

The following tutoring session, the word sort activity is repeated using the same three categories and the same 15 words. As on the first day, Thomas's sorting responses are slow and deliberate, with an occasional error. However, midway through the activity, following one of his errors that the tutor matter-of-factly sorts in a different category, Thomas's eyes light up and he informs the tutor that he has "got it." He does. From that point on, he sorts each word accurately and confidently. At the end of the sort, Thomas and the tutor read aloud the words in each column, agree that they are sorted correctly by vowel sound, and decide that it is time to add something new.

mat	rake	car
sad	name	hard
can	page	start
clap	face	park
rag	made	farm
ham	place	star

The "new" involves introducing a fourth *a* pattern.

mat	rake	car	tail

The tutor keeps the same words used in the three-pattern sort and adds five -*ai* words (*tail, wait, rain, paid,* and *train*), the first three of which are in Thomas's sight vocabulary. Again, the tutor and child take turns reading and sorting each word card into one of four categories. Thomas shows a little confusion on his first turn (sorting *rain* under *rake*), but he quickly picks up on the new visual pattern (CVVC) and proceeds to sort the remaining words with accuracy and a bit more speed.

In subsequent lessons, the tutor introduces reinforcement activities to help Thomas master the *a* patterns. The game of Memory, in which the child searches for pattern matches, is always a popular and effective reinforcement game (see Chapter 5, p. 97 for instructions on how to play Memory).

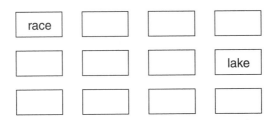

Another fast-paced game is Bingo, a variation of column sorting. Needed materials are (1) two Bingo cards (8.5" × 11"), each containing 20 squares, and (2) a deck of 40 word cards (10 for each pattern) and 6 "wild cards." The same headers are placed in the top row of each Bingo card (see next page).

1. To begin the game, a player draws a word from the deck. If he or she can place it in the appropriate column (e.g., *man* under *bat*) and then read each word in that column, then the word is left on the board. If the player misreads the word or places it in an incorrect column (and the other player challenges), then the word is removed from the board. The players alternate turns.

Thomas's Bingo card

bat	make	car	tail

Tutor's Bingo card

bat	make	car	tail

DECK

2. If a player draws a "wild card" from the deck, he or she can place it anywhere on the board and then take another turn.
3. The game is over when one of the players fills all the squares on his or her Bingo card.

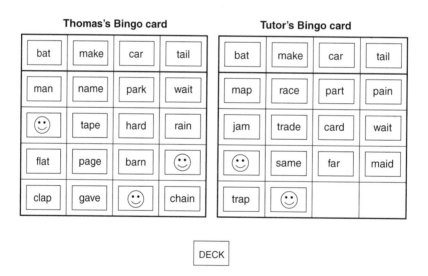

DECK

Another way to reinforce the *a* vowel patterns is through *spelling checks*. After completing a column sort or game, the tutor scoops up all the word cards, leaving only four pattern exemplars across the top of the table:

<u>mat</u>   <u>lake</u>   <u>park</u>   <u>mail</u>

The tutor tells Thomas to number from 1 to 8 on a piece of paper in preparation for a spelling check. Explaining that each spelling word will follow "one of the patterns we have been working on," the tutor proceeds to dictate eight words (from the word cards she has scooped up), one by one. As Thomas spells, he is encouraged to use the exemplars on the table as a pattern reminder. On completion of the test, the tutor immediately goes through the spellings with Thomas, having him self-correct any errors.

1. card	5. star
2. bake	6. ~~fase~~ face
3. flag	7. trap
4. ~~rane~~ rain	8. tail

Timed trials are usually the last game or activity to be introduced when studying a set of vowel patterns. The dual purpose of timed trials is to strengthen the child's automaticity of response and to provide a concrete measure of this automaticity. Needed materials are (1) 40–50 word cards that fit the target patterns (e.g., *sat*, *made*, *hard*, and *rain*); (2) a stopwatch or wristwatch with a second hand; and (3) a progress chart.

1. After shuffling the deck of word cards, the tutor explains to Thomas that she is going to "flash" the words to him one at a time. His task is to read correctly as many words as he can in 1 minute.
2. After noting the starting time, the tutor proceeds to present the words one at a time. If Thomas reads the word correctly, it goes in one pile; if he misreads the word or hesitates for 3 seconds, it goes in a second pile.
3. When 1 minute has gone by, the trial stops. The tutor counts the number of words in the "correct" pile, and Thomas counts the words in the "incorrect" pile. These numbers are then graphed on a progress chart. It is generally appropriate to do two, back-to-back trials in the same lesson.

Each of the activities (column sorting, Memory, Bingo, spelling check, and timed trials) provides the student with needed practice. These activities (1) require little advance planning by the tutor, (2) are enjoyable, and (3) do a good job of strengthening the child's discrimination of, and memory for, basic vowel patterns.

Sorting Patterns of the Other Vowels—I, O, E, *and* U

Individual children will require varying amounts of practice to master the patterns of the vowel *a*. Some will do so after three or four tutoring sessions; others will require hours of column sorting and reinforcement games spread out over a 3- to 4-week period. It should be noted that it is not just the specific *a* patterns that the child is learning, but also the more generalized skill of how to search for and detect orthographic structure (spelling patterns) across any set of words. It is this learned tendency to note pattern relationships among words that will transfer to future word sorts; for example, to Thomas's sorting of patterns across the vowel *i*.

The first three *i* patterns to be sorted (CVC, CVCe, CV-r) are identical to those that were used in the initial *a* sort. Again, six to eight words per pattern are needed, and the child should be able to read 75% of these words before the sort begins. Once the *i* sort is underway, the tutor might notice that Thomas is more accurate, more confident, and somewhat faster in making his sorting decisions than he was at this stage of the *a* pattern sorts. (This is the transfer phenomenon that was mentioned above.) Accordingly, less time or fewer tutoring sessions might be needed for Thomas to achieve proficiency in sorting *i* words into the three major patterns.

big	side	girl
hit	bike	bird
win	time	sir
kid	nine	shirt
swim	slide	first

After the fourth pattern of *i* has been introduced (*-ight*), the various reinforcement games can be played (e.g., Memory, Bingo, timed trials).

big	side	girl	night
kid	time	sir	right
win	bite	first	might
swim	nine	bird	sight
hit	slide	shirt	light
	bike		

After Thomas has mastered the high-frequency *i* patterns, the tutor might decide to collapse the *a* and *i* patterns into one sort before moving on to another vowel. For example:

hat	lake	hit	like
fan	made	pin	mine
sad	race	dig	kite
rag	sale	sick	time

Collapsing a word sort across two vowels allows for a review of previously studied patterns (in this case, *a* patterns), and also highlights pattern regularities across the different vowels (e.g., *hat* and *hit*; *lake* and *like*; *hard* and *bird*).

At this point, assuming accuracy and fluency in Thomas's sorting responses, the tutor can move to a third vowel, possibly *o*. High-frequency patterns of *o* would include:

top	rope	boat	told
rob	joke	coal	cold
shop	pole	foam	fold
jog	stone	float	sold
mop	code	foal	hold

Thomas will master the *o* sort above in a fairly short period of time because *o* is the third vowel across which he has sorted the same patterns (e.g., CVC, CVCe, CVVC). However, the saving of instructional time on later sorts (e.g., *o*, *e*, and *u* patterns) will be contingent on sufficient instructional time having been devoted to the earlier pattern sorts. Again we see the importance of the tutor doing a thorough job of teaching the *a* and *i* vowel patterns. It is on these initial sorts that the child learns, or does not learn, an important transferable reading skill—the tendency to search for and detect pattern regularities in one-syllable words.

A plan for sorting vowel patterns has been illustrated using *a*, *i*, and *o* patterns as examples. Obviously, the *e* and *u* patterns can be sorted using the same basic format. Once the frequently occurring patterns of the five vowels have been sorted, the tutor can go back and have the child work through the less frequently occurring patterns (e.g., *ball*, *bread*, *grew*, *tie*, *hook*, and *glue*).

There is no one best sequence or timetable for moving through the vowel-pattern word sorts with a remedial reader. Children differ in the amount and kind of practice they require to internalize these word patterns. Appendix 6.3 provides a proposed sequence of pattern sorts that spans all five vowels. However, such a sequence should be readily adapted by the tutor (specific sorts added, deleted, or modified) according to the needs of the individual child.

For more extensive discussions of how to teach one-syllable vowel patterns, see Chapter 5 in *The Howard Street Tutoring Manual* (Morris, 2005a), Chapter 7 in *Words Their Way* (Bear et al., 2003), and Chapter 5 in *Word Journeys* (Ganske, 2000). Also see Stage 4 in the classroom instructional program, *Phonics and Phoneme Awareness* (Morris & Bloodgood, 2004).

Two-Syllable Patterns

Many struggling readers in the upper-elementary and middle grades have difficulty reading longer, multisyllable words. These children may possess large sight vocabularies and some decoding skill, yet they are stumped when confronting a new word that contains more than one syllable (e.g., *public*, *termite*, *opinion*, *conductor*). This section on two-syllable patterns has a very narrow purpose: to describe ways that a reader can locate the first syllable break in a multisyllable word, thereby facilitating identification of the word.

Two-syllable patterns should not be introduced in the tutoring lessons until the basic one-syllable patterns (e.g., CVC, CVCe, CV-r) have been mastered. Little is gained by teaching a child to divide *public* and *termite* between adjacent consonants

(b/l and r/m, respectively) if he or she cannot then pronounce "pub-" and "ter-."
On the other hand, if knowledge of one-syllable patterns is in place, the tutor can
teach syllable-division strategies using the following instructional sequence.

An important first step is to introduce the student to the concepts of closed and
open syllables. The tutor explains that a *closed syllable* contains one vowel and
ends with a consonant (the consonant closes off the vowel). The vowel sound in a
closed syllable is short (e.g., *at, met, trip, rock,* and *up*). Conversely, an *open syllable* ends with a vowel (a consonant does *not* close off the vowel). The vowel sound
in an open syllable is long (e.g., *ta, be, tri, ho,* and *pu*).

At this point, the tutor should provide the child with *extended* practice in reading lists of closed and open syllables that are both real words and "nonsense"
words. For example:

Closed syllables		Open syllables	
Real	*Nonsense*	*Real*	*Nonsense*
lad	fil	me	la
pin	jes	go	ti
nod	tam	hi	fe
set	sliv	she	tra
drug	sug	so	spo

Appendix 6.4 contains many more examples of closed and open syllables, along
with word lists that can be used to teach syllable division. The printed syllables can
be put on individual flash cards or practiced in a list-reading format. I suggest practice on the closed syllables separately before moving to the open syllables. It is the
nonsense words in each syllable category (closed and open) that will provide the
biggest challenge to the learner. However, keep in mind that the child's overlearning
(or internalization) of these nonsense syllables is the key to effective syllable-
division instruction (see Adams, 1990; Wilson, 1996).

Once the student can reliably read closed and open syllables, the tutor is ready
to introduce the major syllable-division rules: VC/CV, V/CV, VC/V, and /Cle, in this
order. Explicit explanation is required along with tutor modeling and student practice. The tutor begins by placing a VC/CV pattern (*rabbit)* on the table.

rabbit

Pointing to *rabbit,* the tutor says:

> There are two consonants in the middle of this word, separating the vowels
> *a* and *i*. When this happens, we divide the word between the two conso-
> nants. (*The tutor covers the second syllable,* -bit, *with an index card, leav-
> ing the first syllable,* rab- *exposed.*) What kind of syllable is this, closed or

open? (*Child responds, "Closed."*) Good! Short or long vowel? (*Child responds, "Short."*) Okay, can you read the syllable? (*Child reads, "Rab."*). Good, now read the whole word. (*Tutor uncovers the second syllable, and child responds, "Rabbit."*) Nice job, now let's do some more.

Six more VC/CV words (*slipper, tennis, center, signal, plastic,* and *lumber*) are practiced in the same manner, with the tutor "talking the child through" the division of the words. The short lesson ends with both student and tutor feeling a sense of accomplishment.

One or two lessons later, depending on how quickly the child grasps the VC/CV pattern, the tutor introduces the second syllable-division rule—V/CV. Placing the word, *pilot,* on the table, she says:

<u>pilot</u>

There is one consonant in the middle of this word, separating the vowels *i* and *o*. In this case, let's divide the word *before* the consonant. (*The tutor covers the second syllable, -lot, with an index card, leaving the first syllable, pi- exposed.*) What kind of syllable is this—closed or open? (*Child responds, "Open."*) Good! Short or long vowel? (*Child responds, "Long."*) Okay, can you read the syllable? (*Child reads, "Pi."*) Good, now read the whole word. (*Tutor uncovers the second syllable, and child responds, "Pilot."*) Good work, let's try some more.

After the child has divided and read a half dozen or so open-syllable V/CV words, the tutor places the word cards, *rabbit* and *pilot,* on the table. She explains:

Now we are going to sort some more words into two columns—words that divide like *rabbit* and words that divide like *pilot*. Watch, I'll do the first one. (*The tutor sorts* napkin *under rabbit.*) I placed *napkin* under *rabbit* because both words have two consonants in the middle. I divide between the consonants and I get "nap-kin."

<u>rabbit</u>   <u>pilot</u>
napkin

The child picks up the next word in the deck, *major,* and hesitates.

TUTOR: How many consonants in the middle?

CHILD: One.

TUTOR: Which column does it go in? (*Child tentatively places* major *under pilot.*) Good! Where does it divide?

CHILD: Before the *j*.

TUTOR: Okay, read the first syllable.

CHILD: "Mă-, mă-jor, major."

TUTOR: Well done.

The child proceeds to sort six more words by syllable-division pattern (VC/CV or V/CV), with the tutor providing assistance as needed.

<u>rabbit</u>	<u>pilot</u>
napkin	major
comfort	clover
victim	evil
helmet	Friday

Several lessons are devoted to sorting and reading the VC/CV and V/CV patterns to ensure that they are learned well. At this point, the tutor introduces the third major syllable-division pattern (VC/V) by arraying three word cards on the table.

<u>famous</u>   chapter   robin

TUTOR: Shouldn't the word R-O-B-I-N go under *famous*? It's got one consonant in the middle.

CHILD: Yes.

TUTOR: Let's try it there. (*Moves* robin *under* famous) Where does it divide?

<u>famous</u>   <u>chapter</u>
robin

CHILD: Before the *b*.

TUTOR: (*covering* -bin *with an index card*) Okay, we have an open syllable, right? How do you pronounce it?

CHILD: "Rō-" (*Tutor uncovers second syllable.*) "rō-bin?"

TUTOR: Do you know a word called "rōbin?"

CHILD: No.

TUTOR: Okay, we have a problem. When we divide words into syllables, we need to come up with a real word. In this case, the word doesn't divide *before* the single consonant (*b*) in the middle of the word; it divides *af-*

ter the consonant (*the tutor moves the card to cover the* -in *in* robin). Now how do we pronounce the first syllable?

CHILD: "Rob-, rob-in, robin." Like a bird, robin.

The tutor goes on to explain that when there is a single consonant separating two vowels (as in *robin*), we first divide the word before the consonant and try a long-vowel pronunciation ("rō-bin). If that does not produce a real word, we then divide after the consonant and try a short-vowel pronunciation ("rŏb-in"). The point is that we must be flexible and willing to try it both ways.

Next, the tutor and child take turns sorting two-syllable words into three columns—V/CV (fa/mous), VC/CV (chap/ter), and VC/V (rob/in).

famous	chapter	robin
silent	traffic	habit
shiny	velvet	gravel
robot	fabric	credit
student	insect	limit
pupil	cottage	solid
vacant	pretzel	spinach

Children differ in their ability to grasp the alternating VCV pattern (either long or short). Therefore, this three-column sort will need to be continued across many lessons, using a combination of old and new words. These column contrasts are very important because they (1) capture the open versus closed nature of English syllabication, and (2) illustrate the flexibility that is required, on the learner's part, in dividing words into syllables.

The aforementioned syllable-division principles generalize to many words. For example, words ending in /Cle (really another syllable type) consistently follow the closed- and open-syllable patterns. The rule is to divide *before* the /Cle unit. For example:

Closed	*Open*
jungle	cable
middle	beetle
gamble	bugle
cripple	rifle

In addition, the VC/CV principle covers many *r*-controlled patterns (e.g., par/don, char/coal, her/mit, ser/vice, or/der, bur/den), although the VC/V accounts for others (e.g., tar/iff, per/il, chor/al). A final syllable-division rule, noted by Wilson (1996, p. 62), is also important to keep in mind: "If there are three consonants between two vowels, including a digraph (e.g., *th*, *sh*, *ch*), the digraph stays together (e.g., *bath/tub*, *mush/room*, *pan/ther*, *ker/chief*)."

The explicit teaching of syllable division, because it is isolated from context, can become tedious. Therefore, it is important for the tutor to follow explanation with many opportunities for the child to divide words into syllables. It is also important to show the student how this syllable-division practice can help improve his or her reading. For example, after a couple of principles (e.g., VC/CV and V/CV) have been introduced, the tutor can select words from a text that the child is about to be read. (*Note*: These words should provide recognition challenge but be within the child's meaning vocabulary.) For example:

pitcher	bacon
sopping	demanded
whispered	opened

The child's successful identification of these text-related words (e.g., from Chapter 1 of E. B. White's *Charlotte's Web*), coupled with his or her encounter of the words again when reading the chapter, can drive home the point that syllable division can be a helpful word recognition skill.

Again, this description of syllable-division instruction has had a limited purpose; that is, to help the child locate the first syllable break in a multisyllable word. The idea is that if the reader can isolate and pronounce the first syllable in a long word, he or she is in a better position to attack the rest of the word. In fact, processing the first syllable, along with using sentence context, is often sufficient for word recognition. For example:

1. She found an old chair that had been *dis/carded*.
2. To pick grapes, we went down to Mr. Jones's *or/chard*.
3. He smiled and leaned *la/zily* on the fence.

Comprehension

The goal of reading is to understand or make sense of text. However, the comprehension process is complex and not fully understood. Comprehension is not a set of isolated skills to be mastered (e.g., fact, inference, main idea), nor is it a set of specific strategies that can be drilled into the brain (e.g., QAR, KWL, SQ3R). Rather, it is an internal thinking process, relatively specific to the individual, that can be exercised through good instruction. We do not have to teach a child to think; he or she can do this prior to coming to school. Our job, instead, is to guide and support the child as he or she attempts to make sense of the different types of text encountered in school.

There is a vast research literature on the nature of reading comprehension and the teaching of the process (see reviews by Anderson & Pearson, 1984; Paris,

Wasik, & Turner, 1991; Pressley, 2000). Historically, an interesting thread running through this literature is the concept of *prediction*. Descriptions of how we think (or comprehend) have invariably included the making and testing of predictions—from the philosophical speculations of John Dewey (1916) to early cognitive psychological models of thinking (Miller, Galanter, & Pribrum, 1960) to influential pedagogical approaches (Stauffer, 1970). Recently, the reading educator Gerald Duffy (2003, p. 24) reiterated the importance of prediction in the comprehension process. He stated:

> The task is not one of teaching lots of strategies: as students begin to understand the strategic nature of [reading] comprehension, they use relatively few strategies in various combinations over and over again with slight variation from one reading situation to another. These include:
>
> - Making predictions.
> - Monitoring and questioning what is happening.
> - Adjusting predictions as you go.
> - Creating images in the mind.
> - Removing blockages to meaning.
> - Reflecting on the essence or the significance of what has been read.

In the discussion that follows, I focus on *prediction* and *questioning* as two teaching strategies that a tutor can use to help a student with reading comprehension. The idea is that, with guided practice, the student will internalize these strategies and begin to use them independently in his or her efforts to comprehend text.

Facilitating Comprehension of Narrative Text

Most children have an implicit understanding of how stories work. That is, they realize that at the beginning of a story, the characters and setting are introduced; in the middle, a problem or conflict arises and is addressed; and at the end, the problem is resolved. Nonetheless, children do not always draw on their knowledge of story structure when they read. There can be several reasons for this. The story may be uninteresting; it may contain new information or vocabulary that is outside the child's experience; the plot may be complex or subtle, thereby impeding comprehension; or a child (especially a struggling reader) may have trouble simultaneously concentrating on word processing and meaning as he or she reads.

A tried-and-true method for guiding a child's reading of a narrative text is the Directed Reading–Thinking Activity, or DRTA (Morris, 2005a; Nessel, 1987; Stauffer, 1970). In the DRTA, the child is asked to predict what will happen next in a story, and, as he or she reads on, to confirm or modify the prediction based on information in the text. The best way to understand this process is to experience it. Therefore, as you read the following story (see Figure 6.2 on the next page), make a prediction at each stopping point before proceeding.

Grandpa and the Sea

The summer I was seven was a very happy time for me. That summer Grandpa showed me how to row a boat. "I want you to make friends with the sea," he said.

Grandpa's house was right by the sea, in Maine. Winds often pushed the sea into high waves. The waves came up almost to the rocks in front of the house. At those times, Grandpa said, "Come along, Davy. Let's go meet the sea!" We climbed down over the big rocks together. At times, we went too near the water. Then a wave would knock us down.

I cried the first time this happened. "I'm afraid!" I said. But Grandpa said, "Come along now! You must learn not to be afraid." How brave Grandpa seemed to me! I wanted to be like him.

- **STOP 1** (Make a prediction about what will happen in this story.)

Most men in the town were fishermen. They set out lobster traps in the sea. An old fisherman named Al let us use his boat. Al's strong, heavy boat rode the waves well. Al was very poor. But he would not take money for the boat from Grandpa.

Grandpa found another way to pay him. He knew that Al had to make his lobster traps from old wood. These traps always came to pieces in a storm. So Grandpa made Al some fine lobster traps from new wood. Al liked his new traps very much. He showed them to all the fishermen. Then he set them out in the water.

One day, there was a very big storm. Grandpa and I went down to the sea. The men were standing around, talking. But Al was not with them. Where is Al?" Grandpa asked. "Out there in his boat," one man said. He pointed to the sea. "He's trying to get those traps you made for him. But he lost an oar. He can't get back.

"We must go out and tow him in," Grandpa said. "Who will go with me?" No one answered. Who wanted to go out in such a bad storm?

- **STOP 2** (What do you think will happen next in the story?)

Grandpa walked to a boat. "I'll go with you, Grandpa!" I said. I jumped into the boat beside him. Grandpa started to tell me not to come. Then he picked up the heavy oars. He pushed us out into the deep water.

Grandpa was standing in the boat. He had lost his hat. His white hair was blowing in the wind. He turned and smiled at me. At that very minute, I stopped being afraid. Grandpa pulled on the oars. The waves were high. With each wave, the boat went up in the air. Then it banged down on the water. Up, down, up, down we went.

From the top of a wave, we saw Al. He was trying to use his one oar. But water was filling his boat. Could we get to him in time?

(cont.)

FIGURE 6.2. "Grandpa and the Sea," a second-grade story. From Reader's Digest *New Reading Skill Builders* (1966, pp. 92–98).

- **STOP 3** (What do you think will happen next? Or, how will Grandpa attempt to save Al?)

Yes! Soon Grandpa pulled near enough for Al to throw us a tow rope. We tied the rope to our boat. Then Grandpa began rowing back to land. Big waves followed us in. One of them made Al's heavy boat hit our light one. I thought both of our boats would sink.

Then Grandpa turned our boat around! Were we going back to sea? "We'll have to back in, Davy," Grandpa said. "Then Al's boat will be in front of us. It can't hit us." The waves still came at us, pushing us to land. But now they pushed Al's heavy boat *away* from us. Al got to land first.

At last we climbed out onto the rocks. One fisherman put a coat around Grandpa. The rest stood there shaking their heads over the chance Grandpa had taken. Al came over to shake Grandpa's hand. He knew how brave Grandpa had been. So did I. But Grandpa just said, "Come on, Davy. Let's go home."

FIGURE 6.2 (*cont.*)

PREDICTION. As you read "Grandpa and the Sea," the prediction questions led you to anticipate upcoming events in the story. At Stop 1, or early in the story, your prediction was probably general in kind (e.g., "I think Davy will have an adventure with Grandpa, and the boy will overcome his fear of the sea"). At Stop 2, with the story problem revealed, you may have predicted that Grandpa (and possibly another fisherman) would attempt a sea rescue. At Stop 3, you may have predicted that the rescue would involve Al jumping into Grandpa's and Davy's boat. Or, you may have remembered that Grandpa had mentioned earlier in the story that they "must go out and tow [Al] in." It is doubtful, however, that you would have predicted the problem of a heavy boat being towed through the waves by a lighter boat.

In using the DRTA approach to guide a child's reading of a story (e.g., "Grandpa and the Sea"), the tutor must preread the story and select appropriate stopping (or prediction) points. As the child reads, each of his or her predictions may not turn out to be correct. However, what is important is that the child make reasonable predictions (based on the information given) and then confirm or modify them as further information becomes available. In the DRTA, the tutor is essentially exercising the child's natural thinking process—that is, his or her understanding of cause-and-effect relationships in the world. This approach leads the child to read with concentration, make inferences, and, within limits (i.e., the information given), interpret the story on his or her own terms.

QUESTIONS. There is an important difference between how a mature reader and a child might read "Grandpa and the Sea." With a mature, skilled reader, we can assume that basic, plot-related information is being processed and that predictions are based on this information. But with a child—especially one who struggles with reading—we cannot make this assumption. Moreover, if the child does not process or understand important information as he or she reads, his or her ability to make good predictions at designated stopping points in the story will be weakened.

One way around this problem is to pose one or two questions to the child at each stopping point to check his or her understanding of the passage just read. If the child can answer these plot-relevant questions, then a prediction is called for and the reading continues. If he or she is unable to answer the questions satisfactorily, then some rereading (and possibly some tutor explanation) may be necessary before continuing.

The idea is simple: The child needs to understand one part of a story before moving to the next part. Unfortunately, carrying out the idea is not so simple. On the tutor's part, *it requires spare, thoughtful questioning that addresses central as opposed to peripheral information in the story.* There is a "backbone" to a story—a beginning, middle, and end. In the beginning, characters and setting are introduced; in the middle, a problem emerges requiring action by the characters; and in the end, the problem is resolved. The tutor's questions, as a rule, should relate to these basic parts of the story.

(*Note*: If specific vocabulary words are taught prior to the reading, these words, too, should be related to the central plot.)

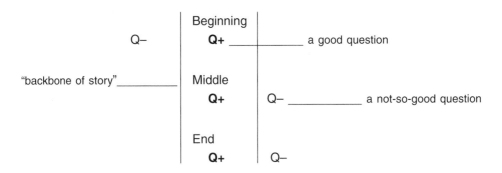

Let us examine a set of questions for "Grandpa and the Sea" (see Figure 6.2). Note that at *Stop 1*, the following questions would be appropriate:

- Where does this story take place? (By the sea)
- Who are the characters? (Grandpa and Davy)
- How does Davy feel about the sea? (He's afraid when the waves knock him down.)
- *Prediction*: What do you think will happen in this story?

Less appropriate questions at Stop 1 might include: Where exactly was Grandpa's house? (Right by the sea.) What time of year does the story take place? (Summer.)

At *Stop 2*, the following questions could be asked:

- Who is Al and what is his relationship with Grandpa? (Al is a fisherman; he lets Grandpa and Davy use his boat, and, in return, Grandpa made Al some new lobster traps.)
- What has happened to Al? (He's out at sea in a bad storm; he only has one oar and can't get back.)
- *Prediction*: What do you think will happen next?

Less appropriate questions at Stop 2 might include: Why were Grandpa's lobster traps better than Al's? (They were sturdier, made of new wood.) What was Al doing out in the ocean? (Trying to get his lobster traps.)

At *Stop 3*, these questions could be posed:

- Who went out to rescue Al? (Grandpa and Davy)
- Was Davy afraid? (At first, yes, but then Grandpa smiled at him.) Why did this help? (Grandpa wasn't afraid, so Davy wasn't afraid.)
- What did they discover when they reached Al's boat? (Al was in danger; he had only one oar, and his boat was filling up with water.)
- *Prediction*: How will Grandpa and Davy attempt to save Al?

The following questions at Stop 3 would be less appropriate: What did Grandpa lose? (His hat.) What trouble did they have getting out to Al? (The waves were high; they made the boat go up and down.)

At the end of "Grandpa and the Sea," further questioning might include:

- How did they rescue Al? (They threw him a rope and towed his boat back to shore.) Why didn't Al just jump into Grandpa's and Davy's boat? (Not easy to do in a storm; also, Al would have lost his boat and all of his lobster traps.)
- As Al's boat was being towed to shore, what problem arose? (Al's boat was heavier than Grandpa's boat, and the waves kept pushing it into the lighter boat). How did Grandpa solve the problem? (Grandpa turned his boat around so that Al's heavier boat would lead the way to shore).

    (*Note*: This is a complex point that might require explanation by the tutor.)
- After this experience, do you think Davy is still afraid of the sea? (It is difficult to anticipate a child's answer to this question, but the question does get at the theme of the story; that is, overcoming fear through action or through emulating the courage of another.)

The preceding questions track the plot of "Grandpa and the Sea" from the beginning of the story to the end.

- *Beginning.* Where does the story take place? Who are the characters? How does Davy feel about the sea? (Prediction?)
- *Middle.* Who is Al and what is his relationship with Grandpa? What has happened to Al? (Prediction?)

    Who went out to rescue Al? Was Davy afraid? What did they discover when they reached Al's boat? (Prediction?)
- *End.* How did they rescue Al? As Al's boat was being towed to shore, what problem arose? How did Grandpa solve the problem? Do you think Davy is still afraid of the sea?

Questions of this kind have an important diagnostic function. That is, the child's answers indicate how closely he or she is following the story line, thereby informing the tutor's next instructional move (e.g., continue with the reading, have the child reread, or provide explanation). The tutor's questions should always be limited in number, closely related to the plot, and posed in a conversational manner. Their judicious use can certainly facilitate a student's comprehension of a given story. But the more important long-term goal is for the child to internalize the "strategies" of prediction and questioning and use them skillfully as he or she reads stories independently.

For more information on this interpretation of the DRTA, see Morris (2005a). For other interpretations of the approach, see Duffy (2003) or Blachowicz and Ogle (2002).

Facilitating Comprehension of Informational Text

Prediction and questioning can also be used to facilitate a child's comprehension of informational or expository text. However, with this type of text, the reader must draw not on knowledge of story structure but rather on his or her knowledge of a specific subject area (e.g., prehistoric animals, the solar system, the Civil War). The tutor's task is to build or activate the child's prior knowledge, elicit predictions, and then, after the child reads a passage, to question him or her about *important* information in the text.

Let us suppose that a tutor is teaching a lesson on why the dinosaurs disappeared. She begins by asking her 10-year-old student Ben the following questions:

TUTOR: Ben, are dinosaurs real or imaginary?

BEN: They're real. I mean, they were real but they died a long time ago.

TUTOR: What kind of animals were they—birds, reptiles, or mammals?

BEN: They were big reptiles, but some of them could fly too.

TUTOR: What does *reptile* mean?

BEN: It means they are big, kind of green, and have rough, bumpy skin.

TUTOR: Do reptiles bear their young alive or do they lay eggs?

BEN: Oh, yeah, they lay eggs—huge eggs.

TUTOR: Ben, why do you think the dinosaurs disappeared?

BEN: I'm not sure.

TUTOR: Well, take a good guess.

BEN: They could have got the flu, like a plague or something, and it wiped them out.

TUTOR: That's a very good prediction. No one is exactly sure what happened to the dinosaurs, but there are some theories or possible explanations. Read the next few pages to see what these are [see Figure 6.3].

Dinosaurs lived on earth for 140 million years. Then, 65 million years ago, they disappeared. Other reptiles disappeared too—flying reptiles and reptiles that lived in the sea. Many other kinds of animals also died out. And many kinds of plants.

No one knows why the dinosaurs disappeared. But there are many theories. A theory is an idea. It is an explanation that might be possible.

Maybe small animals ate dinosaur eggs so only a few eggs were able to hatch. This is one theory. But this theory does not explain why other kinds of animals died out, and many plants as well. Also, some dinosaurs may not have laid eggs.

Maybe a group of dinosaurs got sick and the sickness spread to other groups. That's possible, for even today diseases spread among herds of cattle. But if that happened, chances are the sickness would not have reached reptiles that live in the sea. Also, other kinds of animals would not have caught the sickness, and neither would plants.

Some people have suggested that for a time the sun became cooler and did not shine as brightly. That made the earth cooler, so plants could not grow well. Some dinosaurs were meat eaters—they ate other dinosaurs. But many dinosaurs ate plants. They needed lots of food. If Earth cooled so much the plants could not grow, plant-eating and meat-eating dinosaurs would have starved.

These are some theories to explain what happened to the dinosaurs.

FIGURE 6.3. From *What Happened to the Dinosaurs* (third-grade level), by F. M. Branley (1989, pp. 7–12). Reprinted by permission of HarperCollins.

Following the reading, the tutor acknowledges the child's original prediction and then poses questions regarding central information in the text.

TUTOR: Your prediction was that the dinosaurs may have acquired a disease and thus died out. Was that one of the theories you read about?

BEN: Yep (*proudly*).

TUTOR: What was a problem with this theory?

BEN: What do you mean?

TUTOR: The author said there was a problem with the theory that all the dinosaurs disappeared because of a sickness.

BEN: I don't remember.

TUTOR: That's okay. Let's go back and reread page 11.

BEN: (*Reads page 11, one paragraph, silently.*) The problem was that the disease probably wouldn't have spread to the dinosaurs that lived in the sea. And the disease wouldn't have made the plants die too.

TUTOR: Good job. Do you remember the other two theories about why the dinosaurs died?

BEN: It said mice [small rodent-like animals were pictured] might have eaten the dinosaur eggs before they hatched.

TUTOR: Okay, little animals might have eaten the eggs; the dinosaurs may have died off from disease; there was one more theory.

BEN: (*looking back at a picture of a dinosaur nibbling on a dried-up plant*) Oh, yeah! The sun didn't shine hard enough and the plants couldn't grow. So the dinosaurs didn't get enough to eat. They starved to death.

TUTOR: But I thought some dinosaurs were meat eaters. Why did they starve?

BEN: Because they ate the animals that ate the plants, and the ones that ate the plants weren't there. They had died.

TUTOR: I see, that's interesting.

PREREADING QUESTIONS. The prereading dialogue between tutor and child accomplished several things. It established that dinosaurs were real creatures who died off many years ago; that dinosaurs were egg-laying reptiles; and that there are current theories that attempt to explain why the dinosaurs became extinct. Note that activating this relevant background information prepared the student to read the text. Prior to reading, the tutor also elicited a prediction from Ben as to why the dinosaurs disappeared. Fortunately, the child's common sense prediction (probably based on contemporary fears of contagious diseases) turned out to be one of the three explanations cited in the text.

With an older, more advanced reader, the prereading phase of the lesson could be handled in different ways. For example, the tutor might have the student skim the selection beforehand, using the illustrations and text headings to develop prereading predictions. Or the tutor might use key vocabulary words from the selection and ask the student to predict what the passage might be about. In our "dinosaur" passage, a discussion of the words *mammal*, *disease*, *reptile*, and *disappear* might yield some interesting prereading predictions.

POSTREADING QUESTIONS. In the postreading discussion, the tutor's questions focused on the three theories of why the dinosaurs disappeared. She followed up on several of the child's answers, even having him reread a page to find the answer to one question ("What was the problem with the disease theory?"). However, the tutor did not question the child on minor or trivial details; the emphasis was on important concepts in the text. (See Barr et al., 2002 [Chapter 5], for an interesting discussion of comprehension questions.)

In summary, facilitating a child's comprehension of a text (narrative or informational) requires skill and judgment on the tutor's part. To ask good questions, the tutor must distinguish central from peripheral information in the text. To elicit good predictions, the tutor must choose appropriate stopping points in the text. This skill requires that the tutor read the text *before* the lesson and plan appropriate stopping points and questions (Post-it Notes are helpful here). With an interesting text and sufficient preplanning, the comprehension lesson can become an engaging, give-and-take dialogue between student and teacher regarding the content and implications of the reading selection.

Fluency

Fluency, the ease and efficiency with which one processes text, is a crucial component of reading. As was pointed out in Chapter 1, the processing of printed words (and phrases) needs to be automatic so that the reader can concentrate his or her attention on meaning getting (Perfetti, 1985; Samuels, 2006). Significantly, many struggling readers have problems with fluency. They may read slowly, word by word, or in a halting, erratic manner that violates phrase boundaries and compromises comprehension.

In a revealing study of 604 elementary students referred for Title I reading assistance, Rasinski and Padak (1998) analyzed the children's performance on an IRI. The passage-reading assessment included measures of word recognition accuracy, comprehension, and reading rate (see Table 6.2). When reading at grade level (e.g., a third grader reading a third-grade passage, a fifth grader reading a fifth-grade passage), the Title I-referred students, not surprisingly, tended to score below the accepted minimal criteria on word recognition (95%), comprehension (75%), and rate (varies across grade levels). Notice, however, that whereas the children's word recognition and com-

TABLE 6.2. Grade-Level Reading Performance of Third-, Fourth-, and Fifth-Grade Students Referred for Title I Assistance

Grade	N	Word recognition (95%)	Comprehension (75%)	Reading rate (wpm)
Third	199	90	82	61 (80)[a]
Fourth	118	90	74	63 (95)[a]
Fifth	57	91	62	58 (110)[a]

Note. Data from Rasinski and Padak (1998).

[a]Lowest acceptable rate at the end of the previous school year

prehension scores were in "striking range" of the minimal criteria, their reading rates were well below the minimums and fell lower each year. Rasinski and Padak concluded that reading fluency or rate seems to be a critically important problem for this Title I population. I agree with this conclusion but hasten to point out that, in this study, word recognition may have been a major contributor to the low reading rates. That is, 90% word recognition accuracy—misreading 1 word out of every 10 in running text—undoubtedly contributes to poor reading fluency.

In this book we use *reading rate*, or words read per minute (wpm), as a measure of fluency. Some researchers (e.g., Kuhn & Stahl, 2000; Pinnell et al., 1995; Schreiber, 1991) argue that prosody (proper intonation and phrasing) should also be considered in a measure of fluency. However, rate alone is a fairly reliable indicator of phrasing (see Hendrix & Snow, 2006); moreover, it is unclear what role intonation or expression play in silent reading.

The late Ronald Carver (1990, 2000), who studied reading rate for over 30 years, proposed that each reader has an optimal reading rate. This rate is determined by the reader's word recognition knowledge (store of automatized words) and by his or her overall cognitive or "thinking" speed (the speed with which the individual can process language). The implications of Carver's model are thought provoking. For example, whereas instruction can strengthen a student's word recognition, it can have little influence on his or her cognitive speed. Analogously, Carver's model accounts for the fact that mature readers (all of whom have good word recognition skill) vary in reading rate, presumably due to variation in underlying cognitive speed.

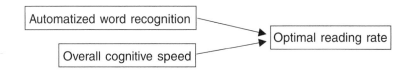

As teachers, what are we to take from Carver's model? First, it is clear that we must help struggling readers develop the automatic word recognition skill that underlies fluent processing of text (see also Samuels, 2006; Perfetti, 1992). Second, at each grade level, we should anticipate a *range* of reading rates that will support comprehension of text. Although struggling readers may read considerably slower than their peers, if they achieve a "threshold" rate at a given grade level (e.g., 100–110 wpm in fourth-grade material), they should be able to progress in reading. See Table 3.3 (p. 51) for average, end-of-year reading rates in grades 1–8.

In the sections that follow, I describe four strategies for improving reading fluency or reading rate. The first three (easy reading, repeated readings, and taped readings) are well known. The fourth strategy (direct word study) has received little attention in the literature on fluency.

Easy Reading

A time-honored way to build reading fluency is to do an ample amount of reading in "easy" materials—in stories containing familiar words and sentence patterns. This task usually involves the child reading material at his or her independent level (½–1 year below his or her instructional level). The instructional goal is obvious: to increase fluency and speed by the experience of comfortable, error-free readings of interesting texts.

There is, however, a potential drawback to easy reading, whether it is done in a tutoring lesson, in the classroom, or at home. That is, the material to be read may be *too easy*. If the child already knows the individual words and syntactic patterns in the text, what is to be gained (from a fluency perspective) from reading it? Surprisingly, we lack good research on this question (see National Reading Panel Report, 2000).

The effectiveness of free, independent-level reading may, in fact, hinge on the difficulty level of the material read. For example, consider a fourth-grade boy who reads fourth-grade material in a slow, halting manner (80 wpm). This child may not benefit, fluency-wise, from reading second-grade stories; they *are* too easy. However, he may well benefit from reading *Encyclopedia Brown* mysteries written at the third-grade level. In reading one of these stories, the child may come across one or two vocabulary words that are new to him, more fully automatize a few words in his sight vocabulary, or develop an interest in mysteries that leads him to read more in his free time. In other words, if the material read is just below the child's instructional level (½–1 year), then easy reading may offer important opportunities for improving reading fluency.

Repeated Readings

In repeated readings (Samuels, 1979), a second method for improving fluency or rate, the student reads aloud the same passage (200–300 words) four times. Each time, he or she reads for 2 minutes, and the number of words read is recorded by the tutor. With successive rereadings, fluency (or number of words read) increases due to a practice or familiarity effect. The improvement in fluency is graphed, providing immediate positive feedback to the child and tutor alike.

Research studies show that the repeated readings method is effective with a wide range of students (National Reading Panel, 2000; Strecker, Roser, & Martinez, 1998). Importantly, the fluency gains made by children in repeated readings trials tend to generalize to their reading of new passages. What could account for this learning, this generalized improvement in reading fluency? Two possibilities come to mind: (1) gains in word knowledge and (2) gains in syntactic awareness. On successive rereadings of a passage, the child has the opportunity to learn a few new words and also to quicken his or her recognition of previously known words or word patterns (e.g., *-able*, *-ly*, *-tion*). Also, rereading the same passage several times allows the child to anticipate or "search out" phrase boundaries that he or she may have been unable to identify on a first reading (Schreiber, 1991). This practice of word recognition—and phrasing, particularly—most likely accounts for the success of repeated readings in improving reading fluency.

Although repeated readings is a fairly straightforward teaching technique, several issues arise regarding its implementation. For example:

- Choosing the passage that the child will read
- Determining the number of repeated readings
- Monitoring the child's oral reading
- Graphing the results

1. *A passage chosen for repeated readings should be at least at the child's instructional level.* If, in guided reading, the child is reading stories written at the late-second-grade level, the tutor can choose a passage (e.g., 250 words) from a 2-2 story that the child has just completed. This will ensure that the repeated readings passage is at the appropriate difficulty level—that it offers some challenge in terms of word recognition and sentence complexity.

It is possible that some children might benefit from rereading passages slightly above their instructional level; for example, using a third-grade story with a late-second-grade reader (see Stahl & Heubach, 2005). The idea here is that the more difficult text exposes the reader to more new vocabulary and more complex sentence patterns. The child should be able to handle the increased difficulty because he or she is able to read the passage several times.

2. *Four repeated readings trials should get the job done.* Four readings of the same passage allow for two trials one day and two additional trials the next day. For example, passage A might be read two times on Monday and then read two more times on Tuesday. On Wednesday, passage B would be introduced.

Monday	Passage A (Readings 1 and 2)
Tuesday	Passage A (Readings 3 and 4)
Wednesday	Passage B (Readings 1 and 2)
Thursday	Passage B (Readings 3 and 4)

Note that more than four rereadings could lead to rote memorization of the passage, which is not the goal of the instructional activity.

3. *During repeated readings trials, the tutor must monitor the quality of the child's oral reading.* Some children tend to hurry through the text, trying to better their previous "number of words read." In so doing, they may ignore punctuation and omit, insert, and substitute words. How should the tutor respond? Two principles provide guidance:

- The reader shall make sense.
- The reader shall read, for the most part, the words on the page.

If either of these principles is violated, the tutor should intervene by having the child stop and reread the sentence. Because stopping and rereading costs the reader valuable time in a repeated readings trial, the child will learn from his or her mistakes and begin to concentrate more closely on reading the text accurately. Regarding the "hurrying through text" issue, it is important to help the child distinguish between reading fast and reading smoothly. At the beginning of a trial, the tutor can remind the child that the goal is to read smoothly. If he or she does so, the number of words read will increase.

4. *Graphing results is an indispensable part of the repeated readings method.* A carefully kept graph not only provides the child with immediate, trial-to-trial feedback, but it also serves as a permanent record of his or her reading performance over time. Children enjoy reviewing and discussing the graphed results, particularly on days when they reach a new performance plateau. The number of words read should be graphed *after each trial*, two times per tutoring session. Precounting the words per page (as in the following illustration) facilitates a quick tally of the child's performance.

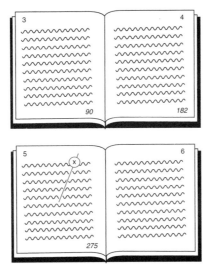

In the preceding trial, the child began reading on page 3 and after 2 minutes had reached the *x* mark on page 5. Having precounted the words on each page, the tutor simply tallies the number of words read by the child on page 5 (*8 words*) and adds this to *182*, the cumulative word total through page 4. The total number of words read (*190*) is then graphed (see second trial, 3/8, in Figure 6.4). Note in the graph that each trial is dated and that information is provided regarding the specific passage being read (title, level). Such record keeping, aside from its motivational function, is important for several reasons:

- It indicates, over time, how consistently the repeated readings technique is being used.
- It indicates if and when a change in reading *level* occurs, for example, from late-second- to third-grade passages.
- It provides an ongoing visual record of patterns of change in the child's oral reading fluency.

Repeated readings is a fairly formal way to work on oral reading fluency. Still, the activity has much to offer; it is effective, it is easy to administer, and it is invariably enjoyed by students.

Taped Readings

Taped readings is a third method for building reading fluency (Carbo, 1981; Chomsky, 1976). The tutor selects a good story written at, or just above, the child's

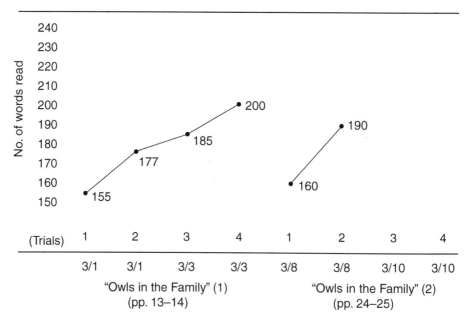

FIGURE 6.4. Results of repeated readings trials (number of words read in 2 minutes).

instructional level, and reads it aloud onto a cassette tape. (The tutor's oral reading is expressive but unhurried, marked by slightly longer pauses at commas and periods.) Then the child, at home or school, practices the story by reading along with the tape.

The recording of six or seven pages in a third-grade chapter book is straightforward and takes less than 15 minutes. Nelson and Morris (1987) suggested the following recording procedure for the tutor:

1. Push the RECORD button on the tape recorder.
2. Read the first page of the story onto the tape before saying "Stop."
3. Pause 5 seconds and then read the next page, again saying "Stop" at the end.
4. Continue this routine until the six-page chapter has been completed.

The tape recorder is never turned off while the story is being recorded. The tutor should read expressively, pausing an extra moment at phrase boundaries so that the child will have a chance to follow along with the tape-recorded reading.

With the story recorded, the tutor carefully explains to the child the "taped reading" procedure:

> You will listen to, or read along with, the tape for one page. When the tape says "Stop," turn off the recorder and go back and reread the page. You will read the rest of the chapter in the same manner; that is, listen to one page, stop the recorder, and then reread that page before moving on. When you finish the chapter, rewind the tape.

The tutor also assigns a specific section of the chapter (perhaps the first two pages) for extra practice.

> I want you to really practice the first two pages of the chapter until you can read them accurately and smoothly. Go back and listen to the tape if necessary. I'm going to check your reading of these two pages at the beginning of our next lesson.

The tutor's check involves a 2-minute oral reading trial on the designated section. Such a check, which includes graphing accuracy and rate performance, motivates the child to work hard on the taped reading assignment.

Taped readings provide an important modeling component. That is, the child is able to listen to an expressive, appropriately phrased reading of a passage *before* he or she attempts to read the passage alone. This modeling or echoic strategy allows the tutor to use reading material that may be slightly above (½ year) the student's instructional level, affording rich opportunities for growth in word knowledge, vocabulary, and phrasing.

This taped echo-reading procedure can be an extremely important supplement to twice-weekly tutorial instruction. Consider that a book could be completed in half the time if the child read every other chapter at home with the tape recorder. The parent's job would be to make sure that the child puts in the time with the tape recorder (15–20 minutes). If the home setting is unworkable, the child's classroom teacher might agree to monitor the child's tape-recorder reading, perhaps during the sustained silent or free reading period (there could be no more meaningful seat-work task). In effect, taped reading allows a struggling reader to read, with support, *away from the tutor.* Such opportunities are rare.

Word Work

A fourth, and often overlooked, way to improve reading fluency is to strengthen the child's knowledge of orthographic or spelling patterns. It stands to reason that inaccurate or slow processing of printed words will limit a student's reading speed. In fact, Carver (2000) argued that increasing a child's store of automatized words and word patterns is the best way to increase his or her reading rate.

In a tutoring setting, the first order of business is to assess the child's word-knowledge level. On the initial reading diagnosis, how did he or she perform on the flash word recognition and spelling tasks (see Chapters 2 and 3)? If the child did not show mastery (80% correct) of the words up to the third-grade level, then a review of one-syllable vowel patterns is called for (see pp. 134–141). If he or she showed mastery through the third grade but faltered on the fourth- and fifth-grade lists, then work on syllable division is appropriate (see pp. 141–146). Finally, if the child scored 80% or higher on the fifth-grade flash word recognition and spelling lists, then systematic word study can probably be omitted. Tutoring time can be better spent on contextual reading and writing.

If instruction is called for, word sorts can be used to introduce a set of patterns (e.g., *crop, spoke, float, snow,* and *fort*), games (e.g., Memory, Bingo) to reinforce learning, and 1-minute speed trials to assess automaticity or mastery. Remember that it is the automatic recognition of the word patterns that will ultimately lead to an increase in reading rate.

Writing

Writing may or not be prioritized in a tutoring plan for an older remedial reader. The decision will be based on several factors, including the student's interest in writing, his or her writing ability, and the time that can reasonably be allotted to writing, given the student's other needs in reading (e.g., comprehension, word recognition, and fluency).

If writing is included in the lesson, the student will write on self-chosen topics, moving through the three phases of the writing process (prewriting, writing, and postwriting; see section, Independent Writing, Chapter 5).

The tutor's goal is to help the older student become more independent as a writer. To this end, in the prewriting phase the tutor may, at first, model the use of a story map to help the student organize his or her thoughts. Over time, however, the student will be expected to construct his or her own prewriting story maps or outlines. Similarly, in the postwriting phase, the tutor may initially lead the child in rereading a completed draft, searching for punctuation and spelling errors. Later, the student will be expected to perform these editing chores by him- or herself.

By allowing the student to choose the topic and by responding openly and honestly to the content of the student's writing, the tutor can create an avenue of free expression that is often denied to children in school. Some will grab at this opportunity and surprise even themselves at what they are able to create.

CLASSROOM APPLICATIONS

The tutoring techniques (word study, comprehension, and fluency) described in the preceding section can be adapted for use in the classroom. In fact, some of the teaching strategies (e.g., the DRTA) are more effective in a small-group than in a one-to-one context. The key to teaching struggling readers in the classroom is to make sure that the students are placed at the appropriate instructional level. Thus we begin this section with the topic of assessment.

Assessment

It is unrealistic and unnecessary for a fourth- or fifth-grade classroom teacher to administer a complete IRI to each child in his or her class. Using comments from the previous year's teachers and end-of-grade test scores, a classroom teacher can usually identify those students who are reading at or above grade level. It is the other below-grade-level readers, perhaps four to eight per classroom, who require an individualized assessment. Time for reading assessment in the classroom is scarce; therefore, I recommend the following course of action:

1. Use test scores and teacher comments from the previous grade to screen for low readers.
2. With the low readers tentatively identified, administer graded oral reading passages to each child, starting two grade levels below the current grade. That is, if the child is in fifth grade, begin the oral reading assessment with the third-grade passage. Move forward or back based on the child's performance. The goal is to find the highest level at which the child can read without being frustrated. (*Note*: The teacher might choose to have the child read just the first 100 words of each IRI passage. This tactic reduces administration time and makes scoring very easy; e.g., *oral reading accuracy* = 1 point

off per error; *oral reading rate* = 6,000 ÷ No. of seconds to read the passage.)

3. Administer the spelling test to the entire class. A fifth-grade teacher would administer a below-grade-level list (fourth), a grade-level list (fifth), and an above-grade-level list (sixth). Scoring these 12-word lists for accuracy will show the teacher how deficient his or her lowest spellers are in word or orthographic knowledge. In fact, the teacher may have to go back and administer additional spelling lists (third or second grade) to her lowest spellers in order to establish instructional levels.

4. Based on the oral reading and spelling results (these often, but not always, go hand in hand), place students in instructional-level groups and plan instruction accordingly. Some teachers may choose to run only two reading groups; others may run three, even four, groups.

Word Study

Although many reading problems in the upper-elementary and middle grades can be traced back to deficient word recognition, ironically, systematic word study is often ignored at this level. Fourth- to sixth-grade teachers generally view phonics instruction as a first- or second-grade issue ("The students should have gotten it back then"), and their stance is unlikely to change. Nonetheless, many of these same upper-elementary-grade teachers do see spelling instruction as part of their responsibility; this is positive because spelling instruction, like phonics instruction, can expose students to the patterns and regularities in the orthography.

Unfortunately, when classroom teachers use commercial spelling programs to teach spelling, they often place their struggling reader/spellers "over their heads" in the curriculum. It makes little sense to assign fifth-grade spelling words each week to a child who spells at the third-grade level. Frustration and confusion usually result (see Morris et al., 1996; Templeton & Morris, 1999). On the other hand, if a fifth-grade student's spelling instructional level (i.e., third grade) was assessed at the start of the school year, and the student was assigned to a developmentally appropriate third-grade spelling group, then good things would happen. He or she would begin to retain the specific words and word patterns that were taught each week and would be in a position to use this new orthographic knowledge in reading and writing texts (Morris et al., 1995). As the student's spelling ability improved over a 4- or 5-month period, he or she could be moved up to a higher spelling level (e.g., fourth grade).

Persuading elementary school teachers to group students by ability for spelling instruction has traditionally been a hard sell. But in this era of heightened attention to reading achievement, perhaps a different argument should be made. That is, developmentally appropriate spelling instruction—teaching spelling at the correct level for the child—builds the orthographic knowledge that underpins successful writing and *reading*. As struggling readers increase their ability to spell words, they will also increase their ability to read with accuracy and fluency (Carver, 2000; Henderson, 1992).

A classroom teacher can use the developmental spelling test described in Chapter 2 (p. 35) to place students in appropriate spelling groups. He or she can use a commercial spelling program (e.g., Houghton Mifflin, Scott-Foresman, Zaner-Bloser) as a source of weekly spelling lists. (*Note*: The grade-level sets of words in these spelling programs mirror the developmental word-knowledge sequence described in this book. That is, second- and third-grade spelling books cover one-syllable vowel patterns; fourth-grade books cover syllable-juncture patterns; and fifth-grade books introduce derivational patterns [e.g., *decide–decision*; *compete–competition*].) Finally, the teacher can develop a weekly instructional routine (activities for Monday, Tuesday, Wednesday, and so on) by consulting the plan in the spelling book or other innovative plans described in the literature (e.g., Bear et al., 2003; Brown & Morris, 2005).

Comprehension

The DRTA is easily adapted for classroom use. Given that a group of readers is placed at the correct instructional level, the teacher can use the DRTA to elicit predictions and ask questions as the students read a story or informational text. In fact, the DRTA works better in a small group than in a tutoring context, because an individual, trying to comprehend a text, benefits from the predictions and speculations of his or her peers.

Management-wise, a fourth-grade classroom teacher could run two reading groups: one group ($N = 18$) reads a fourth-grade novel, the other group ($N = 7$) reads a third-grade novel. The teacher meets with the groups on alternate days, using the DRTA format to guide the discussion. Such an approach calls for careful planning by the teacher (stopping points must be chosen and questions planned for two different novels). However, students in the low group benefit immensely from such differentiated instruction. Because they can read the third-grade text with a reasonable degree of accuracy and fluency, they can concentrate on understanding the story. Both print processing and comprehension are enhanced when students are placed at a text level where they are challenged but not frustrated. Note that no comprehensive "tracking" scheme is being advocated here. My point is that low readers, at some time during the school day, need to work on text that they can comfortably read.

Fluency

Research shows that rereading text is effective in improving fluency and rate. One way to promote rereading in the classroom is to have students practice assigned texts (e.g., story passages, poems, speeches, plays) in preparation for a later "performance" in front of the class. Rasinski (2003) describes several such performance reading activities, including Readers' Theatre, Radio Reading, and the Oral Recitation Lesson. The repeated readings method (see pp. 157–160) could also be tried in the classroom by training pairs of students to time and graph the results of 2-minute reading trials.

Taped reading is another method that can be used to improve reading fluency. Below-grade-level readers benefit in several ways from "reading along" with a taped version of their grade-level textbooks (e.g., science, social studies). In addition, novels or chapter books of varying difficulty can be recorded onto tape by high school students or community volunteers and then used by low readers, in school or at home, to work on reading fluency. The keys to any taped books program are (1) to assign the student a specific part to practice (i.e., to read and reread the passage until he or she has got it down), and (2) to check the child's performance on the assigned part.

In summary, the various tutoring techniques for improving word recognition, comprehension, and fluency can easily be adapted for small-group use in the classroom. However, low readers will benefit from such instruction only if it is presented at the appropriate difficulty level—not too easy, not too hard. Again we see the importance of an accurate diagnosis when working with below-grade-level readers.

In this chapter, I have described instruction that is appropriate for advanced remedial readers. In the next chapter I show how these teaching techniques can be applied to individual cases representing different types of reading problems: word recognition, comprehension, fluency, and severe reading disability.

A Sampling of Reading Materials (Grade-Level Difficulty 2–5) That Appeal to Remedial Readers

Title	Author	Publisher
Second grade		
Buffalo Bill and the Pony Express	Coerr, E.	Harper Trophy
Daniel's Duck	Bulla, C. R.	Harper Trophy
Dolphins	Bokoske, S.	Random House
Drinking Gourd, The	Monjo, F.	Harper Trophy
Dust for Dinner	Turner, A.	Harper Trophy
Girl Named Helen Keller, A	Lundell, M.	Scholastic
Headless Horseman, The	Standiford, N	Random House
Hill of Fire	Lewis, T.	Harper Trophy
Kate Shelley and the Midnight Express	Wetterer, M.	Lerner
Wagon Wheels	Brenner, B.	Harper Trophy
Third grade		
Abraham Lincoln	Colver, A.	Yearling-Dell
Dolphin Adventure	Grover, W.	Beech Tree
J. T.	Wagner, J.	Yearling-Dell
Pompeii: Buried Alive	Kunhardt, E.	Random House
Shark Lady	McGovern, A.	Scholastic
Shoeshine Girl	Bulla, C. R.	Harper Trophy
Stone Fox	Gardiner, J. R.	Harper Trophy
Titanic, The	Donnelly, J.	Random House
To the Top! Climbing the Highest Mountain	Kramer, S. A.	Random House
Wanted Dead or Alive: The True Story of Harriet Tubman	McGovern, A.	Scholastic
Fourth–fifth grade		
Among the Orangutans	Gallardo, E.	Chronicle Books
Best Christmas Pageant Ever, The	Robinson, B.	Harper Trophy
Black Stallion, The	Farley, W.	Scholastic
Bundle of Sticks, A	Mauser, P.	Atheneum

Title	Author	Publisher
Dear Mr. Henshaw	Cleary, B.	Harper Trophy
Gold Cadillac, The	Taylor, M.	Puffin
Hatchet	Paulsen, G.	Puffin
Holes	Sachar, L.	Scholastic
Just Juice	Hesse, K.	Scholastic
Only the Names Remain: The Cherokees and the Trail of Tears	Bealer, A.	Little, Brown
Owls in the Family	Mowat, F.	Yearling-Dell
Rachel Carson: Pioneer of Ecology	Kudlinski, K.	Puffin
Riding Freedom	Ryan, P. M.	Scholastic
Sign of the Beaver, The	Speare, E. G.	Yearling-Dell
Skinnybones	Park, B.	Random House
Taste of Blackberries, A	Smith, D.	Harper Trophy
Trouble River	Byars, B.	Puffin
We Shall Not Be Moved: The Women's Factory Strike of 1909	Dash, J.	Scholastic
Weasel	DeFelice, C.	Avon
Well, The	Taylor, M.	Scholastic

Word Lists from Which to Choose Words for Vowel-Pattern Sorts

A vowel patterns

<u>cat</u>	<u>lake</u>	<u>park</u>	<u>rain</u>	<u>day</u>
ran	race	car	mail	say
dad	tape	hard	wait	may
hat	page	barn	pain	way
cab	same	card	chain	pay
map	made	far	paint	clay
jam	name	part	maid	stay
slam	take	harm	sail	gray
clap	gave	dart	paid	play
back	trade	start	stain	tray
trap	shake	shark	train	spray
grab	space	march	waist	
lamp	grape	smart	praise	

<u>fall</u>	<u>caught</u>	<u>draw</u>	<u>fair/fare</u>
ball	taught	hawk	air
call	fault	saw	chair
wall	cause	law	hair
small	haunt	straw	pair
talk	haul	dawn	bare
walk	launch	slaw	care
chalk	sauce	crawl	share
salt	vault	lawn	scare

E vowel patterns

<u>pet</u>	<u>feet</u>	<u>meat</u>	<u>germ</u>	<u>he</u>
red	deep	team	her	we
beg	meet	lead	clerk	she
get	feel	mean	nerve	me
bell	free	peak	serve	be
less	green	clean	jerk	

nest	seed	beat	term
left	need	dream	herd
desk	queen	beach	verse
step	jeep	leaf	
sled	bleed	wheat	
chest	steep	steam	
swept	screen	speak	

head	learn/clear
bread	heard
dead	earn
deaf	search
death	pearl
breath	fear
spread	hear
threat	near
wealth	spear

I vowel patterns

hit	ride	girl	right	wild
lip	nice	dirt	night	child
win	bike	bird	light	mild
big	five	sir	might	find
kick	mile	first	sight	mind
hid	side	firm	high	kind
pin	dime	shirt	tight	blind
trip	wise	third	fight	climb
chin	shine	birth	bright	grind
swim	smile	stir	flight	
whip	prize	thirst	sigh	
sting	write	twirl	fright	
twist	glide	chirp	thigh	

by	pie/piece
my	tie
cry	die
fly	lie
sky	chief
try	thief
why	field
shy	shield
fry	niece

O vowel patterns

top	rope	boat	corn	blow
job	note	road	fork	snow
pot	hole	soap	for	show
mom	nose	load	torn	row
lock	coke	coal	form	grow
dot	hope	loaf	horn	slow
jog	bone	soak	born	know
shot	stone	float	north	low
chop	close	cloak	porch	growth
pond	spoke	foam	storm	throw
drop	drove	coach	sport	own
crop	smoke	groan	horse	known
spot	froze	throat	force	bowl

told	moon	boil/boy	book/could	ground
cold	roof	coin	good	sound
sold	pool	join	foot	found
gold	boot	point	hook	round
hold	fool	noise	wool	foul
most	shoot	spoil	shook	south
post	tooth	joy	wood	count
ghost	broom	toy	should	cloud
folk	spool	soy	would	doubt

U vowel patterns

bug	cute	hurt	blue	fruit
cup	rule	burn	true	suit
bus	use	fur	glue	juice
fun	huge	turn	flue	bruise
rug	June	curl	due	cruise
club	tune	surf	sue	
drum	fuse	purr	clue	
plug	tube	church		
brush	mule	burst		
much	duke	nurse		
trust	flute	purse		

grew
new
knew
few
dew
chew
flew
screw
threw

A Possible Sequence of Vowel-Pattern Sorts

cat	lake	park	rain
ran	name	car	mail	←——— (sample vowel pattern sort)
bad	made	hard	wait
rag	sale	barn	tail
clap	base	start	chain

cat	lake	day	fall
park	rain	day	fall	←——— (sample headers for next sort)*
cat	caught	draw	fair

pet	feet	meat	germ
pet	feet	he	head
met	germ	he	head
pet	feet	meat	learn

hit	ride	girl	right
hit	ride	wild	by
girl	right	wild	by
hit	ride	pie	piece

top	rope	boat	corn
top	rope	blow	told
boat	corn	blow	told
top	rope	moon	boil
moon	book	could	ground

bug	cute	hurt	blue
bug	cute	fruit	grew
hurt	blue	fruit	grew

---

*Every underlined word on the page (e.g., fall) represents a column header for a potential sort. Under fall might be sorted call, tall, ball, wall, and small. Under rain might be sorted mail, wait, tail, and chain, as shown in the example sort at the top of the page.

From *Diagnosis and Correction of Reading Problems* by Darrell Morris. Copyright 2008 by The Guilford Press. Permission to photocopy this appendix is granted to purchasers of this book for personal use only (see copyright page for details).

Lists of Syllables (Open and Closed) and Lists of Words for Syllable-Division Practice (VC/CV, V/CV, VC/V, and /Cle).

Syllable lists

Closed syllables	Open syllables
cat	be
fish	bri
up	bro
set	chi
hat	de
box	fi
sun	fla
tan	flu
pub	free
lic	fro
com	go
bat	hi
ad	hu
mit	la
bas	le
ket	lo
chap	lu
con	pi
frig	pre
gos	pro
pal	ra
pil	she
pun	shi
rec	so
sel	spo
shiv	tra
tal	tro
tat	tru

Word lists

VC/CV	V/CV	VC/V	/Cle
admit	agent	balance	able
basket	bacon	cabin	angle
blizzard	climate	camel	apple
cactus	crater	closet	battle
channel	evil	dozen	brittle
chapter	famous	driven	bridle
combat	final	finish	bugle
contact	frequent	frigid	candle
dentist	glider	habit	cable
elbow	human	level	crumble
flutter	humid	lizard	cuddle
ginger	ladies	modern	drizzle
gossip	lazy	novel	eagle
helmet	moment	palace	fumble
lantern	notice	planet	gargle
orbit	pirate	prison	hurdle
orchard	private	promise	jungle
pattern	reason	punish	maple
pilgrim	recent	radish	needle
problem	robot	robin	noble
public	rumor	salad	noodle
publish	shiny	shiver	riddle
rescue	siren	shovel	sniffle
shelter	spiral	talent	sprinkle
traffic	spoken	travel	stumble
trumpet	treason	value	title
turkey	vacant	vanish	turtle
whimper	zebra	wizard	whistle

Repeated Readings Chart

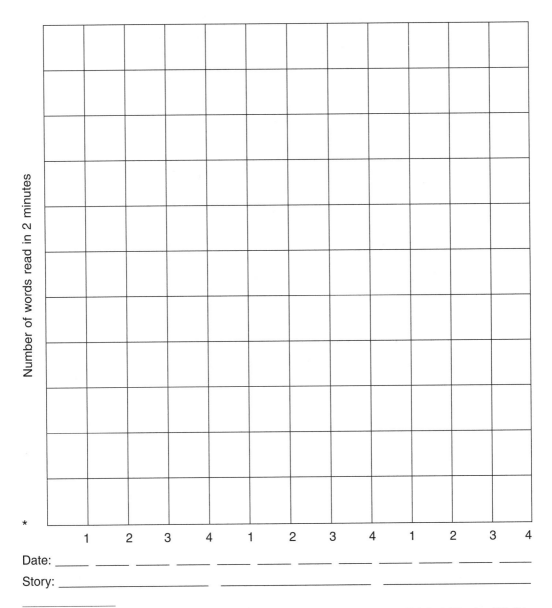

Number of words read in 2 minutes

*

| | 1 | 2 | 3 | 4 | 1 | 2 | 3 | 4 | 1 | 2 | 3 | 4 |

Date: ____ ____ ____ ____   ____ ____ ____ ____   ____ ____ ____ ____

Story: _____   _____   _____

Note. To number the chart, take the student's normal oral reading rate (e.g., 75 wpm) and multiply by 2 (75 × 2 = 150). This base rate of 150 words (in 2 minutes) should be placed at the lower left-hand corner of the chart (see *). Then number by 10 as you move up the chart (e.g., 150, 160, 170, 180, and so on) until you reach the top (250 words).

CHAPTER 7

Correcting Reading Problems in the Later Grades

II. CASE STUDIES

In this chapter we consider representative types of reading problems in the elementary and middle grades (3–8). Most of the chapter is dedicated to *corrective cases*: garden-variety cases of reading disability in the areas of word recognition, comprehension, and fluency. Each of six case descriptions is based on a child we have worked with in the Appalachian State University Reading Clinic and includes (1) an initial reading diagnosis, (2) a lesson plan that draws selectively from the toolbox of teaching techniques described in Chapter 6, and (3) a description of the first two tutoring lessons, along with a 2-month progress report.

At the end of the chapter, I briefly consider *severe cases* of reading disability, describing three types that I have come across in my clinical work.

CORRECTIVE CASES

In the six case descriptions that follow, the context is 1-hour tutoring lessons conducted two times per week. If less time is available for tutoring (e.g., 45 minutes), the lesson parts can be shortened proportionately or the read-aloud activity at the end of the lesson can be omitted.

Case 1: Walter (Word Recognition Problem—Early)

Initial Diagnostic Results

Walter, a fourth-grade child, actually reads at the second-grade level because of a problem with word recognition. His second-grade scores (see Table 7.1) are instructional-level across the board, with the exception of a borderline flash word recognition score (60%) and a slow silent reading rate (62 wpm). Between second and third grade, however, drop-offs in flash word recognition (60–15%) and spelling (50–17%) clearly indicate a serious word knowledge deficiency that undoubtedly contributes to Walter's low oral reading accuracy (91%) and low, frustration-level reading rates at third grade (59 and 44 wpm). Note that although Walter was frustrated reading the third-grade passages, his comprehension remained high.

Second-grade list (50% correct)		*Third-grade list (17% correct)*	
trapped	TRAPED	scream	SKREM
dress	DRASS	count	CONT
stuff	STOFE	caught	COTE
queen	QINE	careful	CAFUL
cloud	CLADE	stepping	STAPEING
shopping	SHOPING	thirsty	THRTE

Walter's flash word recognition and spelling scores go hand in hand. At second grade, his scores of 60% (word recognition) and 50% (spelling) are at, or close to, instructional-level, whereas at third grade, scores of 15% (word recognition) and 17% (spelling) clearly indicate frustration. Walter's specific misspellings on the second- and third-grade lists provide insight into his knowledge of word patterns. Notice that this fourth grader is inconsistent in spelling short vowels (e.g., DRASS

TABLE 7.1. Case Summary Sheet 1: *Walter* (Word Recognition Problem—Early); Grade Level 4; Reading Level 2

Level	Word recognition		Oral reading			Silent reading		Spelling
	Flash	Untimed	Accuracy	Comprehension	Rate (wpm)	Comprehension	Rate (wpm)	
Preprimer	95	100						
Primer	80	100						
First grade	80	100	99	100	86			83
Second grade	60	80	96	100	77	100	62	50
Third grade	15	65	91	92	59	100	44	17

Note. Meaning-change errors: *second grade*—1 of 5; *third grade*—3 of 15.

for *dress*; STOFE for *stuff*; STAPEING for *stepping*), and lacks knowledge of lower-frequency vowel patterns (e.g., *ea* in *scream*; *au* in *caught*; *ou* in *cloud* and *count*). Also notice that when Walter's spelling knowledge was tested by harder, two-syllable words, he tended to omit letter–sounds (e.g., CAFUL for *careful*; THRTE for *thirsty*).

Instructional implications from Walter's reading diagnosis are straightforward. He needs to read for meaning in second-grade-level materials, and he needs to strengthen his knowledge of one-syllable vowel patterns (e.g., short, long, *r*-controlled).

Lesson Plan

Walter's lesson plan draws selectively from the toolbox of teaching techniques described in Chapter 6. The toolbox is reproduced in Table 7.2. For *guided reading*, Walter will start off reading second-grade-level trade books. He expressed an interest in animals, so books on wolves, snakes, dolphins, and sharks should get him off to a good start. These will be followed by second-grade biographies of historical figures, including Christopher Columbus, George Washington, Abraham Lincoln, Harriet Tubman, and Amelia Earhart. These trade books will range in difficulty from early to late second grade. To work on *reading fluency*, Walter will do repeated reading trials (2 minutes) on passages from the aforementioned trade books. The repeated readings will be done on pages he has previously read in guided reading.

Word study is a major component in Walter's lesson plan. He will begin by reviewing the short-vowel patterns (e.g., CVC—*rap*, *led*, *fog*; CCVC—*plan*, *slip*, *drum*; and CVCC—*path*, *list*, *sock*). Once Walter has mastered these patterns (i.e., can read and spell them with accuracy and speed), he will begin a long, systematic study of other one-syllable vowel patterns. For example:

- Long-vowel patterns (e.g., *race*, *paid*, *smile*, *light*, *float*, *told*)
- R-controlled patterns (e.g., *hard*, *shirt*, *fork*, *curb*, *germ*)
- Other vowel patterns (e.g., *fall*, *straw*, *boil*, *moon*, *found*)

TABLE 7.2. Toolbox of Teaching Techniques for Working with Remedial Readers (Reading Levels 2–6)

Word study	Comprehension	Fluency	Writing
One-syllable patterns	Guided reading	Easy reading	Independent writing
Two-syllable patterns	• Narrative text	Repeated readings	
	• Informational text	Taped readings	

Writing is also part of Walter's lesson. He will write for real purposes, and the writing will afford him valuable opportunities to explore and internalize spelling patterns previously introduced in the word study lessons. Finally, time allowing, the tutor will *read to* Walter at the end of each lesson—a good way to reward him for his hard work.

Walter's lesson plan

1. Guided reading (20 minutes)
2. Word study (12 minutes)
3. Fluency building (10 minutes)
4. Writing (12 minutes)
5. Read aloud (6 minutes)

Tutoring Lessons

The First Lesson

1. *Guided reading.* Walter and his tutor preview the first eight pages of the second-grade book, *Wild, Wild Wolves* (Milton, 1992). As they look at the pictures, the tutor poses several prereading questions. Where do wolves live? Do they live alone or in groups? What do they eat? How do they communicate? Are wolves related to dogs? Walter's answers are generally on the mark, and he is eager to start reading.

The tutor reads the first two pages of the book, and then Walter echo-reads these same pages. This process gets him off to a fluent, confident start. The next 10 pages are partner-read; that is, Walter and the tutor alternate reading pages. They stop now and then to discuss the text and provide answers to several of the prereading questions. After 12 pages, Walter begins to read independently, with the tutor providing word recognition assistance as needed. The child does a nice job, reaching page 21 (about halfway through the book) before it is time to quit.

2. *Word study.* The tutor takes out a deck of 36 word cards: 12 short *a* words, 12 short *i* words, and 12 short *o* words. She flashes the word cards to Walter one at a time. If he reads a word correctly, the tutor places it in one pile; if he misreads or hesitates on a word, she places it in a second pile. Walter ends up reading 30 of the words correctly, misreads 3 words (*chin, cob, slid*), and hesitates on 3 more (*mash, pill, lock*). If Walter had read all 36 words accurately and immediately, the tutor may have had second thoughts about the need for short-vowel instruction. However, the fact that the child misread or hesitated on 6 of the 36 short-vowel words means that he can benefit from a careful review of these foundational patterns.

Following the initial flash test, the tutor reassembles the deck of 36 cards and places three of them on the table. (*Note:* These were three words that Walter had recognized immediately on the flash test.)

<u>hat</u>   <u>big</u>   <u>mop</u>

DECK

The tutor and Walter then proceed to sort the words in the deck under the appropriate exemplar. After a word is placed in a given column (e.g., *bag* placed under *hat* and *fan*), the entire column is read from top to bottom. After a dozen or so words have been sorted, the tutor asks Walter to read the *hat* column. She asks, "Walter, what vowel sound do you hear in each of these words? (*The child responds correctly.*) Good, *each word has the /ă/ sound.*" The tutor goes on to have Walter read the big and *mop* columns and to identify the target vowel sound in each column (i.e., /ĭ/ and /ŏ/).

<u>hat</u>	<u>big</u>	<u>mop</u>
fan	sit	shot
bag	trip	rob
slam	pin	jog
fast	lick	sock

Because Walter is quick and accurate in sorting the words, the tutor decides to introduce Memory, a reinforcement game. She places 12 of the short-vowel words, face-down, in a 3" × 4" array. She explains to Walter that the idea is to turn over two word cards, trying to find a matching pair. If a pair is found (e.g., *sit* and *lick*) and he reads the two words correctly, he gets to pick up the two words *and* take another turn. The player who finds the most pairs is the winner. Walter, a competitive sort, wins the game easily and wants to play again.

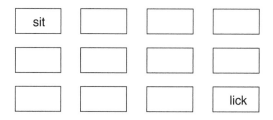

3. *Fluency building.* Repeated readings, to build Walter's fluency and rate, are introduced in the next tutoring lesson.

4. *Writing.* Walter chooses to write about going turkey hunting. With the tutor's help, he constructs the following prewriting story map.

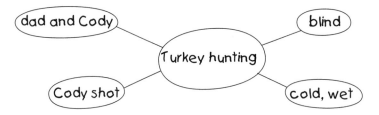

Walter needs help coming up with an opening sentence, but then he begins to write independently.

> I went turkey hunting with my dad and Cody.
> We walked to the blind THRUE the WODS and
> FINSE [fence]. We CLIMDE up in the blind.
> Dads HAED [head] was sticking out of the blind.

At this point, the tutor asks Walter to read back what he has written, and he does so. She then asks the child what he plans to write next, and he says he is going to write about shooting at the turkey. They agree to continue the story in the next lesson.

5. *Read to.* The tutor reads aloud the first chapter of Farley Mowat's *Owls in the Family.* Walter listens attentively, a good sign, as Mowat's book becomes more interesting (more hilarious, one could say) with each succeeding chapter.

The Second Lesson

1. *Guided reading.* Walter and the tutor begin by paging through the first half of *Wild, Wild Wolves,* briefly recounting what occurred on these pages. Then they proceed to partner-read (two pages at a time) the second half of the book. The tutor's slowed-down but expressive reading provides an important model for Walter. On his two-page sections, he reads with few errors and improved fluency. At the end of the book, the prereading questions posed in the first lesson are addressed (e.g., Where do wolves live? What do they eat? How do they communicate?). Walter answers each question accurately and seems pleased with his newly gained knowledge.

2. *Word study.* Walter sorts and reads the same short-vowel patterns (*hat, big,* and *mop*) that were introduced in the previous lesson. After the three-column sort and a quick game of Memory, he takes a short spelling test.

1. trap	4. slam
2. fit	5. shot
3. rob	6. ~~leck~~ lick

Based on Walter's performance, the tutor decides that in the next lesson, she will substitute short *u* patterns for short *a* patterns.. She also decides to include more blends (e.g., *cl-, dr-, sp-*) and digraphs (e.g., *ch-, sh-, th-*) in the sort to provide needed challenge. For example:

big	mop	rug
rip	log	bus
this	job	much
pin	drop	nut
rich	shot	rush
spin	clock	cub

3. *Fluency building.* In this second lesson, the tutor introduces repeated readings. Walter is to read the first 200 words from *Wild, Wild Wolves*, a passage he encountered the previous day in guided reading. Before beginning, the tutor explains that the idea is "to read smoothly, not to race." Walter nods in agreement but then proceeds to read too quickly on the first 2-minute trial, making several careless errors that disrupt his fluency. On the second trial, he slows down a bit, his reading accuracy improves, and his rate goes up—from 144 to 168 words read. Figure 7.1 shows Walter's performance on the two repeated readings trials. (*Note*: He will complete trials three and four on the same passage in the next tutoring lesson.)

4. *Writing.* Walter continues the "turkey hunting" story that he began in the previous lesson.

> I went turkey hunting with my dad and Cody.
> We walked to the blind THRUE the WODS and
> FINSE [fence]. We CLIMDE up in the blind.
> Dads HAED [head] was sticking out of the blind. //
> The turkey NOO something was RONG
> but he just STOD there. Dad called more turkeys. Cody
> shot at a big one and missed. We got cold and wet
> and DASIDID to come home.

The tutor congratulates Walter on a job well done, and the child seems genuinely pleased with his effort. The tutor recognizes several opportunities for revision (e.g., Who is Cody? What is a blind? How do you "call" turkeys?), but these can wait till the next tutoring lesson.

5. *Read to.* The tutor reads aloud Chapter 2 of *Owls in the Family* (Mowat, 1981). Walter is hooked.

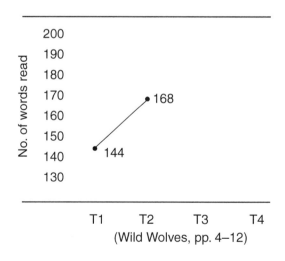

FIGURE 7.1. Walter's performance on the first two repeated reading trials.

Two Months Later

After 16 tutoring lessons, Walter is reading comfortably in late-second-grade material. About one-third of his reading is done silently now, and his comprehension is excellent in both the oral and silent reading modes. In word study, Walter has progressed through the *a* and *i* vowel patterns (e.g., *flat, rake, hard, tail; ship, mile, dirt, night*). He can read these patterns automatically and is beginning to spell them consistently. Finally, the repeated readings have helped Walter with his reading fluency. He reads approximately 10 wpm faster on *first* trials (85 wpm vs. 75 wpm), and his improved fluency is clearly noticeable in the guided reading part of the lesson.

By the end of the school year, Walter should be a strong third-grade (possibly early-fourth-grade) reader. His success will result from a blend of instructional-level reading, systematic word study, and fluency drill.

Case 2: Wendy (Word Recognition Problem—Late)

Initial Diagnostic Results

Entering seventh grade, Wendy reads, at best, at the fourth-grade level. As with *Walter* (Case 1), the underlying problem is word recognition, but this time at a more advanced level.

On the IRI (see Table 7.3) Wendy's scores clearly show frustration at the fifth-grade level. She has little sight vocabulary at this level (flash word recognition— 10%), which leads to a very slow oral reading rate (86 wpm). The fifth-grade silent rate (131 wpm) is probably misleading, because Wendy could answer only two of six questions (33%) about the passage.

TABLE 7.3. Case Summary Sheet 2: *Wendy* (Word Recognition Problem—Late); Grade Level 7; Reading Level 4

Level	Word recognition		Oral reading			Silent reading		Spelling
	Flash	Untimed	Accuracy	Comprehension	Rate (wpm)	Comprehension	Rate (wpm)	
Preprimer	100	—						
Primer	100	—						
First grade	90	100						92
Second grade	85	100						100
Third grade	60	90	94	83	118	75	148	75
Fourth grade	45	90	94	75	115	67	149	42
Fifth grade	10	60	90	83	86	33	131	17

Note. Meaning-change errors: *fourth grade*—3 of 9; *fifth grade*—7 of 18.

Wendy's fourth-grade scores are borderline instructional. Her word knowledge at fourth grade (flash word recognition—45%; spelling—42%) is relatively weak, but her reading rates (oral—115; silent—149) are acceptable. Wendy's other fourth-grade scores—oral reading accuracy (94%) and comprehension (75 and 67%)—"walk the line" between instructional and frustration level.

Wendy's problem with word recognition is revealed clearly at the fourth- and fifth-grade levels. On the fourth-grade word recognition list, she couldn't read or she misread the following two-syllable words on the flash presentation:

tobacco	*no response*
liberty	liber
coward	crowd
opinion	*no response*
miracle	*no response*
explode	explore

Even when given time to decode words on the fifth-grade word recognition list, Wendy still misread or didn't read the following words:

dissolve	desolve
evidence	advance
rampaging	*no response*
assorted	absorted

Finally, she misread or didn't read several two-syllable words on the fifth-grade reading passage:

staple	stample
intense	instant
throbbing	*no response*

To sum up, the initial diagnosis indicates that Wendy's instructional level is fourth grade. She needs to read for meaning at this level. Regarding skill instruction, she needs to improve her ability to decode multisyllable words.

Lesson Plan

Wendy's lesson plan includes *guided reading* of fourth-grade narrative text. (On the interest inventory, she expressed an interest in adventure stories.) In *word study*, the emphasis will be on decoding multisyllable words. Repeated readings will be used as a *fluency* technique, but as much to develop Wendy's word reading accuracy as to increase her reading speed. Finally, *writing* will be included in the initial lesson plan to see if she needs help in this area.

Wendy's lesson plan

1. Guided reading (25 minutes)
2. Word study (13 minutes)
3. Repeated readings (10 minutes)
4. Writing (12 minutes)

Tutoring Lessons

The First Lesson

1. *Guided reading.* From an array of fourth-grade novels, Wendy selects *Trouble River* by Betsy Byars (1969). *Trouble River* is a well-written adventure story set in pioneer days. It contains 106 pages divided into 11 chapters.

The tutor begins by reading aloud the first three pages of Chapter 1. He asks Wendy a few questions about the setting and characters, and then tutor and child proceed to partner-read the rest of the chapter. Wendy's oral reading is erratic at first (poor phrasing and a few word recognition errors), but as she becomes familiar with the author's style, her reading smooths out. Wendy has no trouble answering the tutor's comprehension questions (one or two per page). At the end of the chapter, the child makes a good prediction about what may happen next in the story. All in all, this is a good start. Wendy is interested in the story, and it seems to offer an appropriate reading challenge.

2. *Word study.* On the initial reading diagnosis, Wendy showed good mastery of one-syllable spelling patterns. However, she had difficulty reading and spelling multisyllable words. Word study is focused on this area of weakness.

The tutor begins by introducing the concepts of closed and open syllables (see Two-Syllable Patterns, pp. 141–146). In a closed syllable (e.g., *hot*), a final consonant letter "closes off" the vowel, yielding a short-vowel sound (/hŏt/). In an open syllable (e.g., *so*), the vowel letter is not closed off by a consonant (it is "open"), yielding a long-vowel sound (/sō/). Wendy quickly grasps the closed–open distinction. She also is able to read a list of closed syllables, making only one error ("clēv" for *clev*).

pat	min	flut
led	clob	sim
cop	reg	dag
slip	tram	(clev)
drug	shud	trop

However, when open syllables are mixed in with closed syllables, she misreads more than half of the open syllables (see italics). Her most common mistake is to substitute the short- for the long-vowel sound (e.g., /ră/ for /rā/; /brŭ/ for /brū/).

cop	(*bru*)	(*fe*)
reg	fla	prob
(*ra*)	med	bet
nim	spo	ti
(*sli*)	(*fu*)	plus

The tutor quickly recognizes that Wendy will require more practice reading closed and open syllables before moving forward in the syllable-division sequence.

3. *Fluency building.* On the initial reading diagnosis, Wendy's oral reading accuracy was a concern. She read with only 94% accuracy at both the third- and fourth-grade levels. The tutor decides to use the repeated readings method to help Wendy improve her contextual reading accuracy.

Amazing True Stories, by Don Wulffson (1991), is chosen for repeated readings. Of fourth-grade difficulty, the book contains two-page selections of "stranger than fiction" stories, ranging across several topic areas; for example, crime, disasters, science, politics, sports.

The tutor explains that Wendy will be reading a story four times, each time trying to *decrease* her number of oral reading errors. To get the child off to a good start, the tutor models a reading of the first paragraph of the selection "Grand Theft." Then Wendy goes back and oral-reads for 2 minutes, at which point the tutor says "Stop." As Wendy reads, the tutor marks a slash (/) for each oral reading error (substitution, omission, insertion, self-correction, or teacher help). At the end of the trial, the tutor counts up how many words Wendy read in 2 minutes. He then records, on a repeated readings chart (see Figure 7.2), the number of words read (225) and the number of oral reading errors made (12).

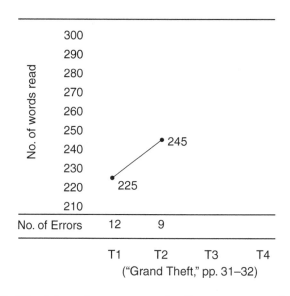

FIGURE 7.2. Wendy's performance on the first two repeated reading trials.

Before beginning the second repeated readings trial, the tutor tells Wendy not to rush and to concentrate on reading accurately. Wendy follows this advice and shows improvement on the second trial. She decreases her errors by 3 (from 12 to 9), and she increases her number of words read from 225 to 245 (see Figure 7.2). Trials 3 and 4 on "Grand Theft" will be done in the next tutoring lesson.

4. *Writing.* Wendy decides to write about her girl's basketball team at school. She is the starting point guard. Wendy has no trouble coming up with ideas for the prewriting story map.

Once she begins to write, Wendy does so with surprising fluency, pausing only once to look back at the prewriting map. After 8 minutes, the tutor, who has been writing his own baseball story, asks Wendy to stop and read back what she has written.

> I play point guard on my school basketball team. THEIR are 12 girls on the team. THEIR are three positions on a basketball team, guard, forward and SENTER. My best friend is a forward on my team. She is five feet, 6. Our first game is on Friday AGANST MOUNTAN City.

Pleased with her effort, Wendy says that next time she will write about the Mountain City game.

The Second Lesson

1. *Guided reading.* Having preread Chapter 2 in *Trouble River,* the tutor places yellow Post-it Notes, each containing one or two comprehension questions, at four places within the chapter (at the end of pages 2, 5, 8, and 10). These prediction/question points will guide today's reading.

The tutor and Wendy alternate reading the first two pages aloud, at which point two comprehension questions are addressed. For the next six pages (up to page 8), a 1+1+1 procedure is followed. That is, the tutor oral reads one page (1), Wendy oral-reads the next page (1), and then she silently reads the third (1). Questions are asked and a prediction made at the end of each three-page sequence. On reaching stopping point 3 at the end of page 8, Wendy makes a prediction about how the chapter will end. She then silently reads the final two pages of the chapter.

The 1+1+1 procedure offers several advantages. First, Wendy is doing two-thirds of the reading. Second, the tutor is able to monitor word recognition and fluency when the child reads orally, and comprehension when she reads silently. And third, the tutor's oral reading of every third page not only provides Wendy with a fluent reading model, but also helps to move the lesson along.

2. *Word study.* Word study continues with more practice on closed and open syllables. The tutor brings out a deck of 40 word cards: 20 closed syllables (e.g., *ran, fill, las, pid*) and 20 open syllables (e.g., *go, she, plo, re*). After reviewing the distinction between closed and open syllables (vowel closed by consonant = short sound; vowel open = long sound), the tutor leads Wendy through three practice activities. First, they sort the syllable cards into three columns. After each card is sorted, the player reads down the column to check on the vowel sound ("Is it short or long?").

mat	so	she
reg	pi	plo
cup	he	fla
pil	ga	bro
les	lu	sta
wrig	ro	cru

Next, they play Memory with only two patterns (closed and open). Notice, below, that *lo* and *sta* are an open-syllable match.

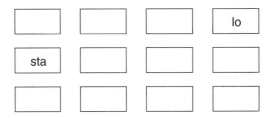

Finally, the tutor conducts a timed trial. After shuffling the deck, he flashes the syllable cards, one by one, to see how many Wendy can read in 1 minute. She reads 33 correctly and misreads 4. Of the misses, 3 are open syllables. The tutor decides that more work is needed on these foundational syllable patterns.

3. *Fluency building.* Wendy does the third and fourth trials on the initial repeated readings passage, "Grand Theft." Notice in Figure 7.3 how number of words read (272) increases significantly on trial 3, whereas word recognition errors (4) stay low. She becomes a little careless on the fourth trial (word recognition errors go up slightly), but still she maintains a strong reading rate.

4. *Writing.* Wendy continues with the "basketball" story she began in the preceding lesson. Again, she writes confidently and fluently.

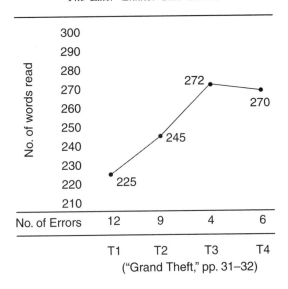

FIGURE 7.3. Wendy's performance on all four repeated reading trials.

Two Months Later

Wendy has made good progress over the first 2 months (17 lessons) of tutoring. In guided reading she is midway through her second, fourth-grade-level novel, *Shiloh*, by P. R. Naylor (1991). The 1+1+1 reading procedure is still used, but Wendy now does about one-half (as opposed to one-third) of her reading silently. Her comprehension remains strong.

In word study, after a lengthy and necessary review of closed and open syllables, Wendy worked through the basic, syllable-division patterns: VC/CV, V/CV, and VC/V (see Two-Syllable Patterns, pp. 141–146). Now, *prior* to guided reading, the tutor often picks a few words from the text for syllable-division practice. For example:

de/pos/it   cat/a/log   Rip/pen/tuck   li/ma   com/plain/ing

Wendy enjoys this activity, because she has gotten good at dividing words into syllables. More important, the tutor observes that Wendy is beginning to apply the skill in contextual reading. When reading orally, no longer does she routinely guess at long, multisyllable words; instead she tries to figure them out.

After 10 lessons, the repeated readings activity, having served its purpose, was discontinued. The graphing of word recognition errors across repeated readings of a passage eventually led Wendy to attend more closely and, thus, read more accurately. Again, the tutor saw this positive tendency carry over into the guided reading part of the lesson.

Priorities in Wendy's tutoring program shifted over the 2 months, as her current lesson plan shows:

Wendy's current lesson plan

1. Guided reading (35 minutes)
2. Word study (5 minutes)
3. Writing (12 minutes)
4. Read to (8 minutes)

Time-wise, guided reading has assumed prominence, especially because Wendy will soon start reading more difficult fifth-grade material. Word study now involves maintenance practice on syllabication skills. Writing is still a part of Wendy's program, but not a high priority (sentence combining and creating paragraphs are two skills presently receiving attention). Finally, the tutor often finds 8–10 minutes at the end of the hour to read to Wendy. Good literature provides a fitting reward for 50 minutes of hard work.

By the end of the school year, Wendy should be a strong, fifth-grade-level reader, with improved word attack skills that will serve her well in the future.

Case 3: Cory (Comprehension Problem—Early)

Initial Diagnostic Results

Cory, a midyear third grader, is having problems with comprehension, especially when reading silently. On the IRI (see Table 7.4), Cory's third-grade scores are at or near instructional level, with the exception of low scores on silent comprehension (33%) and silent rate (81 wpm). Looking back at second grade, the pattern

TABLE 7.4. Case Summary Sheet 3: *Cory* (Comprehension Problem—Early); Grade Level 3; Reading Level 3

Level	Word recognition		Oral reading			Silent reading		
	Flash	Untimed	Accuracy	Compre-hension	Rate (wpm)	Compre-hension	Rate (wpm)	Spelling
Preprimer	100	—						
Primer	100	—						
First grade	90	100	98	80	96			100
Second grade	80	95	97	100	89	42	87	75
Third grade	65	90	95	75	86	33	81	58
Fourth grade	35	80	92	50	79			33

Note. Meaning-change errors: *third grade*—2 of 7; *fourth grade*—5 of 12.

repeats itself; that is, he has surprisingly low scores in silent comprehension and rate.

Cory clearly has the requisite word knowledge to read third-grade material (flash word recognition—65%; oral reading accuracy—95%; spelling—58%). Moreover, his third-grade oral reading rate, though a little low, is acceptable. Cory's problem is in the area of silent reading—not an unusual occurrence for 8-year-olds, who often lack experience reading silently.

Lesson Plan

Cory's initial lesson plan includes *guided reading* at the third-grade level, with an emphasis on silent comprehension. The *word study* component focuses on low-frequency vowel patterns (e.g., *claw, bread, tie, coin, knew*). To build *fluency*, Cory will do some easy reading at the late-second-grade level and repeated readings at the third-grade level. Finally, he will *write* on topics of his choice.

Cory's lesson plan

1. Guided reading (25 minutes)
2. Word study (10 minutes)
3. Easy reading/repeated readings (10 minutes)
4. Writing (10 minutes)
5. Read to (5 minutes)

Tutoring Lessons

The First Lesson

1. *Guided reading.* The tutor chooses Margaret Davidson's (1976) *Nine True Dolphin Stories* for guided reading. These third-grade stories are short (five or six pages), interesting, and lend themselves to the DRTA format.

In the first selection, "The Story of Pelorus Jack," the tutor and child partner-read the first four pages, orally, stopping at several points to check comprehension. (The tutor mentally notes that this seems to be a good instructional level for Cory.) After making a prediction, Cory reads the final page silently. He reads very slowly, and, when asked a few questions, has difficulty recalling central information. The tutor has him go back and reread one paragraph to find the answer to a question. Cory does better the second time around.

2. *Word study.* The tutor's overall plan is to review the less frequently occurring, one-syllable vowel patterns with Cory. To this end, she decides to work across each vowel (i.e., *a, i, o, e,* and *u*), contrasting high-frequency patterns with lower-frequency patterns. Today, she and Cory start off with an *a* pattern sort:

flag	bake	saw	taught
sad	race	draw	caught
grab	grape	fawn	fault
pan	plate	claw	daughter
scrap	tame	lawn	

Cory has no difficulty sorting the words by visual pattern. He stumbles in reading a few words (e.g., *fawn*, *fault*, and *daughter*), but, with practice, should do well with this sort.

3. *Easy reading.* Cory and the tutor partner-read the first half of a content book about dolphins (second-grade level). Cory does about two-thirds of the reading and seems to enjoy learning more about the characteristics and habits of dolphins.

4. *Writing.* Cory talks about three topics he would be willing to write about: baseball, fishing, and his dog, Benny. Next lesson, he will choose one of these topics and begin writing.

The Second Lesson

1. *Guided reading.* Cory reads the next selection, "The Story of Opo," in *Nine True Dolphin Stories*. The first three pages of the story are partner-read, orally. Then, Cory reads the last three pages, silently, while being guided by the tutor's questions. He reads only two paragraphs silently (about a half page) before stopping to answer a question posed by the tutor (e.g., "Why did people come to see Opo?" or "Tell me what happened in that section."). The idea is to help the child concentrate more closely as he reads, to hold him accountable for comprehending. The tutor notes that the strategy is partially successful; although Cory is not always able to answer a question, he is beginning to concentrate harder, at times subvocalizing the words as he reads silently.

2. *Word study.* The word sort from the previous lesson (-at, -ake, -aw, and -au) is repeated, with Cory sorting two words to the tutor's one. They then play a quick game of Memory, which Cory wins. In the next lesson, the tutor will introduce a spelling component to the activity. As the tutor dictates a word to be spelled, Cory's task will be to write it under the correct pattern exemplar. For example:

trap	made	draw	caught
fan	page	fawn	taught
	space	law	

3. *Writing.* After brainstorming some favorite antics of his dog, Benny, Cory gets a good start on his first writing sample.

> Benny is a big brown MUT. He likes CHACEING cats and SCWERLS. He never CATCHS one but

he likes doing it. Benny does not like dog food. He
likes to eat MEET.

4. *Read to.* The tutor realizes that Cory needs to read away from the tutoring lessons if he is to improve his silent comprehension and rate. She has located a third-grade book—*Shark Lady* by Ann McGovern (1978)—that she is sure Cory will enjoy. The book contains 13 short chapters, each five or six pages in length.

The tutor makes a deal with Cory. She will read a chapter of *Shark Lady* to him each lesson if he will work on the next chapter at home. Part of the homework chapter, the tutor explains, will be tape-recorded for him; the other part he will read by himself. Then, in the following tutoring lesson, Cory and the tutor will discuss what happened in the home-assigned chapter before moving on to the next chapter of *Shark Lady.* Cory seems to like the idea, and the tutor commences her reading of the first chapter of the book.

Two Months Later

Cory has made important progress in the first 2 months of tutoring. In guided reading, after finishing *Nine True Dolphin Stories*, he began reading stories in *Encyclopedia Brown, Boy Detective* (by Donald Sobol, 1978). His love for these detective stories led to motivated silent reading lessons (DRTAs) with the tutor. Cory's silent reading rate now approximates his oral rate (90+ wpm), and his silent comprehension is improving.

Undoubtedly contributing to this improvement has been Cory's home reading of *Shark Lady.* His mom makes sure he practices the tape-recorded chapter, and the tutor checks his reading of the home-assigned pages at the beginning of each lesson. An added bonus is that Cory can use *Shark Lady* for a required book report at school.

In word study, Cory has worked through the *a*, *i*, and *o* vowel patterns and is ready to begin the *e* patterns. This is an area of strength for Cory; he is learning to both read and spell these low-frequency orthographic patterns.

By the end of the school year, Cory should be firmly on grade level in reading. Originally caught in the tricky transition from oral to silent reading, this third-grade child has benefited greatly from the targeted tutoring lessons. One year of reading tutoring should be enough for him to catch up with his peers.

Case 4: Carol (Comprehension Problem—Late)

Initial Diagnostic Results

Carol is a fifth-grade student who struggles with reading comprehension. She achieved a low score on the end-of-fourth-grade state reading test, and she is experiencing academic difficulties in fifth grade.

Carol's performance on the IRI (see Table 7.5) reveals her problem with com-

TABLE 7.5. Case Summary Sheet 4: *Carol* (Comprehension Problem—Late); Grade Level 5; Reading Level 4

| Level | Word recognition | | Oral reading | | | Silent reading | | Spelling |
	Flash	Untimed	Accuracy	Compre-hension	Rate (wpm)	Compre-hension	Rate (wpm)	
Preprimer	100	—						
Primer	100	—						
First grade	100	—						100
Second grade	100	—						100
Third grade	95	100	99	75	125	50	137	83
Fourth grade	90	100	98	50	118	42	128	83
Fifth grade	75	85	98	58	115	25	122	67
Sixth grade	55	80	94	42	94	33	108	42

Note. Meaning-change errors: *fourth grade*—1 of 3; *Fifth grade*—2 of 4.

prehension. Her isolated word knowledge (flash word recognition and spelling), oral reading accuracy, and oral and silent reading rates are all relatively strong up to the fifth-grade level. However, her reading comprehension scores begin to falter as early as third grade (50%—silent) and remain consistently low through sixth grade. Because of this contrast between print-processing and comprehension performance, it is difficult to pinpoint Carol's instructional level (fourth grade is probably a decent estimate). One thing is for sure, though; comprehension needs to be addressed in the tutoring lessons.

Lesson Plan

The workhorse activity in Carol's lesson plan will be *guided silent reading* for comprehension. Over time, she will read and discuss both narrative and informational texts. Based on the initial diagnosis, neither word study (the study of orthographic patterns) nor fluency building will be emphasized in Carol's program. *Writing* will be used—at times, to enhance reading comprehension, at other times, for personal expression. Finally, both *easy reading* and *reading to* will be staples of the lesson plan. These will serve to strengthen comprehension and promote interest in reading.

Carol's lesson plan

1. Guided reading (35 minutes)
2. Writing (10 minutes)
3. Easy reading (or read to) (15 minutes)

Tutoring Lessons

The First Lesson

1. *Guided reading.* The tutor chooses *Louis Braille: The Boy Who Invented Books for the Blind* (by Margaret Davidson, 1971) as the first book for guided reading. This informative, 80-page biography, divided into 10 chapters, is written at a late-third to early-fourth-grade level.

The tutor starts off by asking Carol if blind children go to school, and if so, how do they do their lessons? Carol responds that they go to school but that they "probably learn things by listening to the teacher, because they can't read." The tutor explains that, in this book, they are going to learn about a very important blind man, Louis Braille, who grew up in France almost 200 years ago.

After partner-reading the first few pages of Chapter 1, the tutor asks Carol to read silently the final two pages and be prepared to answer a few questions (these pages describe how 5-year-old Louis injured his eyes). Carol reads the two pages with concentration, but, on being questioned, shows only a vague understanding of what occurred. The tutor has her reread with a specific purpose in mind: "Carol, read from here to here [two paragraphs] to see if Louis immediately became blind or if it happened over time." Carol rereads the section and, afterward, shows a fuller understanding of the accident that led to Louis Braille's blindness.

Reflecting on the guided reading, the tutor determines that *Louis Braille* offers Carol appropriate challenge, comprehension-wise. He wonders if shortening the sections she reads silently would help her with comprehension.

2. *Writing.* Carol chooses three topics she would be willing to write about, then launches into an animated monologue on topic 1: "My Sister Learns to Drive."

3. *Easy reading.* With 15 minutes left in the hour, the tutor brings out a good fourth-grade version of *Ichabod Crane and the Headless Horseman* (retold by C. B. York, 1980). Carol has never heard the story. The tutor reads the first four pages to introduce the characters and the long-ago setting. Then he and Carol begin to partner-read (orally), one page at a time, stopping now and then to discuss the plot. The pace is leisurely, though the emphasis is on following the story line and making predictions. They finish half the story before time runs out.

The Second Lesson

1. *Guided reading.* After a brief review of the first chapter, Carol and the tutor begin to read Chapter 2 of *Louis Braille.* The tutor reads a half page orally, Carol reads a half page orally, and then the child reads a full page silently. The tutor questions her closely on the silent reading, on two occasions sending her back to reread paragraphs when she lacks comprehension. Carol still has trouble recalling important information when she reads silently. Nonetheless, she seems to enjoy the Braille biography and puts forth a good effort in the guided reading.

On finishing Chapter 2, the tutor asks Carol to write down three ways that

Louis showed he was a smart little boy. She is free to look back at Chapter 2 if necessary. Carol quickly writes the following sentences, without looking back.

1. Louis helped his dad polish the LETHER.
2. He helped his mother set the table.
3. He could tell people a part by LISSENING to their voices.

This becomes the first entry in her *Reading/Writing Notebook*: "How Little Louis Was Smart."

2. *Writing.* Carol maps a few ideas for her story, "My Sister Learns to Drive," and begins to write. She writes easily and with good concentration for almost 10 minutes. Writing could well turn out to be an area of strength.

3. *Easy reading.* Carol and the tutor review the first half of *Ichabod Crane* by looking back through the pictures. Then they begin to partner-read where they left off the previous lesson. As the plot thickens in the second half of the story, the tutor finds that he has to provide more explanation. Still, Carol is engrossed in the story and makes several good predictions. As the story reaches its climax (Ichabod riding home in the dark with somebody following him), the tutor has Carol read silently. On questioning, she misses some details, but still shows decent understanding of how the story ends.

Two Months Later

Progress is a little harder to track in a reader with Carol's profile; that is, a child who can read the words on the page but has difficulty with comprehension. Still, over the first 20 tutoring lessons, Carol has shown improvement. She is definitely more interested in reading, and she is beginning to self-monitor her comprehension when she reads silently.

The tutor's goal in the guided reading lessons is simple enough. He wants Carol to become a more active reader who assumes responsibility for monitoring meaning as she reads. To this end, the tutor has the child (1) make a prediction before reading a passage silently, (2) answer questions about what she has read, and (3) reread parts of the passage if her answers prove to be inaccurate or incomplete. This pattern of predicting, reading, answering questions, and rereading is a type of guided practice. (Think of a football team practicing plays, making mistakes, and then repracticing plays until they get it right.) Over time, the goal, of course, is for Carol to *internalize* the practice procedure. That is, she will begin, on her own, to predict, pose and answer questions, and stop and reread when her comprehension is interrupted.

An advantage of working with a fourth-grade-level reader is that there is an abundance of good material to read. As Carol was completing *Louis Braille*, the tutor considered following up with a fourth-grade biography of Helen Keller. Instead, he chose *Riding Freedom*, a fourth-grade novel written by Pam Ryan (1998). Carol read the first half of this book (five chapters) with the tutor. Once she was thoroughly familiar with the story line and the author's style, she began to read every other chapter at home. The tutor provided a few questions for Carol to think about as she read the home-assigned chapter. This combining of tutorial and home reading worked out well, and the tutor plans to continue the practice with the next guided reading book, *Dear Mr. Henshaw*, by Beverly Cleary (1983).

In the easy reading part of the lesson, Carol is reading an early-fourth-grade book, *Greek and Roman Myths* (Ware & Sutherland, 1952). The book introduces the various gods and goddesses and includes a few famous tales (e.g., Prometheus, Atlas, Atalanta, and Jason and the Golden Fleece). Carol enjoys reading and discussing these ancient stories. Moreover, she is building background knowledge that in the future will enable her to read a more challenging fifth-grade text, *Hercules and Other Tales from Greek Myths*, by Olivia Coolidge (1960).

By the end of the school year, Carol will be a stronger reader. Specifically, she will be better able to comprehend fourth- and fifth-grade material when she reads silently. This was the goal of tutoring.

Case 5: Faye (Fluency Problem—Early)

Faye, a fourth grader, is experiencing difficulty in the area of reading fluency or rate. All of her third-grade scores (see Table 7.6) meet instructional-level criteria, with the exception of oral and silent reading rate. In other words, at third grade, she reads accurately (97%) and with good comprehension (100%), but does so at a very slow pace (70 wpm, orally; 58 wpm, silently). It is relatively rare for a child with such good word knowledge (at third grade, flash word recognition = 70%; spelling = 67%) to read so slowly. Nonetheless, it does happen, and slow, halting reading of this kind can be a devastating problem. Imagine a student who reads only half as fast as her classmates, who takes twice as long to finish a reading assignment, at school or home. Why would such a child pick up a book and read for enjoyment when the process is so slow and arduous?

Given Faye's very slow reading rates, setting her instructional level at third grade can be questioned. Still, she has the requisite word knowledge to read third-grade material, and partner reading (alternating pages with tutor) can provide a fluent model for Faye to emulate. Fourth grade is the clear frustration level. Here, Faye's word knowledge runs out (see flash word recognition and spelling scores), adversely affecting her oral reading accuracy.

Lesson Plan

On the surface, Faye's lesson plan appears similar to those used in the preceding case studies (e.g., guided reading, word study, and repeated readings). However, her lessons are focused on building reading fluency. Note that writing is omitted from her plan to provide more time for reading practice.

TABLE 7.6. Case Summary Sheet 5: *Faye* (Fluency Problem—Early); Grade Level 4; Reading Level 3

Level	Word recognition		Oral reading			Silent reading		Spelling
	Flash	Untimed	Accuracy	Compre-hension	Rate (wpm)	Compre-hension	Rate (wpm)	
Preprimer	100	—						
Primer	100	—						
First grade	90	100						100
Second grade	85	95	98	100	75	100	65	83
Third grade	70	90	97	100	70	100	58	58
Fourth grade	45	75	92	92	63	83	52	33

Note. Meaning-change errors: *third grade*—1 of 4; *fourth grade*—3 of 11.

In truth, all parts of Faye's lesson plan should lead toward more fluent reading. In *guided reading* of third-grade stories, she should benefit from hearing the tutor's fluent reading of alternate pages of the text. In *word study*, her ability to automatize recognition of low-frequency, one-syllable vowel patterns should enhance text-processing speed. Finally, three different *fluency-building* activities (easy reading, repeated readings, and tape-recorder reading) should combine to produce noticeable gains in Faye's reading rate.

Faye's lesson plan

1. Guided reading (25 minutes)
2. Word study (10 minutes)
3. Fluency building: easy reading, repeated readings, tape-recorder reading (15 minutes)
4. Read to (10 minutes)

Tutoring Lessons

The First Lesson

1. *Guided reading.* After a brief picture walk, Faye and the tutor partner-read the first half of *Kate Shelley and the Midnight Express* (by Margaret Wetterer, 1990), an early-third-grade story. On Faye's reading turns, word recognition is not a problem, nor is comprehension; however, she does read in a slow, halting mono-tone. On one page, the tutor employs an echo-reading strategy. He says, "Faye, I'm going to read this page with expression. Then I want you to go back and read it just like I did." The echo reading does seem to help; when Faye echo-reads, there is a noticeable improvement in her phrasing.

2. *Word study*. Faye's first word sort contrasts high- and low-frequency patterns of the vowel *a* (see Case 3, *Cory*).

tap	late	draw	taught
bag	tame	paw	caught
crab	shake	claw	fault
plan	race	straw	daughter
trash	crate	lawn	

She has no trouble sorting or reading the words, although she does hesitate in pronouncing *paw* and *fault*.

3. *Easy reading*. The tutor drops down to second grade for easy reading. Choosing a "pioneer days" theme for fourth grader Faye, he brings out *The Long Way Westward* by Joan Sandin (1989). On page 1, the tutor and child look over a map of the trail the American settlers took westward. Then they begin to partner-read the story, two pages at a time. Even though the book is written at a second-grade level, several of the concepts are new to Faye (e.g., emigrants, Philadelphia, homestead, Minnesota). These new elements lead to a good discussion and frequent map checks. Faye and the tutor read about 20 pages (half of the book).

4. *Read to*. The tutor reads aloud the first chapter of the third-grade book *Stone Fox* (by J. R. Gardiner, 1980). If Faye likes this story of a legendary Wyoming dog-sled race, then it can be used for tape-recorder reading at home.

The Second Lesson

1. *Guided reading*. After a "picture walk" to review what happened in the first half of *Kate Shelley*, Faye and the tutor partner-read the second half. Near the end of the story, the tutor asks Faye to make a prediction and then read the following two pages silently. He notices that her silent reading is even slower than her oral reading. The tutor speculates that Faye is losing her train of thought as she reads silently and thus has to go back frequently and reread. Still, Faye enjoys reading *Kate Shelley and the Midnight Express*, and the tutor is confident she will also enjoy the next guided reading selection, *Wanted Dead or Alive: The True Story of Harriet Tubman* (by Ann McGovern, 1965).

2. *Word study*. After Faye sorts and reads the low-frequency *a* patterns introduced in the previous lesson, the tutor scoops up the 26 word cards and places them in a shuffled deck. He explains to Faye that they are going to do a "speed trial." He will flash the words to her one at a time, and at the end of 1 minute, they will count up how many words she was able to read. On the first speed trial, Faye reads the 26 words in 42 seconds. The tutor reshuffles the deck, and they do a second trial. This time, Faye reads the words in 35 seconds.

3. *Easy reading*. Faye and the tutor partner-read the second half of *The Long Way Westward*, this time with the child doing about two-thirds of the reading.

Again, they refer frequently to the map in following the story line. Aside from practicing fluent reading in easy text, Faye learns much from this second-grade story; for
example, that some emigrants came across the ocean from a place called Sweden,
that emigrants were poor, and that both child and adult emigrants were full of spirit
and hope.

At the end of the activity, the tutor shows Faye the next book for easy reading,
Buffalo Bill and the Pony Express (by Eleanor Coerr, 1995), also written at the
second-grade level.

4. *Read to.* The tutor reads the second chapter of *Stone Fox* to Faye. After they
discuss what happened in the first two chapters, the tutor brings out a second copy
of the book, along with an audiotape. He explains that he has tape-recorded the
third chapter of *Stone Fox*, and that Faye's homework is to listen to Chapter 3,
reading along with the tape. Then she is to go back and practice the first two pages
of the chapter (250 words) until she can read them smoothly. This may involve several rereadings. Finally, in the next tutoring lesson, Faye will read aloud the first
two pages of Chapter 3, and the tutor will graph the number of words she reads in
2 minutes. If she has practiced, her reading fluency and speed should be good.

Two Months Later

Over 18 lessons, Faye has read five third-grade books, including *Kate Shelley*,
Wanted Dead or Alive, *Stone Fox*, *The Courage of Sarah Noble* (Dalgliesh, 1986),
and *Vanished . . . Amelia Earhart* (Kulling, 1986). Some of this material was read at
home (with tape-recorder support), but most was read with the tutor.

In *guided reading*, Faye and the tutor continue to partner-read orally; however,
Faye is also beginning to read some passages silently, usually in high-interest parts
of a chapter. About once every three lessons, the tutor takes a reading rate measure.
Within the guided reading activity, he simply records the number of seconds it takes
Faye to read a given passage. Later, he goes back and computes her reading rate (60
× No. of words read ÷ No. of seconds). Happily, the tutor finds that Faye's reading
rate is improving. She is now reading at 79 wpm, orally, and 72 wpm, silently. Although these rates are still low for a fourth-grade child reading third-grade material, they are significantly higher than her third-grade rates on the initial reading diagnosis (70 wpm, oral; 58 wpm, silent).

The four fluency-building activities—word study, easy reading, repeated readings, and tape-recorder reading—have undoubtedly contributed to Faye's gains in
reading rate. In *word study*, she has worked through the low-frequency patterns of
the vowels *a, i,* and *o,* and will soon be starting the *e* patterns (*seat, breath; germ,
clerk*). She can read and spell these patterns accurately; more important, her pattern
recognition speed is improving (see speed trials).

In the tutoring lessons, Faye has alternated between *easy reading* at the second-
grade level and *repeated readings* at the third-grade level. She spends 3 weeks on
one activity and then 3 weeks on the other. At present, Faye seems to benefit,

fluency-wise, from reading easy second-grade material. However, as she continues to improve, easy reading will probably be phased out of the lessons in favor of repeated readings at the third-grade level. Finally, the *tape-recorder reading* has been a real success. Encouraged by her mom, Faye has been consistent in reading along with the tape recorder at home. Moreover, she enjoys the tutor's "rate checks" of her home-assigned passages at the beginning of each tutoring lesson. Interestingly, even with tape-recorder support and several practice readings at home, Faye's 2-minute rate checks hover around 80–85 wpm (see Figure 7.4).

At the end of the school year, we can measure Faye's improvement in reading fluency informally, through rate checks in the guided reading lessons, or more formally, through the administration of an IRI. Reading rate is definitely a problem area for this child, possibly due to cognitive speed factors (see Carver, 2000). Still, given 50 or more lessons with an emphasis on fluency development, we might expect Faye, at the end of the year, to be reading third- and fourth-grade material at 90+ wpm, both orally and silently. Such a performance would represent significant improvement and constitute a foundation for future reading growth.

Case 6: Frank (Fluency Problem—Late)

Initial Diagnostic Results

In the middle of his sixth-grade year, Frank is a determined but struggling reader. His problem is in the area of fluency. On the IRI (see Table 7.7), Frank's oral and silent reading rates drop at fourth grade, in spite of a strong flash word recognition score at this level (80%). Relistening to the tape, the examiner notes that the slow, fourth-grade oral reading rate (95 wpm) is due not to a word recognition problem (see 97%), but rather to choppy, sporadic reading that features lots of word and phrase repetitions. As he reads orally, Frank does not honor phrase boundaries and often reads through sentence-ending periods. At fifth-grade, Frank's flash word rec-

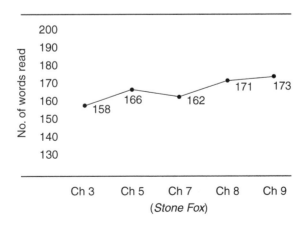

FIGURE 7.4. Faye's performance on 2-minute rate checks of home-assigned reading.

TABLE 7.7. Case Summary Sheet 6: *Frank* (Fluency Problem—Late); Grade Level 6; Reading Level 4

Level	Word recognition		Oral reading			Silent reading		Spelling
	Flash	Untimed	Accuracy	Compre-hension	Rate (wpm)	Compre-hension	Rate (wpm)	
Preprimer	100	—						
Primer	95	100						
First grade	90	100						100
Second grade	95	100						83
Third grade	90	100	96	100	121	100	117	75
Fourth grade	80	100	97	100	95	100	96	58
Fifth grade	40	100	95	100	92	100	95	25
Sixth grade			94	100	79	100	83	

Note. Meaning-change errors: *fourth grade*—2 of 4; *fifth grade*—5 of 10.

ognition score (40%) drops precipitously, but note that, given time, he can decode fifth-grade multisyllable words. In addition, Frank's fifth-grade contextual reading scores (accuracy, comprehension, and rate) actually mirror his fourth-grade scores. Given Frank's strong comprehension scores, his grade level in school, and his evident determination, the tutor decides to begin reading instruction at the fifth-grade level. She is aware, given the IRI results, that fourth grade may be a more defensible instructional level. Therefore, she resolves that if Frank experiences difficulty at the fifth-grade level, she will quickly move back to fourth grade.

Lesson Plan

Frank's lessons are focused primarily on reading fluency and secondarily on word recognition. Comprehension, of course, will be monitored, but this does not appear to be an area of weakness.

In *guided reading*, the tutor will use the 1+1+1 procedure (see Case 2, p. 187). Working in fifth-grade material, the tutor will read a passage orally, then Frank will read the next two passages—the first, orally; the second, silently. The cycle is then repeated. Frank will benefit from trying to emulate the tutor's fluent oral reading model. Moreover, the 1+1+1 procedure will afford him both oral and silent practice.

Word study will be focused on division of longer words into syllables. The initial diagnosis showed that Frank can decode multisyllable words, both in isolation and context. The goal in tutoring will be to help him recognize these words (and their component parts) more quickly.

Finally, *repeated readings* will play a major role in Frank's tutoring program.

Rereading fifth-grade passages several times will help him build sight vocabulary and improve his ability to read (or chunk) text in meaningful phrases.

Frank's lesson plan

1. Guided reading (30 minutes)
2. Word study (10 minutes)
3. Repeated readings (10 minutes)
4. Read to (10 minutes)

Tutoring Lessons

The First Lesson

1. *Guided reading.* The tutor's first book choice is *Weasel* (by Cynthia DeFelice, 1990), a "can't miss" novel for a 12-year-old boy such as Frank. Written at the fifth-grade level, this 117-page book tells the realistic and frightening story of an Ohio pioneer family in the mid-1800s. Themes of good and evil, and fear and courage, are deftly explored in this short, coming-of-age book.

The tutor begins by reading aloud the first chapter of *Weasel*, only three pages. In an unusual way, it introduces three of the main characters in the story. After some discussion and speculation, the tutor and Frank proceed to read Chapter 2. They use the 1+1+1 procedure, reading about a half page (or three paragraphs) per turn. The tutor notes three things about Frank's reading. First, when he reads orally, he lacks cadence or rhythm, repeating a word or a phrase on almost every line. Second, when he reads silently, he progresses very slowly, at times appearing to be lost in the middle of a short passage. And third, whether Frank reads orally, silently, or listens to the tutor read, he comprehends everything.

2. *Word study.* The tutor introduces the concepts of closed and open syllables, the first step in two-syllable word sorts (see case study 2, p. 185). Frank grasps the concepts quickly and, to the tutor's delight, is able to read a randomized deck of closed and open syllables (e.g., *pat, reg, ta, nim, ti, sup, spo, fu, hos, le*) with only one error (/fŭ/ for *fu*).

3. *Read to.* The tutor brings out *Buffalo Hunt* (by Russell Freedman, 1988), a beautifully illustrated 50-page book that describes how American Indians hunted buffalo in the mid-1800s. The book is written at the fifth-grade level. The tutor reads aloud the first three pages of Chapter 1, "A Gift from the Great Spirit," and she and Frank discuss the text.

4. *Repeated readings.* Frank really likes *Buffalo Hunt*, and the tutor decides that the expository text would be a perfect source for repeated readings passages. She quickly counts the words on the first two pages, wishing she had done this prior to the lesson, and then explains the repeated readings procedure to Frank. On the first repeated readings trial, he reads 189 words in 2 minutes (95 wpm); on the sec-

ond trial, he reads 205 words (103 wpm). The tutor notes a few less repetitions on the second trial.

The Second Lesson

1. *Guided reading.* Frank and the tutor pick up where they left off in the preceding lesson. Using the 1+1+1 procedure, they read and discuss nine pages of *Weasel*. Today, Frank reads orally with a little more fluency, but he still makes frequent repetitions (i.e., goes back and repeats words or phases). The tutor suggests that Frank track the print with his finger to see if that helps with oral reading. A sixth grader, he is initially hesitant to do this. However, the tutor points out that *she* is running her finger under the line as she reads orally, and it doesn't slow her down. Frank tries finger tracking and it does help; he makes fewer repetitions and begins to honor periods at the end of sentences. He also begins to use his finger when reading silently, and, again, this method seems to reduce repetitions and increase reading rate.

That *Weasel* has captured Frank's imagination is important. His interest in the story will spur the concentrated mental effort that is needed if he is to improve his reading skill.

2. *Word study.* After reviewing the distinction between closed and open syllables, Frank takes a speed trial on 30 syllables. His responses are quick, and he misses only 2 of 30 (both open syllables). The tutor decides that they will do a speed trial each lesson until Frank is 100% accurate in recognizing the closed and open syllables.

Because Frank does show mastery of the closed-syllable pattern (CVC, CCVC), the tutor introduces the first syllable-division rule (VC/CV). Placing the word card *rabbit*, on the table, the tutor says:

<u>rabbit</u>

There are two consonants in the middle of this word, separating the vowels *a* and *i*. When this happens, we divide the word between the two consonants. *(The tutor covers the second syllable,* -bit, *with an index card, leaving the first syllable,* rab-, *exposed.]* Frank, what kind of syllable is this, closed or open? *(The child responds, "Closed.")* Good! Short or long vowel? *(The child responds, "Short.")* Okay, can you read the syllable? *(The child reads, "Rab.")* Good, now read the whole word. *(The tutor uncovers the second syllable, and the child responds, "Rabbit.")* Nice job, now let's do some more.

They practice six more VC/CV words (*slipper, tennis, center, signal, plastic,* and *lumber*) in the same manner, with the tutor "talking the child through" the division of each word. Frank catches on quickly.

3. *Repeated readings.* Frank takes his third and fourth trials on the *Buffalo Hunt* passage from the previous lesson. His fluency or rate (number of words read in 2 minutes) really improves on these trials. He increases 27 words from trial 2 to 3, and another 14 words from trial 3 to 4 (see Figure 7.5). On trial 4, the tutor notices a qualitative difference in Frank's oral reading. He makes only a few repetitions, he stops at periods, and his phrasing is much improved. Repeated readings, an activity which Frank really enjoys, could play a major role in helping him to improve his reading fluency.

4. *Read to.* The tutor reads aloud the next three pages of *Buffalo Hunt.* She and Frank discuss the information, enjoying the beautiful paintings and illustrations that accompany the text. Frank's next repeated readings passage will be drawn from these pages. In this way, he is able to listen to a passage in one lesson before starting repeated readings of the passage in a later lesson.

Two Months Later

After 17 lessons Frank is still reading fifth-grade material, but . . . he is reading it better. In guided reading, the 1+1+1 procedure is still being used, but now Frank reads from two-thirds to a full page on his turns. His comprehension continues to be strong, and importantly, his fluency is starting to improve. A recent rate check (see Case 5, p. 200) showed Frank to be reading around 105 wpm, both orally and silently. This represents a rate gain of 10 wpm in just 2 months (see Table 7.7). Qualitatively speaking, Frank's oral reading is now characterized by fewer word repetitions and more attention to punctuation. Interestingly, he still benefits from tracking the print with his finger, particularly when reading silently.

After completing *Weasel* and *Buffalo Hunt,* Frank wanted to continue to read about Indians. He is currently halfway through a fifth-grade biography, *Osceola: Patriot and Warrior* (Jumper & Sonder, 1993), and the tutor plans to follow up

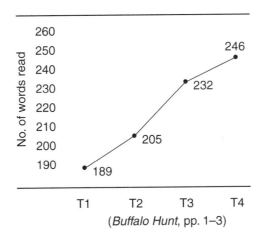

FIGURE 7.5. Frank's performance on all four repeated readings trials (2 minutes each).

with *The Sign of the Beaver* (by Elizabeth G. Speare, 1983). This American Indian theme is helping to build Frank's knowledge base and also allows for interesting book discussions.

The work on dividing longer words into syllables continued for eight lessons before being phased out. Frank was good at this task. He now has a systematic and, hopefully, quicker way to attack the difficult, multisyllable words he confronts in his reading.

Repeated readings, on the other hand, continue to be used in Frank's lessons. Frank loves the competitive nature of repeated readings—the timing and graphing of results. He can now read up to 135 wpm on his fourth reading of a passage. The tutor has recently lengthened the individual trials from 2 to 3 minutes to provide even more of this concentrated practice on reading fluency.

Frank's lesson plan has changed a bit over the 2 months. With word study discontinued, guided reading and repeated readings are now sandwiched around a 10-minute period in which the tutor reads aloud to Frank. Presently, she is reading the book *Unsolved! Famous Real-Life Mysteries*, by George Sullivan (1992).

Frank's current lesson plan

1. Guided reading (35 minutes)
2. Read to (10 minutes)
3. Repeated readings (15 minutes)

By the end of the school year, Frank should be reading at the sixth-grade level. Reasonable end-of-year goals for rate are 125 wpm, orally, and 135 wpm, silently. Although these rates are still below average for a sixth-grade reader, for Frank they would represent significant improvement.

SEVERE CASES OF READING DISABILITY

What is common to the six corrective cases described in the preceding section is that each child benefited from traditional, balanced reading instruction. This instruction included guided reading and word study at the appropriate level, along with fluency practice and sometimes writing. Nonetheless, in my experience, there are a few children—perhaps 3% of the school-age population—who do not respond adequately to such traditional instruction and therefore require a different approach. I do not claim to be an expert in working with such severe cases, but over 27 years I have crossed paths with a few dozen of them. In this section I briefly describe my work with three children, each of whom, I believe, represents a distinct type of severe reading disability.

A Problem with Letters and Sounds

Greg came to our reading clinic at the beginning of his fourth-grade year. An obliging, freckle-faced 9-year-old, he read, at best, at a late-first-grade level. Moreover, he could neither read nor spell short-vowel words consistently. We placed him in late-first-grade reading material and began a systematic review of the short-vowel patterns.

After 40 tutoring lessons (two per week), Greg had made only minimal progress. Now in fifth grade, he could read, with support, at an early-second-grade level (see Table 7.8). However, his sight vocabulary was still weak, and the intensive work on short- and long-vowel patterns (using the word sort approach) did not seem to be transferring to either his contextual reading or writing. Most discouraging was the fact that Greg's reading progress seemed to have stalled after 1 year of tutoring.

A teacher must be willing to acknowledge when his or her instruction is not working. I had given the traditional clinical approach (guided reading and systematic, analytic phonics) a fair chance, and it had come up short. It was time to try something different. Clearly, Greg's problem area was word recognition (sight vocabulary and word attack). I decided to try a more synthetic, piecemeal approach to phonics instruction.

I pulled out an old manual for teaching severely disabled readers (Gillingham & Stillman, 1960), and carefully studied the phonics sequence. (*Note:* At this point, I was not formally trained in this approach.) Then, in the word study part of Greg's tutoring lesson, he and I began to review the short-vowel patterns, this time using the Gillingham–Stillman procedures. These involved:

- Drill on saying the individual letter–sound associations until they were "burned" into memory (e.g., b = /b/; g = /g/; t = /t/; a = /ă/; i = /ĭ/).
- Drill on blending the letter–sounds into short-vowel words (e.g., *t-a-g* =

TABLE 7.8. Greg's Reading Performance at the Beginning of Fifth Grade; Grade Level 5; Reading Level 2 (Early)

Level	Word recognition		Oral reading			Silent reading		Spelling
	Flash	Untimed	Accuracy	Compre-hension	Rate (wpm)	Compre-hension	Rate (wpm)	
Preprimer	90	90						
Primer	80	95						
First grade	70	90	95	100	91	100	80	75
Second grade	25	75	94	100	73	100	67	17
Third grade			84	75	64	—		

"tag"; *b-i-g* = "big"; *f-l-a-t* = "flat"); and the reverse, drill on spelling short-vowel words from dictation ("tag" = *tag*; "big" = *big*).

• Speed trials (1 minute) to automatize the short-vowel patterns in memory.

Greg responded well to the new phonics instruction. Step by step he progressed, and I sensed that he was starting to develop more complete mental representations of the foundational short-vowel patterns. More important, after a couple of months, Greg began to use this new phonics knowledge in contextual reading. This was a first. Before, on coming upon a new word in his reading, he simply guessed, using sentence context and random letter cues (e.g., "starting" for *strange*; "ladder" for *lantern*). Now he was systematically "sounding through" the word (left to right) and often coming up with the pronunciation. I could only attribute this new word-attack behavior to the synthetic nature of the Gillingham phonics instruction.

As his word recognition skill improved, Greg began to make reading progress. In guided reading, he advanced from second- to third-grade material, and his end-of-year testing showed improvement across the board (see Table 7.9). The 1 year of reading progress (second to third grade) he made in fifth grade must be weighed against the 1.5 years of progress he had made *in the previous four grades*. Moreover, Greg's contextual reading gains in fifth-grade were undergirded by significant improvement in his weak area, word recognition.

In summary, traditional, balanced reading instruction was only minimally effective in helping Greg with his serious word recognition problem. However, when multisensory, synthetic phonics instruction was introduced in the tutoring lessons, Greg began to decode words more effectively, becoming a much stronger reader. He did not fully "catch up" in reading achievement, however; at the end of fifth grade, he was reading at a third-grade level. Still, Greg's confidence was bolstered, and he now had a solid word recognition foundation on which to build.

Had the Gillingham–Stillman phonics approach been introduced earlier—say,

TABLE 7.9. Greg's Reading Performance at the End of Fifth Grade; Grade Level 5; Reading Level 3

Level	Word recognition		Oral reading			Silent reading		
	Flash	Untimed	Accuracy	Compre-hension	Rate (wpm)	Compre-hension	Rate (wpm)	Spelling
Preprimer	95	95						
Primer	90	100						
First grade	85	95						92
Second grade	75	85	97	100	92	100	88	75
Third grade	55	80	95	92	88	100	80	33
Fourth grade	25	70	90	83	74	67	82	

in second grade—would Greg have fallen so far behind in reading? Very possibly not. However, before jumping to the conclusion that multisensory, synthetic phonics is *the* remedy for all cases of severe reading disability, let us consider the next case study.

A Problem with Word Retrieval

Jason came to our summer reading clinic after his first-grade year in school. He did not know all the alphabet letters, he could recognize fewer than 10 printed words, and he was frustrated. That summer we taught Jason in a conventional manner (see The Emergent Reader, pp. 109–113), with little success. Convinced that he needed a more intensive program, in September I began tutoring the child, two times per week, using the Orton–Gillingham approach. (*Note:* By this time, I had been formally trained to use this method.) I was optimistic about Jason's chances because we were intervening early—at the start of his second-grade year.

In the first year of tutoring, Jason advanced very slowly through the Wilson Reading Program (Wilson, 1996), a materials-based offshoot of the Orton–Gillingham approach. Jason spent 45 lessons learning the alphabet letters, "hearing" the individual sounds in one-syllable short-vowel words, blending letter–sounds into words, and reading very simple, decodable texts. By the end of the school year, he had developed rudimentary phoneme awareness, and he could, if given time, decode and spell short-vowel words comprising three or four letters.

Jason's program was intensified in the second year. He received multisensory, synthetic phonics instruction 4 days per week—2 days with me and 2 days at school. Still, his progress was excruciatingly slow. By the middle of this year, I realized that Jason had a significant problem with *word retrieval*, that is, accessing the pronunciation of printed words. To read, we must "see individual words and say them fast" (Denckla, 2004). Jason could not do this. Although he could now decode or sound out almost any short-vowel word, he was not perceiving these words as "chunks" or immediately recognizable wholes. This is a devastating problem, for progress in contextual reading is stifled when a child has to stop and sound out almost every word in a sentence. We forged on, but I was fully aware that it was going to be a long journey.

In our third and fourth years, we continued to work on word recognition. Jason reviewed the short-vowel patterns, working on speed of recognition, and then moved to the high-frequency long-vowel patterns (e.g., *make, ride, spoke, tail, coat, heat*) and *r*-controlled patterns (e.g., *card, bird, short, burn, clerk*). Progress was slow; nothing came easy.

By this time, I had decided that, given Jason's problem with word recognition speed, he might benefit from supported contextual reading in natural-language (as opposed to decodable) texts. Learning to use passage and sentence context skillfully might facilitate his word recognition. We began to echo- and partner-read a number of late-first- and early-second-grade texts, selected stories from the *New Reading*

Skill Builders (Readers Digest, 1966) and *Pal Paperbacks* (Xerox, 1977). Jason enjoyed reading these more realistic stories. Unfortunately, the impact of passage and sentence context on his reading was not as great as I had hoped. Unless Jason had almost memorized a passage, he still had difficulty reading it fluently. It seemed as if his word processing speed was so slow that the benefits of context were compromised.

In the midst of this rather somber pedagogical story, I need to inject two points of light. First, Jason never gave up on learning to read. He had his up and down days, but overall, resilience and determination characterized his efforts. Second, Jason loved to be read to; we would work for 45 minutes, and then in the last 10–15 minutes of the lesson, I would read the best books I could find to him. Over the years, these included: *Stone Fox* (Gardiner, 1980), *Shoeshine Girl* (Bulla, 1975), *The Best Christmas Pageant Ever* (Robinson, 1972), *Trouble River* (Byars, 1969), *The Hobbit* (Tolkein, 1999), *The Lion, the Witch, and the Wardrobe* (Lewis, 1978), *Weasel* (DeFelice, 1990), *Tom Sawyer* (Twain, 1986), *The Watsons Go to Birmingham* (Curtis, 1995), *The Black Stallion* (Farley, 1969), and *Good Old Boy* (Morris, 1980). I honestly do not know who enjoyed these read-alouds more—the child who was read to, or the tutor who did the reading.

At the beginning of our fifth year, the year in which I am writing this account, I administered an informal word recognition test to Jason (lists preprimer, primer, first, and second). The pattern of Jason's word recognition scores (see Table 7.10) was not surprising; it fit a student with a word-retrieval problem. Notice that he could decode words through the second grade (see untimed second-grade score of 85%). On the other hand, his flash word recognition (or sight vocabulary) score fell below 50% as early as the primer or mid-first-grade level. Significantly, on the first three lists, almost one-half of Jason's errors (18 of 40) on the flash presentation were *hesitations*. That is, after a word was flashed, he would hesitate for a second or more before correctly identifying the word. Jason knew the word but he could not retrieve it instantaneously.

To further check out this word-retrieval problem, I administered the Rapid Digit Naming and Rapid Letter Naming subtests from the *Comprehensive Test of Phonological Processing* (Wagner, Torgesen, & Rashotte, 1999). Jason's task was to name, as fast as he could, 72 digits (or 72 letters), arrayed in rows on the page. Not

TABLE 7.10. Jason's Word Recognition Scores at the Beginning of his Fifth Year of Tutoring

Level	Flash (%)	Untimed (%)
Preprimer	55	95
Primer	40	90
Late first grade	10	85
Second grade	20	85

surprisingly, his performance placed him at the 4th percentile on each subtest. In other words, 96% of children Jason's age could perform these letter and digit naming tasks at a faster rate.

Despite the low word recognition scores and strong evidence of an underlying word-retrieval problem, year 5 has actually ushered in some hope. Whether due to maturation, the accumulated effects of 4 years of tutoring, divine intervention, or a combination of the above, Jason's reading has undergone a positive change. Simply stated, *context now helps Jason.* As he reads second-grade material, he is better able to orchestrate sight-word recognition, decoding, and contextual anticipation. Where before he was battling the text, word-by-painful-word, now there is a hint of fluency (or phrasing) in his reading. Yes, he still needs support (echo and partner reading), lacks stamina (150 words is about his limit), and gets frustrated. Nonetheless, there has been a qualitative change in Jason's reading; he is more skillful and more independent. For a child and a tutor who have struggled, this indeed is reason for hope.

The cases of Greg and Jason warrant comparison. Both children had severe difficulty with word recognition (contrast with Case 1 [*Walter*], pp. 177–183), and both required a multisensory, synthetic phonics approach that "pounded away" at the problem area. However, their responses to such intensive phonics instruction were different. Greg responded quickly, improving his decoding of single words and soon thereafter his contextual reading. Jason, on the other hand, responded slowly, only gradually demonstrating proficiency at phoneme segmentation and single-word decoding. Once Jason could "hear" the individual sounds in words and blend letter–sounds into words, he faced another roadblock. He had difficulty getting "whole" words (decodable and irregular words) into and out of memory. This word-retrieval problem stunted his reading development, particularly in the area of fluency. Jason, then, faced two problems: a "double deficit" in phonological decoding and word retrieval (Felton, 1995; Wolf & Bowers, 1999). This double deficit placed him further to the edge on a continuum of reading disability (see Figure 7.6), making remediation difficult but not impossible. If both Greg and Jason fall into the 3% of students with severe reading disabilities, and I think they do, I would argue that Greg is at the 3rd percentile whereas Jason is at the 1st, or lowest, percentile.

A Problem with Patterning

My third example of severe reading disability is a bit of an enigma. Although patterning problems are seldom mentioned in the reading disability literature, I come across a few such cases each year in my clinical work. Henderson (1981, p. 136) described the syndrome in the following manner:

> Popularly, [patterning difficulty] is much less widely recognized, yet in my experience, it is relatively common and often far more devastating to the learner. The critical inability in this syndrome appears to lie in activities requiring serial or patterned responses. The

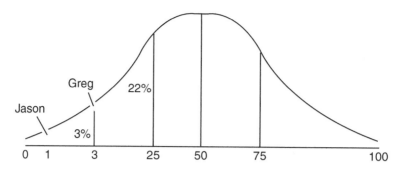

FIGURE 7.6. Positions of Greg and Jason along a continuum of reading disability (print-processing skill).

impact on the learner of reading appears to be a breakdown in his attempt to maintain a temporal–spatial match or coordination.

Henderson discusses how a patterning deficiency might affect the reader's internal analysis of words. That is, the child might know his or her letters and sounds but be unable to pattern—or sequence—the letter–sounds within the word.

My own experience with patterning problems is that the temporal–spatial match, noted by Henderson, can also be disrupted at the syntactic or across-words level. When you think about it, oral reading entails matching the temporal flow of a spoken sentence onto its fixed, unmoving representation on the page—in essence, an orchestration of letter–sounds, words, and syntax that is particularly difficult for a subgroup of disabled readers. The reading scores of Robby (see Table 7.11) illustrate this problem.

The first point we notice in this fourth grader's profile is the low oral reading accuracy and oral rate scores at second grade, 88% and 64 wpm, respectively. We quickly look over at the flash word recognition column, expecting a correspond-

TABLE 7.11. Robby's Diagnostic Results: Indications of a Patterning Problem; Grade Level 4; Reading Level 2

| Level | Word recognition | | Oral reading | | | Silent reading | | |
	Flash	Untimed	Accuracy	Compre-hension	Rate (wpm)	Compre-hension	Rate (wpm)	Spelling
Preprimer	100	—						
Primer	90	100						
First grade	90	95	96	100	91	75	73	83
Second grade	80	95	88	92	64	75	69	75
Third grade	75	85	85	75	55	67	60	58
Fourth grade	45	75						33

ingly low score at second grade. To our surprise, there is strength in this column, with scores of 90% at first grade, 80% at second grade, and 75% at third grade. How can this be? How can a child show strong word recognition in isolation yet read so poorly in context? Notice that this pattern occurs at both the second- and third-grade levels.

On relistening to Robby's oral reading of the second-grade passage, we note that it is devoid of cadence or rhythm. His reading is halting in some spots, fitful in others. He repeats words and phrases, misreads long words, omits short words, and sometimes does not stop at periods. Paradoxically, context, for Robby, seems to be the "enemy"; instead of facilitating the reading process, it confounds it.

Scores and qualitative description notwithstanding, we are still left with the question *why?* What causes the patterning problem? Is it a problem of orthographic processing, of syntactic processing, or of intermodal timing? I do not know. What I do believe, based on clinical experience, is the following:

1. An initial diagnosis in which flash word recognition scores exceed oral reading accuracy and rate scores, is a good indicator of a potential patterning problem.
2. Intensive phonics approaches (e.g., Orton–Gillingham, Wilson), by themselves, do not address the contextual nature of patterning problems. If used, they need to be accompanied by lots of supported contextual reading (guided reading, repeated readings, tape-recorder reading) at the student's instructional level.
3. A patterning difficulty can disrupt silent reading as well as oral reading (see Robby's scores in Table 7.11).
4. Patterning problems, like word recognition problems, seem to fall along a continuum. Some cases are mild and susceptible to remediation (see Case 6 [Frank] in this chapter, pp. 201–206); others are severe and resistant to instructional intervention.

In summary, severe reading disability—or dyslexia, as it is sometimes called—is real. In the past, it has often been ignored, resulting in some students reaching high school reading at the first- or second-grade level. Today, there is more focus on students with severe reading problems and a growing awareness that they require a different type of instruction; that is, a multisensory synthetic approach to building decoding skill. Nonetheless, there are many unanswered questions in this area (see patterning problem, above). Moreover, there has been an unhealthy tendency to generalize from what works for a small group of severely disabled readers (3%) to what should be tried with the much larger group of garden-variety, poor readers (22%). In other words, the belief seems to be "If it works for the most disabled, it should work for everyone." Such reasoning is sloppy and deserves to be challenged. Intensive multisensory phonics, accompanied by the reading of decodable text, is not the answer to every reading problem. As I have tried to show in this chapter, many struggling readers will benefit more from conventional reading instruction, carefully tailored to meet their individual needs (see Corrective Cases 1–6).

In this chapter, we considered case studies illustrating different types of reading problems. For each case, there was a *context*—a specific set of instructional activities—that facilitated the child's learning. In the next chapter we consider a different type of context—a training context that addresses the needs of teachers who work with struggling readers.

PART III

TRAINING READING TEACHERS

CHAPTER 8

Clinical Training
for Teachers of Reading

Children learn to read in a variety of contexts: at home in a parent's lap, at school in a first-grade reading circle, or sometimes, if necessary, in a one-to-one setting with a skillful tutor. But what is the optimal context for an adult who is learning how to teach a child to read? Certainly the information on reading diagnosis and instruction found in the preceding seven chapters bears on this question. And, a college methods class—that is, an instructor, a textbook, and 20 or so students—would seem to be the obvious context for transmitting this information. However, over the years, I have come to question the value of the traditional methods class in training teachers to work successfully with struggling readers. Interestingly, it was the work of a young political scientist, J. M. Fraatz, that stimulated—or, more accurately, reinforced—my thinking on this matter.

THE GOALS OF CLINICAL TRAINING

In a large-scale interview study, Fraatz (1987) found that elementary-grade teachers experience professional uncertainty about reading instruction, particularly the instruction of low-achieving readers. Following are two representative quotes from the interviewed teachers:

> "Teaching reading is such a complex skill. We just don't know why some things work and why others don't. One teacher told me once that she thinks that for some of her

---

This chapter is adapted, in part, from Morris (1999) and Morris (2003b).

kids she could stand on her head and speak Swahili, and they would still learn to read. We just don't know how youngsters put together the skills necessary to learn to read. Our best efforts seem to be to instruct children in the skills that have some obvious relevance to learning to read." (White-collar suburb teacher, p. 29)

"Even in a small, almost individualized group of four or five children working at this table with me, some kids are just not getting it, and some kids are having trouble focusing on it. . . . I'm sure there are reasons but they are not always apparent." (Blue-collar suburb teacher, p. 29)

Both of these teachers are expressing a sense of uncertainty or lack of control in teaching reading. They view reading acquisition as a complex, mysterious process and are not sure how their pedagogical actions actually influence student learning. This professional uncertainty may not affect the majority of their students who learn to read given sensible, "obviously relevant" instruction. However, it does affect those students who progress slowly or experience difficulty with reading—children who need specific instruction geared to their individual needs.

Fraatz (1987) believes that professional uncertainty is a "fact of life" for teachers of reading. She states:

Despite decades of research and reflection, no one is sure exactly how children learn to read or how best to teach them. Teachers confront this problem daily on both a theoretical and a practical level. Uncertainty and inconclusiveness in the theoretical scholarship on learning and instruction is a fact of life for educational practitioners. Debate continues on the broadest of questions, such as whether differences among teachers matter for student achievement or whether differences in instructional methods matter. (pp. 26–27)

Twenty years later, in 2007, the debate over "the best way to teach reading" continues. Although careful research has advanced our understanding of both the beginning reading and fluent reading processes (see reviews by Adams, 1990; Snow et al., 1998; Rayner et al., 2001), research per se is incapable of offering a "technical" solution to the problem of reading pedagogy. William James (1899/1958) addressed this issue more than a century ago in his famous *Talks to Teachers*:

I say moreover that you make a great, a very great mistake, if you think that psychology, being the science of the mind's laws, is something from which you can deduce definite programs and schemes and methods of instruction for immediate schoolroom use. Psychology is a science, and teaching is an art; and sciences never generate arts directly out of themselves. *An intermediate, inventive mind must make the application by using its originality.* (p. 3, emphasis added)

If research cannot provide a final answer to the problem of reading failure, where then are we to turn? Following James's lead, I believe that our only alternative is to invest in "intermediate, inventive minds," that is, *teachers'* minds. We must fashion training schemes that produce knowledgeable, problem-solving teachers who have confidence in their ability to teach low-achieving readers. The goals or outcomes of such clinical training are as follows:

1. The teacher will possess a coherent theory of the developmental reading process. That is, he or she will understand how specific knowledge or skill areas (e.g., word recognition, fluency, vocabulary, and comprehension) unfold and interrelate in reading acquisition.
2. The teacher will be skillful in assessing where a student is along a continuum of reading development.
3. The teacher will have mastery of a basic set of instructional methods and be able to selectively apply specific methods to meet the reading needs of individual students.
4. The teacher will be a "reflective practitioner" who plans carefully but also is capable of making reasoned, "on-the-run" adjustments to facilitate the student's learning.

Designing and implementing training programs that fulfill these goals is not easy. However, it can be done if we acknowledge, from the start, three important factors. First, empirical research does contribute, albeit indirectly, to the teaching enterprise. Whereas careful studies of the reading process cannot prescribe a technology or set procedure for teaching reading, they can define the boundaries within which teachers must work. Philosophical differences notwithstanding, serious teachers cannot ignore substantive, well-replicated research findings that increase our knowledge of the reading process. For example, a first-grade teacher needs to understand how phoneme awareness (Liberman & Liberman, 1992) influences the beginner's attempts to read words. Similarly, a second- or third-grade teacher needs to understand how both automatized word recognition (Perfetti, 1992) and background schemata (Pressley, 2000) contribute to the comprehension of text. Although such research-based constructs do not dictate a specific method of teaching reading, they must be accounted for in any serious instructional design.

Second, although we will always lack a science of teaching reading, in training teachers we can draw upon a century-old "wisdom of practice," a body of craft knowledge that has stood the test of time. It is true that the field of reading education, notorious for ignoring its history, reengages in methodological warfare at least once per decade. Still, a set of pedagogical concepts (e.g., sight vocabulary, decoding, informal assessment, instructional level, fluency, background knowledge, prediction) seems to survive across the years and is handed down to each new generation of teachers. A crucial task for teacher training is to present these core pedagogical concepts or strategies in a coherent manner that highlights the developmental nature (what comes first, what comes next) of the learning-to-read process.

Third, teachers-in-training need, along with course work in reading diagnosis and pedagogy, a carefully supervised practicum experience in which they tutor one or more struggling readers while receiving feedback from an experienced mentor or coach. It is to this idea of a clinical practicum that I now turn.

THE PRACTICUM: A CONTEXT FOR TRAINING TEACHERS OF READING

In his seminal work on preparing professionals for the demands of practice, Donald Schön (1987) opens with the following statement:

> In the varied topography of professional practice, there is a high, hard ground overlooking a swamp. On the high ground, manageable problems lend themselves to solution through the application of research-based theory and technique. In the swampy lowland, messy, confusing problems defy technical solution. The irony of this situation is that the problems of the high ground tend to be relatively unimportant to individuals or society at large, however great their technical interest may be, while in the swamp lie the problems of greatest human concern. (p. 3)

Of course, the effective practitioner (doctor, lawyer, teacher) must descend into the swamp of messy, everyday problems; he or she has no other choice. What is of interest to Schön is the professional training provided to these practitioners—its relevance and ultimate usefulness.

Schön (1987) argues that professional schools in modern universities are based on technical rationality: the idea that practical competence should be grounded in systematic or scientific knowledge. There exists in these schools, he states, a hierarchy of knowledge (basic science → applied science → technical skills of practice), with general theoretical knowledge enjoying a privileged station. Regarding professional training, it is assumed that practitioners should first receive a grounding in theory and theory-based applications. They will then be able to solve specific problems by selecting and applying appropriate technical procedures.

The difficulty with this perspective, Schön points out, is that real-world problems rarely present themselves to the practitioner as well-formed structures. In fact, the problems or problematic situations are often messy and indeterminate and, therefore, resistant to quick diagnosis and procedural solution. Consider the doctor trying to diagnose and treat an unusual collection of symptoms, the lawyer trying to plan strategy in a convoluted legal matter, or the teacher trying to help an intelligent youngster with a seemingly intractable reading problem. In such cases, the practitioner cannot look up the answer in a textbook; the case may not be "in the book." Instead, the practitioner must first frame the problem, hypothesize a suitable plan of action, and then act, always remaining ready to adapt thoughts and actions according to the feedback received from working with the problem. Viewed in this way, professional practice becomes a creative, craft-like activity (Schön, 1987).

To produce practitioners who can solve the messy but important problems found in the real world, Schön calls for a wholly different type of professional training. He argues that if practitioners are eventually to work "in the swamp" with indeterminate problem situations, then, in their training, they must experience these problems and attempt to solve them under the guidance of an experienced coach or mentor. This leads Schön (1987) to the concept of a *practicum*, which he describes as follows:

> A practicum is a setting designed for the task of learning a practice. In a context that approximates a practice world, students learn by doing. . . . They learn by undertaking projects that simulate and simplify practice; or they take on real-world projects under close supervision. . . . The practicum is a virtual world, relatively free of the pressures, distractions, and risks of the real world, to which, nevertheless, it refers. . . . It is also a collective world in its own right, with its own mix of materials, tools, languages, and appreciations. It embodies particular ways of seeing, thinking, and doing that tend, over time, as far as the student is concerned, to assert themselves with increasing authority. (p. 37)

In a practicum, students learn by doing under the guidance of an experienced practitioner. This instructor may sometimes impart information or theory to the students, but his or her main function is to coach; to guide the practice situation through demonstrating, advising, and questioning. The coach's role is critical in Schön's conception of a reflective practicum. The students are not set free to practice or apply, on their own, procedures learned in a previous course. Rather, the coach is integrally involved in the ongoing practicum experience, helping students to frame problems, create possible solutions, act purposefully, and reflect on the outcome of their actions. The ultimate goal of the practicum is to produce professionals who can problem-solve effectively in the indeterminate zones of real-world practice.

To illustrate his idea of a reflective practicum, Schön uses examples from the training of architects, performance musicians, psychoanalysts, and even city planners. However, in reading his book, I was struck by how directly his analysis applies to issues of teacher training, particularly to the training of reading teachers.

Learning to read and learning how to teach reading are complex processes; both are learned in the doing, and both are facilitated by performance feedback. One-to-one tutoring offers the best learning opportunity for a struggling reader (Clay, 1993; Wasik & Slavin, 1993). Tutoring is also the optimal context for learning to teach reading because a tutor, unlike a classroom teacher, can give his or her full attention to observing, interpreting, and intervening purposefully in a child's reading development. Here, then, are the ingredients for what Schön terms a reflective practicum. A small group of teachers-in-training gather to tutor children with reading problems under the watchful eye of a skilled clinician. The tutors teach, the coach observes, and there is dialogue based on the shared activity.

A TWO-COURSE CLINICAL SEQUENCE

Most graduate programs in reading education allot two courses to training teachers to work with struggling readers: a diagnosis and correction course and a supervised teaching practicum. Our graduate reading program at Appalachian State follows this plan. In this section, I describe our two clinical courses. There are many ways "to skin a cat," and I make no claims for the superiority of our clinical training sequence. If anything makes it different, it is its adherence to tradition—to the ghosts of famous clinics at Temple University (1940s), University of Delaware (1950s and 1960s), and the University of Virginia (1970s and 1980s).

Diagnosis and Correction Course

This course (3 semester hours [sh]), taught over 15-weeks, introduces basic diagnostic and correction procedures and prepares students for the teaching practicum that will follow.

Diagnosis

The first 7 weeks of the course are dedicated to reading diagnosis. The goal is for the students to become competent at administering and interpreting a small number of informal diagnostic instruments: word recognition, passage reading, and spelling inventories. The emphasis is not on "learning about" reading diagnosis but rather on "learning how to do" it.

In the first 2 weeks, along with lecturing about the developmental nature of reading, the instructor models the administration of a word recognition inventory, including how to flash each word for ¼ second. The students practice the flash procedure in class and at home. One week later they meet with the instructor, individually, to fine-tune their technique, and the following week they are tested on their ability to administer (or flash) a word list. Teaching the word recognition flash procedure in this manner is tedious and time consuming. However, the instruction accomplishes two things. First, it introduces the students, in a concrete way, to the important concept of automatized word knowledge. Second, it shows them, from the start, that reading diagnosis is a craft that is learned through concentrated effort. (*Note*: Although the flash technique can be difficult for some students to master, once it is learned it becomes an effortless motor skill that can be performed at will.)

The next order of business is learning to score an oral reading sample. First, the students are taught a system for coding oral reading errors (see pp. 23–24). Then, in class with the instructor, they listen and relisten to audiotapes of various children reading IRI passages. Precise, careful scoring of errors is emphasized, and borderline scoring decisions (e.g., a true mispronunciation versus a dialectical difference) are discussed with the instructor. Double-scoring for meaning-change errors and how to compute reading rate are also covered. Up to two class sessions are spent learning to score oral reading samples for accuracy, rate, and comprehension. For many students, even veteran teachers, this is a new and important experience. It is often the first time they have carefully listened to, and reflected on, a child's oral reading performance, the first time they have thought analytically about the developing reading process.

After covering the administration and scoring of silent reading and spelling, it is time to move to *interpretation* of results. A summary or cover sheet (see Table 8.1) is put on the overhead, and the instructor guides the class through the interpretation of the scores. The dual goal is to (1) establish the child's instructional and frustration levels and (2) identify his or her specific area(s) of strength and weakness. Again, learning to interpret summary sheets takes place over several weeks, with the cases progressing from easy to difficult (see order of cases in Chapter 3). Some students pick up on this problem-solving skill more quickly than others. Therefore, summary sheet interpretations are continued throughout the semester to make sure that all students eventually master the process.

At about the midpoint of the semester, the students take an in-class quiz on reading diagnosis. The quiz involves scoring two oral reading passages, interpreting two summary sheets, and answering a few short-answer questions. This quiz provokes a bit of anxiety (especially in teachers who have not taken one in a while), but it serves a purpose. Preparing for the quiz leads the students to review 6 weeks of diagnostic training and readies them to go out and administer the assessments to children. (*Note*: One of the students' assignments in the second half of the course is to administer and hand in [to be graded] two full reading assessments—word recognition, oral and silent reading, and spelling.)

Correction

The second half of the course is devoted to the correction of reading problems. The discussion is organized around three case studies that represent three levels of read-

TABLE 8.1. Sample Summary Sheet (*Clint*, a Third Grader Reading at the Primer Level)

| Level | Word recognition | | Oral reading | | | Silent reading | | |
	Flash	Untimed	Accuracy	Compre-hension	Rate (wpm)	Compre-hension	Rate (wpm)	Spelling
Preprimer	95	100						
Primer	55	75	93	100	77	—	—	
First grade	15	50	91	90	46	—	—	50
Second grade	—	—	77	67	28	—	—	8
Third grade								

Note. Meaning-change errors: *primer*—1 of 7; *first grade*—2 of 9.

ing development: the *emergent reader* (early first grade), the *primary-grade reader* (mid-first through third grade), and the *upper-elementary-grade reader* (fourth grade and above). One to two weeks are spent on each case study, during which the instructor describes teaching strategies (e.g., word recognition, comprehension, and fluency) that are appropriate for an individual child. These strategies were described in some detail in Chapters 5, 6, and 7, and the information need not be repeated here. Suffice it to say that the three case studies help students to see how reading instruction can be organized to meet the needs of children functioning at different developmental levels.

Although reading instruction is the focus in the second half of the course, diagnosis is not forgotten. As the graduate students begin to hand in the cases of children they have tested, the instructor chooses interesting summary sheets to discuss each week in class. The discussion of these cases—of children with whom the teachers are actually working—lends real-world credibility to the diagnosis and correction course.

Near the end of the course, the instructor explains that the diagnostic and teaching strategies that have been covered are appropriate for about 97% of the school-age population. The remaining 3% of severely disabled readers, he or she points out, will require a different, more intensive type of code-emphasis instruction. The instructor briefly overviews the Orton–Gillingham approach and suggests that the students might want to pursue such training. (*Note*: Our graduate program accepts as an elective course [3 sh] the successful completion of Orton–Gillingham or Wilson training).

In summary, this first course in a two-course clinical sequence imparts important information about the diagnosis and correction of reading problems. By the end of 15 weeks, most of the students are adept at administering, scoring, and interpreting the diagnostic instruments. They also understand a set of basic teaching strategies and how they fit within a developmental framework. However, understanding a teaching strategy (e.g., support reading, word sort, DRTA, repeated readings) and skillfully implementing it can be two different things. With regard to instruction, the diagnosis and correction course promotes understanding; the teaching practicum that follows leads to skill, or what Schön refers to as "knowledge-in-action."

The Teaching Practicum

There is a seamless transition between the diagnosis and correction course and the teaching practicum, the first course serving as the foundation for the second. In the practicum, there are few lectures, little outside reading, and no quizzes. The purpose of the practicum is straightforward: to help teachers develop skill and confidence in working with struggling readers.

Organization of the Practicum

The practicum is directed by a reading professor who has expertise and interest in clinical teaching. This instructor, who is a full participant in the practicum, is assisted by one to three clinical supervisors, enough to ensure that the tutoring is carefully carried out. An experienced clinical supervisor (a skilled doctoral student or a reading specialist from the local school district) can observe five tutor–child pairs in a 1-hour session.

Ten to twenty graduate students, usually practicing teachers, enroll in the practicum each semester. They come to the reading clinic after school on Monday and Wednesday afternoons. Each teacher tutors one child from 4:00 to 5:00, and then another from 5:00 to 6:00. Thus, if there are 15 teachers in the practicum, there are 30 tutor–child pairs (see Figure 8.1). The tutoring lessons are observed, and a tutor and his or her assigned supervisor meet after each lesson to discuss what occurred and what needs to be done next. Facilitating this post-lesson dialogue is a *lesson plan notebook* that the tutor keeps for each child. Each page in the notebook represents a single tutoring lesson and includes a *plan* going into the lesson, and an *evaluation* afterward (more on this later).

On Wednesday evenings, after the tutoring and follow-up conferences are completed, the practicum instructor conducts a 1-hour seminar. The first three or four seminars are used to review teaching strategies that were introduced in the diagnosis and correction course. This review is essential and well received by the teachers, because now they are actually *using* these strategies with struggling readers. The next five seminars are used to staff (or discuss) the cases of children who are presently in the practicum. Two cases are staffed each week in the following manner. First, the child's diagnostic summary sheet is put on the overhead and discussed by the group. Next, the child's tutor stands up and describes the teaching plan he or she has devised (e.g., guided reading, word study, fluency building, writing) and tells how the child is pro-

4:00–5:00 P.M.	Practicum instructor observes five tutor–child pairs.
	Clinical supervisor A observes five tutor–child pairs.
	Clinical supervisor B observes five tutor–child pairs.
5:00–6:00 P.M.	Practicum instructor observes five tutor–child pairs.
	Clinical supervisor A observes five tutor–child pairs.
	Clinical supervisor B observes five tutor–child pairs.
6:00–7:00 P.M.	Supervisors meet with teachers, individually, to discuss the just-completed lessons and plan for the next session. Teachers waiting to meet with a supervisor evaluate the current lesson in their lesson plan notebook.
7:00–8:00 P.M. (Wednesday only)	Practicum instructor leads a seminar in which teaching techniques are reviewed and, later in the semester, clinic cases are staffed.

FIGURE 8.1. Organization of a reading practicum (30 children, 15 teachers, and 3 supervisors) that meets on Monday and Wednesday afternoons.

gressing in each area. Finally, after questions or comments from the class, the instructor leads a discussion of how this child's reading problem might be addressed in a school context; for example, in the classroom or resource room.

The weekly staffings of children in the clinic provide rich learning opportunities. Each practicum teacher can work directly with only two struggling readers. However, the seminar staffings allow a teacher to learn about 10–12 additional children in the practicum. These cases are real, they are being reported by a peer, and there is ample time for both formal and informal discussion. The staffings also provide the practicum instructor with chances to compare and contrast various cases (nature of problem, severity, prognosis) from both a theoretical and practical perspective. The final two or three Wednesday seminars often deal with the following topics: (1) how to implement a volunteer- or paraprofessional-staffed tutoring program in a school; (2) how to adapt tutoring techniques for small-group instruction; and (3) how to write a brief student progress report for parents (see Appendix 8.1).

The organization of our practicum is far from perfect. It would be better if the tutoring occurred three or four times per week; better still if the practicum extended over two semesters instead of one. Nonetheless, the 1-semester, 2-days-per-week practicum does afford important opportunities for a teacher-in-training to (1) learn about the reading process, and (2) develop confidence in his or her ability to enhance a student's reading skill.

Off-Campus Reading Practicums

Clinical training in the teaching of reading need not take place on the college campus. At Appalachian State, we offer our graduate reading program in an urban area (Winston–Salem) 90 minutes from campus. Regarding the two-course clinical sequence, in the spring semester a professor travels to the off-campus site once per week to teach the diagnosis and correction course. Then, the same professor, with a cadre of skilled assistants, supervises a 4-week summer practicum in an elementary school in the Winston–Salem area. Participating teachers tutor two children on a daily basis and attend twice-weekly seminars. The summer practicum makes up in intensity for what it lacks in length. That is, 18–20 tutoring lessons, with each of two children, is enough for a teacher to master the strategies emphasized in the summer practicum. Such a training model benefits the local school district in two important ways. First, it provides 18 hours of quality, one-to-one reading assistance to 40 or more low-achieving students. Second, it provides intensive staff development in teaching reading to the participating teachers.

I continue to marvel at the effectiveness of the off-campus summer practicum: 40 children, 20 teachers, 1 professor, and 3 clinical supervisors come together on neutral ground and accomplish so much in such a short time. It shows that a reading clinic is not so much a physical setting as it is the purposeful gathering of struggling readers, teachers-in-training, and experienced coaches.

THE PRACTICUM AND THE TEACHER-IN-TRAINING

To illustrate pedagogical issues that surface in a practicum, let us examine the case of Clint, a third-grade boy who reads at a mid-first-grade level. In reviewing Clint's initial testing at the beginning of the semester (see Table 8.1, p. 223), the tutor and her supervisor agree that Clint should start out reading primer-level stories and, in word study, working through the short-vowel word families. (Note that Clint could spell only 50% of the short-vowel words on the first-grade list.) The supervisor suggests a set lesson plan for the tutor to follow (see Figure 8.2). This lesson plan, which in outline, remains constant across the semester, becomes the *frame* within which the child and tutor negotiate learning to read, and the tutor and supervisor negotiate learning how to teach reading.

Plan	Evaluation
1. Guided reading • *Pepper's Adventure* Rigby (primer level)	1. First we did a picture walk to get familiar with the story. We then echo-read the first page and partner-read (alternated pages) the rest of the story. Clint made a number of oral reading errors. Sometimes I had him try to sound out the word, but this was difficult for him; sometimes I just gave him the word. I'm not sure how I should handle his mistakes. Also, should Clint be doing some silent reading? Gosh, I don't know how many mistakes he would make then. By the way, his comprehension was excellent.
2. Word study • Sort word families (-*at*, -*an*, -*it*)	2. This was our third day on *a* and *i* rhyming words. He sorted the words quickly and read down the column accurately. When we played the memory game, which he loves, Clint misread one word ("bat" for *bit*). On the spell check, he spelled correctly five of the six words.
3. Easy reading • Reread 2× the first 100 words in *Cave Boy* (primer level), a book we finished two lessons ago.	3. Clint read the first 100 words in *Cave Boy*, concentrating on not making errors. Then he read the same 100 words again. First reading = 6 errors; second reading = 3 errors. Second reading was much smoother.
4. Writing • Continue working on "My Dog" story.	4. His story is great but his spelling is atrocious. He misspelled two short *i* words—HET for *hit* and STEK for *stick*. We'll revise and edit next time.
5. Read to: • *The Terrible Mr. Twitmeyer*	5. Second day on Twitmeyer; Clint listened intently to this story about a mean dogcatcher.

FIGURE 8.2. Sample lesson plan (*Clint*, a third grader reading at the primer level).

The parts of the lesson plan (guided reading, word study, fluency building, and writing) provide distinct opportunities for the tutor and supervisor to interact, particularly around the issues of teaching technique and instructional pacing. For example, with regard to technique, consider the guided reading part of Clint's lesson. A third grader, Clint reads first-grade-level stories quickly but inaccurately. He consistently skips over and substitutes words as he reads. His tutor should have in mind, or be led to consider, the following questions:

- Should Clint do most of his reading orally or silently?
- Should I worry about Clint's word-reading errors as long as he is comprehending the story?
- Should I intervene immediately when Clint misreads a word, or should I give him an opportunity to self-correct his error? What if he does not self-correct?

In helping the tutor address these questions, the supervisor can provide feedback with an accompanying explanation. For example:

> Oral reading is still appropriate for Clint. For the most part, hold him accountable for reading the words that are on the page. Once in while you can let a substitution or omission go by, but remember that his weakness is word recognition, and this will not improve unless he begins to attend closely to individual words as he reads.

Or, the supervisor might sit down and partner-read a few pages with Clint to demonstrate how to let a child read past an error so that he or she has a chance to go back and self-correct. Obviously, performance feedback and model teaching by the supervisor are also called for in other parts of the lesson, particularly word study and writing.

Instructional pacing is always an issue in teaching a child to read. The student needs to work consistently at his or her optimal instructional level, not below or above it. However, over time, the child's ability changes, and the ever-present question facing the tutor is, "Should we move forward today or stay at this level a while longer?" It is here that the supervisor can be of great help. Again, consider Clint's case. In word study, he moved through the short-vowel word families with little difficulty. After 5 weeks, he could consistently read rhyming words by changing the beginning consonant (e.g., "bat," "mat," "sat"; "big," "wig," "twig"), and he seemed to have committed a number of these words to sight memory. Nonetheless, Clint is still inconsistent in spelling short-vowel words and often misreads these patterns upon meeting them in text. The supervisor, therefore, suggests that the tutor keep Clint at the short-vowel level and try working with the words in a different manner: by having him "take apart" and "put together" short-vowel words, letter by letter. The supervisor explains that Clint needs to focus his attention on the individual letter–sounds in the short-vowel words if he is ever to master these patterns (see p. 98). In this case, the instructional pacing decision is to keep the student at the same conceptual level but to vary the teaching strategy. In another case, the decision may be to move forward.

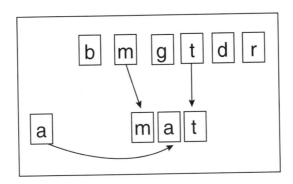

The supervisor, unlike the tutor-in-training, has an experience-tested theory or "sense" of how word knowledge and contextual reading ability develop. He or she can therefore judge what level of mastery is necessary for the student to move successfully to the next level, be it from short- to long-vowel patterns in word study, or from late-first- to second-grade stories in guided reading. By cueing the tutor when the student is ready to advance or stay put (and offering a reason as to why), the supervisor or coach is performing an essential function.

A major goal of the practicum is to help the teacher-in-training recognize what constitutes good practice. This recognition comes only from *doing*—from sensing, in the act of teaching, something that works, and why it works. It might involve the tutor helping a child figure out an unknown word in text; modifying a word sort activity on the spot so that the child can grasp a needed concept; or asking a question that helps the child discover an important meaning in a story. In establishing good practice, different teachers will require different amounts of guidance from the supervisor. Some will require modeling, extensive practice, and ongoing performance feedback. Others, possessing a more intuitive feel for teaching, may require little overt intervention on the supervisor's part. Even in the latter cases, however, the coach's role is important. His or her words of approval or nods of agreement, in the presence of good practice, provide affirming feedback to the teacher who is doing it right.

In bringing this section to a close, I am reminded of a confident young teacher in one of my practicum courses a few years back. I assigned her two disabled readers, an 8-year-old boy and a 38-year-old man, and helped her get started. After a few weeks, she was teaching so effectively that in observing her, I, the coach, was beginning to refine some of my own understandings about clinical teaching. This young teacher was a "natural" who seemed to be gliding so effortlessly through the practicum that I questioned whether she really needed the supervision. I was somewhat surprised then upon reading the following paragraphs in her master's thesis, completed some 2 years later.

In studying for a Masters degree in reading education, I took courses in the teaching of beginning reading, reading assessment and correction, and even a seminar with a focus on reading disability. However, the course that had the greatest influence on my understanding of the reading process and indeed the course which prompted me to write this thesis was a practicum in the clinical teaching of reading. In this semester-long practicum, I worked with two different clients, meeting with each of them twice per week. My clinic supervisor monitored my lesson plans, observed tutoring sessions, and discussed with me what he saw happening in the lessons. Before I began this practicum, I felt that I had a sound understanding of the reading process; however, when I was engaged in the practicum, the reading process took on a whole new shape. Reading instruction was no longer an abstract sequence of skills, but now a very real conversation. Through these tutoring lessons, I learned how it is that people learn to read. Through discussions with my supervisor, I was given the language to understand and to think about how this process was occurring. (Mock, 1996, pp. 83–84)

THE PRACTICUM AND THE READING PROFESSOR

We have seen what a practicum experience can offer to the teacher-in-training. But what does it offer to the supervising instructor, who must invest significant time and energy in such a course? Obviously, the practicum context affords the supervising clinician ongoing opportunities to observe children with reading problems and to test remediation hypotheses. But more basically, the practicum grounds the university professor in reality. Theory remains important, of course, but only to the degree that it can help explain the reading problems facing real children in the clinic. Two examples illustrate this point.

Edmund Henderson, my clinical mentor, was trained in the language-experience tradition in the late 1950s. This pedagogical tradition, which might be labeled holistic or child-centered, emphasized dictated stories, DRTAs, and creative writing. When Frank Smith's top-down, psycholinguistic model of reading burst onto the scene in the early 1970s, Henderson was quite taken by the model, as were many other reading educators. Smith's theory matched Henderson's philosophy of instruction. Nonetheless, in my graduate school years in the late 1970s, I saw my professor begin to question Smith's (1971) popular explanation of reading as a "psycholinguistic guessing game." It is true that Henderson was reading experimental literature that countered the "guessing game" model, but it was his hands-on experience with children in the McGuffey Reading Center that gnawed at his initial acceptance of Smith's position. Henderson (1981) realized that it was accurate, automatic word recognition that these disabled readers lacked, not the ability to guess or anticipate upcoming words in text. His insight about the crucial importance of automatized word knowledge put Henderson directly at odds with the prevailing whole language movement of the 1980s and 1990s. However, he did not care. He knew from his clinical work—and his reading of the research evidence—that the centrality of word knowledge could not be ignored in any serious explanation of the reading process.

My second example comes from my own experience and involves the area of severe reading disability or dyslexia. In graduate school, I learned that dyslexia does exist in perhaps 2–3% of the population, but that the condition is very difficult, if not impossible, to treat. The best we could do, I was taught, was to apply traditional methods (a balance of supported contextual reading and direct phonics instruction) and hope for the best.

We remember our graduate school lessons; in fact, they produce a theoretical orientation that guides our later work in the field. After assuming directorship of my own reading clinic at National–Louis University in Chicago, I worked with several children and adults who had severe reading problems. I steadfastly used traditional, balanced reading instruction, but with little success. Later, after moving to Appalachian State University in rural North Carolina, I began to encounter more and more cases of severe reading disability in my clinical work. I could no longer tolerate my ineffectiveness in teaching these children to read. Abandoning long-held theoretical biases, I and a few colleagues began to search for alternative approaches to teaching dyslexic readers. We pursued training in multisensory systematic phonics approaches (e.g., Orton–Gillingham), and, though we have not discovered a panacea, we are convinced that we are now on a better track in working with the problem of severe reading disability. My point is that it was the face-to-face encounter with dyslexia in the clinic that led me to rethink what I had been taught in graduate school and search for better ways to help students with this devastating problem.

THE FATE OF CLINICAL TRAINING FOR TEACHERS OF READING

In this chapter I have argued that teachers in the elementary and middle grades need specialized training if they are to provide effective help to struggling readers. This training should include information on a basic set of diagnostic and teaching methods and the opportunity to apply these methods in a supervised practicum. The goal is to produce classroom and specialist teachers who possess a coherent understanding of the learning-to-read process and confidence in their ability to help students with reading problems.

In its particulars, my argument can be questioned on several grounds. For example, is it reasonable to expect teachers to become expert at reading diagnosis and remediation by taking a single diagnosis and correction course and a follow-up practicum? The answer is no. Expertise is gained over years of experience working with low-achieving readers. What clinical courses can do, however, is provide teachers of reading with needed tools and "ways of thinking." Although the teacher-in-training may diagnose only two students in the diagnosis course and tutor only two students in the practicum, these initial clinical experiences are of crucial importance. Carefully undertaken, they enable the teacher to develop and sharpen technique; they also enter the teacher's memory as well-thought-out cases against which future ones can be compared.

A second and prevalent criticism of clinical training pertains to its emphasis on one-to-one diagnosis and instruction. After all, critics state, most school-based reading instruction occurs in groups (small or large), and the dynamics of individual versus group instruction are very different. True enough, but one must keep in mind that the purpose of clinical training is not to teach teachers how to manage or conduct group lessons. Rather, such training is intended to help the teacher see a complicated process up close and gain understanding of it (Kibby & Barr, 1999). This kind of seeing and understanding, which occurs more easily in a one-to-one than in a small-group context, can lead thoughtful teachers to rethink and experiment with traditional classroom instructional routines. For example, a third-grade teacher might create a separate reading group so that her six lowest readers can read and discuss a novel written at their instructional level (early second grade); a fourth-grade teacher might provide second-grade spelling instruction to three students who are clearly functioning at that level; or a fifth-grade teacher may take the time to record third-grade chapter books onto tapes so that her four lowest readers can read with support at their instructional level. Clinical training that provides a model of good practice can lead dedicated teachers to make such accommodations in the classroom. Thus, the criticism of *one-to-one* clinical training, I believe, needs to be turned around. Can we afford *not* to provide such quality training to elementary and middle school teachers entrusted with the responsibility of teaching children to read?

A third question relates to the content of clinical training. That is, are the traditional instructional strategies I have described in this book effective with *all* low-achieving readers? Unfortunately, the answer is no. As noted previously, there are a few students (perhaps 3%) at the extreme end of the reading disability continuum who have severe phonological processing deficits, word-retrieval deficits, or both (Felton, 1995). To learn to read, these students require a different type of code-intensive instruction. Having said this, I believe that reading teachers need to be able to distinguish between severely disabled readers (3%) and garden-variety remedial readers (perhaps 22%), and to provide instruction accordingly. Whereas it can be ineffective to provide traditional instruction to severely disabled readers, it can be inefficient—indeed, inappropriate—to provide intensive, step-by-step phonics instruction to remedial readers who do not require it. In other words, it is simplistic and dangerous to think that "one size fits all." Teachers need to be able to distinguish between reading types and to provide instruction that fits the individual case. (*Note*: Probably the best way to identify a severe reading disability is to observe, over time, the student's response to sound reading instruction provided in a one-to-one context.)

If clinical training can help teachers do a better job with their low-achieving readers, then what are the barriers to providing such training? Time and cost certainly come into play. Clinical training in teaching reading involves concentrated work over a large block of time, usually a full school year. Even a month-long summer practicum can involve a tremendous time investment on the trainee's part, with daily tutoring lessons, lesson plan evaluations, and seminars. Cost is also a factor. To ensure adequate supervision of a practicum, a ratio of one coach to every five tutor–child pairs (per hour) is needed. Otherwise, observation and supervision of the tutoring sessions become problematic. Thus, if 15 teachers are enrolled in a practicum, each tutoring 2 children, the resulting 30 tutor–child pairs would require 3 coaches (each coach would observe two, 1-hour sessions, with five tutor–child pairs in each session). Even if one of the three coaches is the professor assigned to the practicum (and this should be the case), funds must be found to pay the other two. Time and money, then, are potential obstacles to providing teachers with quality clinical training. However, there is a third and, I believe, much more serious obstacle that involves the availability of coaches.

From the 1920s through the mid-1970s, graduate training in reading often revolved around the university-based reading clinic (Morris, 2003b; Pelosi, 1977). Major figures such as Gates at Columbia, Gray and Robinson at Chicago, Betts at Temple, and Stauffer at Delaware were deeply involved in clinical work, and their students, in turn, carried the tradition to universities throughout the country. Over the past three decades things have changed. A groundswell of interest in literature-based instruction in the 1990s, and a more recent focus on "scientifically based" reading programs, have diverted the reading field's attention from clinical practice to classroom practice. (*Un*coincidentally, the major clinical reading initiative of the past 20 years, Reading Recovery, was introduced not by an American but by a New Zealand developmental psychologist, Marie Clay.) No longer does every college of education house a reading clinic, no longer is the directorship of such a clinic considered a prestigious position, and no longer is carefully supervised clinical work the central focus in training reading teachers. The tradition of the reading clinic, and the wealth of knowledge and experience it encompasses, are teetering at the brink of oblivion.

In the current professional environment, what seems, to me, to be most at risk is the passing down of the clinical craft of teaching reading to the next generation; or, to use Schön's terminology, the future development of coaches. If clinical training is not highly valued by the profession, then it will not be supported in colleges of education. If respected senior professors are not actively engaged in clinical work, then it will not be appreciated or seriously undertaken by their doctoral students. And eventually, if there are not enough new clinical professors or coaches in our colleges to train teachers, then important pedagogical knowledge will not find its way into the schools.

In bringing this chapter and book to a close, I would again like to quote Edmund Henderson. Because Henderson deeply respected the complexities of teaching reading, he often used metaphors to drive home important but subtle points. One afternoon in a graduate seminar he said:

Just the other day I saw an older man working a garden. As I watched, I suddenly realized that the handling of the spade was a thing of vast skill and artistry. I wish that something as fine as that might happen in our schools. If we could but develop a taste for such quality, I do think that literacy would thrive. (1981, p. 156)

Engrossed as I was in the serious business of theory and research, I paid little attention to what seemed like an offhand comment. Several days later it dawned on me that Henderson had been comparing the old gardener to a reading teacher. How quaint, I thought at the time. Now, many years later, I better appreciate the wisdom in my professor's deceptively simple statement. The old gardener of Henderson's acquaintance dignified his humble work by taking it seriously, doing it right, and striving for quality in every movement; his years of patient diligence showed in the supreme skill with which he used his tools. Like Henderson, I now hope to see teachers of reading strive for, and attain, such skill.

If we are ever to make a difference with the 25% of children who experience difficulty with reading, the reading field must develop a "taste for quality." Quality does not come effortlessly, of course. Like everything else of real importance, it requires getting down in the swamp, along with your students, on a regular basis. It cannot be found in books, courses, seminars, or contemplation; the core of good reading instruction resides in the careful, reflective doing of it. I know of no better way to proceed toward quality than by bringing reading professors and teachers together to work with struggling readers; that is, to resurrect our clinical tradition.

Sample Progress Reports to Parents of Children Attending a Reading Clinic

A. First-grade boy reading at the preprimer 3 level

Dear parent,

It has been a pleasure to work with *Brad* this spring semester. He has worked hard and been cooperative during the tutoring lessons.

Brad's instructional reading level is *preprimer 3* (approaching mid-first grade). This means that he is challenged by preprimer 3 materials but has adequate word recognition, fluency, and comprehension to learn and move forward at this reading level. Brad has read in preprimer 2 and preprimer 3 materials this semester at the Reading Clinic. For example:

Mrs. Wishy Washy, Wright Group (preprimer 2)
Tom Is Brave, Rigby (preprimer 2)
Blackberries, Rigby (preprimer 3)
Lucky Goes to Dog School, Rigby (preprimer 3)

One area of strength for Brad is comprehension. He is able to follow the story line and make good predictions forward as he reads. With repeated readings of a story (he reads each story three times), Brad is able to improve the fluency and accuracy with which he reads.

One area Brad needs to improve is his word recognition. He needs to increase his store of known (or sight) words and improve his decoding skill. To this end, we have been working on the *a*, *i*, and *o* short-vowel word families (e.g., *cat, hat, flat; man, pan, plan*), and he has made progress in reading these short-vowel words. By reading preprimer 2 and 3 stories this semester, Brad has also increased his sight vocabulary, which is now up to 60+ words.

Our recommendation is that Brad return to the Reading Clinic in the summer. He will continue to benefit from the one-to-one instruction we are able to offer. You can support Brad at home by (1) reading aloud good books to him (consult your local librarian for suggestions), and (2) having Brad read to you books his tutor sends home this summer.

Sincerely,

Reading tutor

B. Fourth-grade girl reading at a third-grade level

Dear parent,

It has been a pleasure to work with *Daisy* this spring semester. She has worked hard and been cooperative during the tutoring lessons.

Daisy's instructional reading level is *third grade*. This means that she is challenged by third-grade materials but has adequate word recognition, fluency, and comprehension to learn and move forward at this reading level. Daisy has read in late-second-grade and third-grade materials this semester at the Reading Clinic. For example:

Christopher Columbus, Random House (2-2)
The True Story of Pocahontas, Random House (2-2)
Helen Keller, Scholastic (3rd)
The Titanic . . . Lost and Found, Random House (3rd)

One area of strength for Daisy is comprehension. She understands what she reads and shows ability to make good predictions and draw inferences. Daisy's word recognition—ability to decode new words she meets in text—is also a strength, at least when reading third-grade text.

One area Daisy needs to improve is her reading fluency or reading rate. When reading a text orally the first time, she reads haltingly with many repetitions of words and phrases. We have worked on her fluency using "repeated readings." In this activity, she reads the same 200–250 word passage four times, each time trying to improve her reading fluency (accuracy and phrasing). Daisy has shown improvement in this oral reading area (she can now read 110 wpm on her final trials), and I believe that the fluency gains are carrying over to silent reading. I have searched for chapter books (late-second-grade and third-grade levels) that she can read at home for enjoyment. Such free reading will eventually improve her fluency and her confidence as a reader.

Our recommendation is that Daisy return to the Reading Clinic in the summer. She will continue to benefit from the one-to-one instruction we are able to offer. You can support Daisy at home by (1) taking her to the public library and having her choose late-second- and third-grade books that are of interest to her (ask the librarian for suggestions), and (2) setting aside a regular time at home for Daisy to read for enjoyment.

Sincerely,

Reading tutor

References

Adams, M. (1990). *Beginning to read: Thinking and learning about print.* Cambridge, MA: MIT Press.

American Heritage College Dictionary. (1997). Boston: Houghton Mifflin.

Anderson, R., & Pearson, P. D. (1984). A schema-theoretic view of basic processes in reading comprehension. In P. D. Pearson (Ed.), *Handbook of reading research* (Vol. 1, pp. 255–291). New York: Longman.

Barr, R., Blachowicz, C., Katz, C., & Kaufman, B. (2002). *Reading diagnosis for teachers: An instructional approach.* Boston: Allyn & Bacon.

Bear, D., Invernizzi, M., Templeton, S., & Johnston, F. (2003). *Words their way: Word study for phonics, vocabulary, and spelling instruction.* Englewood Cliffs, NJ: Merrill.

Betts, E. (1946). *Foundations of reading instruction.* New York: American Book Company.

Blachman, B. (2000). Phonological awareness. In M. Kamil, P. Mosenthal, P.D. Pearson, & R. Barr (Eds.), *Handbook of reading research* (Vol. 3, pp. 483–502). Mahwah, NJ: Erlbaum.

Blachowicz, C., & Ogle, D. (2002). *Reading comprehension: Strategies for independent learners.* New York: Guilford Press.

Bloodgood, J., & Kucan, L. (2005, November). *Oral and silent reading norms for groups of second, third, and fourth graders.* Paper presented at the annual meeting of the National Reading Conference, Miami, FL.

Bond, G., & Tinker, M. (1973). *Reading difficulties: Their diagnosis and correction.* Englewood Cliffs, NJ: Prentice Hall.

Brown, J., & Morris, D. (2005). Meeting the needs of low spellers in a second-grade classroom. *Reading & Writing Quarterly, 21,* 165–184.

Calfee, R. (1982). Literacy and illiteracy: Teaching the nonreader to survive in the modern world. *Annals of Dyslexia, 32,* 71–93.

Carbo, M. (1981). Making books talk to children. *Reading Teacher, 34,* 186–189.

Carver, R. (1990). *Reading rate: A review of research and theory.* San Diego, CA: Academic Press.

Carver, R. (2000). *The causes of high and low reading achievement.* Mahwah, NJ: Erlbaum.

Chall, J. (1983). *Stages of reading development.* New York: McGraw-Hill.

Chomsky, C. (1971). Write first, read later. *Childhood Education, 47,* 296–299.

Chomsky, C. (1976). After decoding, what? *Language Arts, 53,* 288–296.

Clay, M. (1979). *The early detection of reading difficulties.* Auckland, NZ: Heinemann.

Clay, M. (1991a). *Becoming literate: The construction of inner control.* Portsmouth, NH: Heinemann.

Clay, M. (1991b). Introducing a new storybook to young readers. *Reading Teacher, 45,* 264–273.

Clay, M. (1993). *Reading Recovery: A guidebook for teachers in training.* Portsmouth, NH: Heinemann.

Cunningham, J., Koppenhaver, D., Erickson, K., & Spadorcia, S. (2004). Word identification and text characteristics. In J. Hoffman & D. Schallert (Eds.), *The texts in elementary classrooms* (pp. 21–37). Mahwah, NJ: Erlbaum.

Denckla, M. (2004, November). *Neurology of reading.* Paper presented at the annual meeting of the International Dyslexia Association, Philadelphia, PA.

Dewey, J. (1916). *How we think: A restatement of the relation of reflective thinking to the educative process.* Boston: Heath.

Duffy, G. G. (2003). *Explaining reading: A resource for teaching concepts, skills, and strategies.* New York: Guilford Press.

Ehri, L. (1989). The development of spelling knowledge and its role in reading acquisition and reading disability. *Journal of Learning Disabilities, 22,* 356–365.

Ehri, L. (1998). Grapheme–phoneme knowledge is essential for learning to read words in English. In J. Metsala & L. Ehri (Eds.), *Word recognition in beginning literacy* (pp. 3–40). Mahwah, NJ: Erlbaum.

Elkonin, D. B. (1973). U.S.S.R. In J. Downing (Ed.), *Comparative reading* (pp. 551–580). New York: Macmillan.

Felton, R. (1995). *Teaching reading to students with reading disabilities: What we know about what works.* Report prepared for the North Carolina Partnership Training System, Winston–Salem, NC.

Fraatz, J. M. (1987). *The politics of reading.* New York: Teachers College Press.

Frye, E. (2004). *Measure of word-level automaticity and its relation to reading fluency.* Unpublished doctoral dissertation, Appalachian State University, Boone, NC.

Frye, E. (2007). *Word-level automaticity and its relation to reading fluency.* Manuscript submitted for publication.

Ganske, K. (2000). *Word journeys: Assessment-guided phonics, spelling, and vocabulary instruction.* New York: Guilford Press.

Gayán, J., & Olson, R.K. (1999). Reading disability: Evidence for a genetic etiology. *European Child and Adolescent Psychiatry, 8,* 52–55.

Gillingham, A., & Stillman, B. (1960). *Remedial training for children with specific disability in reading, spelling, and penmanship.* Cambridge, MA: Educators Publishing Company.

Harcourt Assessment, Inc. (2002). *Stanford Achievement Test* (10th ed.). San Antonio, TX: Harcourt.

Harris, A., & Jacobson, M. (1982). *Basic reading vocabularies.* New York: Macmillan.

Hasbrouck, J., & Tindal, G. (2006). Oral fluency norms: A valuable assessment tool for reading teachers. *Reading Teacher, 59,* 636–644.

Henderson, E. (1981). *Learning to read and spell: The child's knowledge of words.* DeKalb, IL: Northern Illinois University Press.

Henderson, E. (1990). *Teaching spelling.* Boston: Houghton Mifflin.

Henderson, E. (1992). The interface of lexical competence and knowledge of written words. In S. Templeton & D. Bear (Eds.), *Development of orthographic knowledge and the foundations of literacy* (pp. 1–30). Hillsdale, NJ: Erlbaum.

Henderson, E., & Beers, J. (1980). *Developmental and cognitive aspects of learning to spell: A reflection of word knowledge.* Newark, DE: International Reading Association.

Hendrix, M., & Snow, A. (2006, December 9). *The relationship between reading rate and measures of reading fluency.* Paper presented at the annual meeting of the American Reading Forum, Sanibel Island, FL.

Holdaway, D. (1979). *Foundations of literacy.* Auckland, NZ: Heinemann.

Hoover, H., Dunbar, S., & Frisbie, D. (2001). *Iowa Test of Basic Skills.* Rolling Meadows, IL: Riverside.

Huey, E.B. (1968). *The psychology and pedagogy of reading.* Cambridge, MA: MIT Press. (Original work published 1908)

Invernizzi, M., & Hayes, L. (2004). Developmental-spelling research: A systematic imperative. *Reading Research Quarterly, 39,* 216–228.

James, W. (1958). *Talks to teachers on psychology and to students on some of life's ideals.* New York: Norton. (Original work published 1899)

Johnson, M., Kress, R., & Pikulski, J. (1987). *Informal reading inventories.* Newark, DE: International Reading Association.

Kibby, M., & Barr, R. (1999). The education of reading clinicians. In D. Evensen & P. Mosenthal (Eds.), *Advances in reading/language research: Vol. 6. Reconsidering the role of the reading clinic in a new age of literacy* (pp. 3–40). Stamford, CT: JAI Press.

Kuhn, M., & Stahl, S. (2000). Fluency: A review of developmental and remedial practices. *Journal of Educational Psychology, 95,* 3–21.

Leslie, L., & Caldwell, J. (2005). *Qualitative Reading Inventory–4.* Boston: Allyn & Bacon.

Lewkowicz, N. (1980). Phoneme awareness training: What to teach and how to teach it. *Journal of Educational Psychology, 72,* 686–700.

Liberman, I., & Liberman, A. (1992). Whole language versus code emphasis: Underlying assumptions and their implications for reading instruction. In P. Gough, L. Ehri, & R. Treiman (Eds.), *Reading acquisition* (pp. 343–366). Hillsdale, NJ: Erlbaum.

MacGinitie, W., MacGinitie, R., Maria, K., Dreyer, L., & Hughes, K. (1999). *Gates–MacGinitie Reading Tests* (4th ed.). Rolling Meadows, IL: Riverside.

Markwardt, F. (1998). *Peabody Individual Achievement Test—Revised.* Circle Pines, MN: American Guidance Service.

Miller, G., Galanter, E., & Pribrum, K. (1960). *Plans and the structure of behavior.* New York: Holt.

Mock, D. (1996). *Systematic instruction of students with severe reading disability: Two case studies.* Unpublished master's thesis. Appalachian State University Reading Clinic, Boone, NC.

Morris, D. (1999). The role of clinical training in the teaching of reading. In D. Evenson & P. Mosenthal (Eds.), *Advances in reading/language research: Vol. 6. Rethinking the role of the reading clinic in a new age of literacy* (pp. 69–100). Stamford, CT: JAI Press.

Morris, D. (2003a). Reading instruction in kindergarten. In D. Morris & R. Slavin (Eds.), *Every child reading* (pp. 8–32). Boston: Allyn & Bacon.

Morris, D. (2003b). Of Studebakers and reading clinicians. *American Reading Forum Online Yearbook.* Available at *www.americanreadingforum.org/03_yearbook/volume03toc.htm.*

Morris, D. (2005a). *The Howard Street tutoring manual: Teaching at-risk readers in the primary grades.* New York: Guilford Press.

Morris, D. (2005b). A Title I reading success story. *Reading Research and Instruction, 45,* 1–17.

Morris, D., Blanton, L., Blanton, W., Nowacek, J., & Perney, J. (1995). Teaching low spellers at their "instructional level." *Elementary School Journal, 96,* 163–177.

Morris, D., & Bloodgood, J. (2004). *Elements of reading: Phonics and phoneme awareness.* Austin, TX: Steck-Vaughn.

Morris, D., Bloodgood, J., Lomax, R., & Perney, J. (2003). Developmental steps in learning to read: A longitudinal study in kindergarten and first grade. *Reading Research Quarterly, 38,* 302–328.

Morris, D., Ervin, C., & Conrad, K. (1996). A case study of middle-school reading disability. *Reading Teacher, 46,* 368–377.

Morris, D., Nelson, L., & Perney, J. (1986). Exploring the concept of "spelling instructional level" through the analysis of error-types. *Elementary School Journal, 87,* 181–200.

Morris, D., & Perney, J. (1984). Developmental spelling as a predictor of first-grade reading achievement. *Elementary School Journal, 84,* 441–457.

Morris, D., Shaw, B., & Perney, J. (1990). Helping low readers in grades 2 and 3: An after-school volunteer tutoring program. *Elementary School Journal, 91,* 133–150.

Morris, D., & Slavin, R. (Eds.). (2003). *Every child reading.* Boston: Allyn & Bacon.

Morris, D., Tyner, B., & Perney, J. (2000). Early Steps: Replicating the effects of a first-grade reading intervention program. *Journal of Educational Psychology, 92,* 681–693.

National Reading Panel. (2000). *Teaching children to read: An evidence-based assessment of the scientific research literature on reading and its implications for reading instruction (reports of the subgroups).* Washington, DC: National Institute of Child Health and Human Development.

Nelson, L., & Morris, D. (1987). Echo reading with taped books. *Illinois Reading Council Journal, 16,* 39–42.

Nessel, D. (1987). The new face of comprehension instruction: A closer look at questions. *Reading Teacher, 40,* 604–606.

Olson, R.K. (2006). Genes, environment, and dyslexia: The 2005 Norman Geshwind Memorial Lecture. *Annals of Dyslexia, 56,* 205–238.

Paris, S., Wasik, B., & Turner, J. (1991). The development of strategic readers. In R. Barr, M. Kamil, P. Mosenthal, & P.D. Pearson (Eds.), *Handbook of reading research* (Vol. 2, pp. 609–640). Mahwah, NJ: Erlbaum.

Pelosi, P. (1977). *The origin and development of reading diagnosis in the United States.* Unpublished doctoral dissertation, State University of New York, Buffalo, NY.

Pinnell, G. S., Pikulski, J., Wixon, K., Campbell, J., Gough, P., & Beatty, A. (1995). *Listening to children read aloud.* Washington, DC: Office of Educational Research and Improvement, U.S. Department of Education.

Perfetti, C. (1985). *Reading ability.* New York: Oxford University Press.

Perfetti, C. (1992). The representation problem in reading acquisition. In P. Gough, L. Ehri, & R. Treiman (Eds.), *Reading acquisition* (pp. 145–174). Hillsdale, NJ: Erlbaum.

Pressley, M. (2000). What should comprehension instruction be the instruction of? In M. Kamil, P. Mosenthal, P.D. Pearson, & R. Barr (Eds.), *Handbook of reading research* (*Vol. 3*, pp. 545–561). Mahwah, NJ: Erlbaum.

Rasinski, T. (2003). *The fluent reader.* New York: Scholastic.

Rasinski, T., & Padak, N. (1998). How elementary students referred for compensatory reading instruction perform on school-based measures of word recognition, fluency, and comprehension. *Reading Psychology, 19,* 185–216.

Rayner, K., Foorman, B., Perfetti, C., Pesetsky, D., & Seidenberg, M. (2001). How psychological science informs the teaching of reading. *Psychological Science in the Public Interest, 2,* 31–74.

Rayner, K., & Pollatsek, A. (1989). *The psychology of reading.* Englewood Cliffs, NJ: Prentice Hall.

Read, C. (1971). Pre-school children's knowledge of English phonology. *Harvard Educational Review, 41,* 1–34.

Richgels, D. (2001). Invented spelling, phonemic awareness, and reading and writing instruction. In S. Neuman & D. Dickinson (Eds.), *Handbook of early literacy research* (pp. 142–155). New York: Guilford Press.

Roe, B., & Burns, P. (2007). *Informal reading inventory* (7th ed.). Boston: Houghton Mifflin.

Samuels, S. J. (1979). The method of repeated readings. *Reading Teacher, 32,* 403–408.

Samuels, S. J. (2006). Toward a model of reading fluency. In S. J. Samuels & A. Farstrup (Eds.), *What research has to say about fluency instruction* (pp. 24–46). Newark, DE: International Reading Association.

Santa, C., & Hoien, T. (1999). An assessment of Early Steps: A program for early intervention of reading problems. *Reading Research Quarterly, 34,* 54–79.

Schlagal, R. (1989). Constancy and change in spelling development. *Reading Psychology, 10,* 207–232.

Schlagal, R. (2007). Best practices for teaching spelling and handwriting. In S. Graham, C. MacArthur, & J. Fitzgerald (Eds.), *Best practices in writing* (pp. 178–201). New York: Guilford Press.

Schön, D. (1987). *Educating the reflective practitioner.* San Francisco: Jossey-Bass.

Schreiber, P. (1991). Understanding prosody's role in reading acquisition. *Theory into Practice, 30,* 158–164.

Smith, F. (1971). *Understanding reading.* New York: Holt, Rinehart & Winston.

Snow, C., Burns, M., & Griffin, P. (1998). *Preventing reading difficulties in young children.* Washington, DC: National Academy Press.

Spear-Swerling, L., & Sternberg, R. (1998). *Off track: When poor readers become "learning disabled."* Boulder, CO: Westview Press.

Stahl, S., & Heubach, K. (2005). Fluency-oriented reading instruction. *Journal of Literacy Research, 37,* 25–60.

Stauffer, R. (1970). *The language-experience approach to the teaching of reading.* New York: Harper & Row.

Stauffer, R., Abrams, J., & Pikulski, J. (1978). *Diagnosis, correction, and prevention of reading disabilities.* New York: Harper & Row.

Strecker, S., Roser, N., & Martinez, M. (1998). Toward understanding oral reading fluency. *National Reading Conference Yearbook, 47,* 295–310.

Templeton, S., & Bear, D. (1992). *Development of orthographic knowledge and the foundations of literacy: A memorial festschrift for Edmund H. Henderson.* Hillsdale, NJ: Erlbaum.

Templeton, S., & Morris, D. (1999). Questions teachers ask about spelling. *Reading Research Quarterly, 34,* 100–112.

Tyner, B. (2004). *Small-group reading instruction: A differentiated teaching model for beginning and struggling readers.* Newark, DE: International Reading.

Wagner, R., Torgesen, J., & Rashotte, C. (1999). *Comprehensive Test of Phonological Processing.* Austin, TX: Pro-Ed.

Wasik, B., & Slavin, R. (1993). Preventing early reading failure with one-to-one tutoring: A review of five programs. *Reading Research Quarterly, 28,* 178–200.

Wiederholt, J., & Bryant, B. (2001). *Gray Oral Reading Tests* (4th ed.). Austin, TX: Pro-Ed.

Wilson, B. (1996). *Wilson reading system: Instructor's manual.* Millbury, MA: Wilson Language Training Corporation.

Wolf, M., & Bowers, P. (1999). The double-deficit hypothesis for the developmental dyslexias. *Journal of Educational Psychology, 91,* 415–438.

Woodcock, R., Mather, N., & Schrank, F. (2006). *Woodcock–Johnson III Diagnostic Reading Battery.* Rolling Meadows, IL: Riverside.

Woods, M. L., & Moe, A. (1977). *Analytical Reading Inventory.* Columbus, OH: Merrill.

Woods, M. L., & Moe, A. (2007). *Reader's passages to accompany Analytical Reading Inventory.* Upper Saddle River, NJ: Pearson.

Zutell, J., & Rasinski, T. (1989). Reading and spelling connections in third and fifth grade students. *Reading Psychology, 10,* 137–155.

Reading Materials Cited in Text

Chapter 5

Bang, M. (1987). *Wiley and the hairy man.* New York: Aladdin Books.

Cowley, J. (1986a). *In the mirror.* Bothell, WA: Wright Group.

Cowley, J. (1986b). *Yuk soup.* Bothell, WA: Wright Group.

Eller, W., & Hester, K. (1980). *Toothless dragon* (pp. 28–43). River Forest, IL: Laidlaw Brothers.

Randell, B. (1996a). *Father bear goes fishing.* Crystal Lake, IL: Rigby.

Randell, B. (1996b). *Pepper's adventure.* Crystal Lake, IL: Rigby.

Randell, B. (1996c). *Seagull is clever.* Crystal Lake, IL: Rigby.

Chapter 6

Branley, F. M. (1989). *What happened to the dinosaurs?* New York: Harper Trophy.

Curtis, C. P. (1995). *The Watsons go to Birmingham—1963.* New York: Yearling-Dell.

Spinelli, J. (1990). *Maniac Magee.* Boston: Little, Brown.

White, E. B. (1980). *Charlotte's web.* New York: Harper Trophy.

Woodbury, D. (1966). Grandpa and the sea. *New Reading Skill Builder* (pp. 92–98). Pleasantville, NY: Reader's Digest.

Chapter 7

Bulla, C. R. (1975). *Shoeshine girl.* New York: Harper Trophy.

Byars, B. (1969). *Trouble river.* New York: Puffin.

Cleary, B. (1983). *Dear Mr. Henshaw.* New York: Harper Trophy.

Coerr, E. (1995). *Buffalo Bill and the pony express.* New York: Harper Trophy.

Coolidge, O. (1960). *Hercules and other tales from Greek myths.* New York: Scholastic.

Dalgliesh, A. (1986). *The courage of Sarah Noble.* New York: Aladdin.

Davidson, M. (1971). *Louis Braille: The boy who invented books for the blind.* New York: Scholastic Book Services.

Davidson, M. (1974). *Nine true dolphin stories.* New York: Scholastic.

DeFelice, C. (1990). *Weasel.* New York: Avon.

Farley, W. (1969). *The Black Stallion.* New York: Random House.

Freedman, R. (1988). *Buffalo hunt.* New York: Scholastic.

Gardiner, J. R. (1980). *Stone fox.* New York: Harper Trophy.

Jumper, M., & Sonder, B. (1993). *Osceola: Patriot and warrior.* New York: Steck-Vaughn.

Kulling, M. (1996). *Vanished! The mysterious disappearance of Amelia Earhart.* New York: Random House.

Lewis, C. S. (1978). *The lion, the witch, and the wardrobe.* New York: Harper Collins.

McGovern, A. (1965). *Wanted dead or alive: The true story of Harriet Tubman.* New York: Scholastic.

McGovern, A. (1978). *Shark lady: The adventures of Eugenie Clark.* New York: Scholastic.

Milton, J. (1992). *Wild, wild wolves.* New York: Random House.

Morris, W. (1980). *Good old boy.* Oxford, MS: Yoknapatawpha Press.

Mowat, F. (1981). *Owls in the family.* New York: Yearling-Dell.

Naylor, P. R. (1991). *Shiloh.* New York: Yearling-Dell.

Robinson, B. (1972). *The best Christmas pageant ever.* New York: Harper Trophy.

Ryan, P. M. (1998). *Riding freedom.* New York: Scholastic.

Sandin, J. (1989). *The long way westward.* New York: Harper Trophy.

Sobol, D. (1978). *Encyclopedia Brown: Boy detective.* New York: Bantam Skylark.

Speare, E. G. (1983). *The sign of the beaver.* New York: Yearling-Dell.

Sullivan, G. (1992). *Unsolved! Famous real-life mysteries.* New York: Scholastic.

Tolkien, J. R. (1999). *The hobbit.* New York: Harper Collins.

Twain, M. (1986). *Tom Sawyer.* New York: Penguin Books.

Ware, K., & Sutherland, L. (1952). *Greek and Roman myths.* St. Louis: Webster.

Wetterer, M. (1990). *Kate Shelley and the midnight express.* Minneappolis: Lerner.

Wulffson, D. (1991). *Amazing true stories.* New York: Scholastic.

York, C.B. (1980). *Ichabod Crane and the headless horseman.* New York: Troll.

Chapter 8

Cowley, J. (1998). *Mrs. Wishy-Washy.* Bothell, WA: Wright Group.

Dubowski, C., & Dubowski, M. (1988). *Cave boy.* New York: Random House.

Davidson, M. (1969). *Helen Keller.* New York: Scholastic.

Donnelly, J. (1987). *The Titanic: Lost . . . And found.* New York: Random House.

Krensky, S. (1991). *Christopher Columbus.* New York: Random House.

Moore, L., & Adelson, L. (1988). *The terrible Mr. Twitmeyer.* New York: Scholastic.

Penner, L. (1994). *The true story of Pocahontas.* New York: Random House.

Randell, B. (1996a). *Lucky goes to dog school.* Crystal Lake, IL: Rigby.

Randell, B. (1996b). *Tom is brave.* Crystal Lake, IL: Rigby.

Randell, B. (2006). *Blackberries.* Austin, TX: Rigby.

Index